CREATING THE NATIONAL HEALTH SERVICE

CASS SERIES: BRITISH POLITICS AND SOCIETY
SERIES EDITOR: PETER CATTERALL
ISSN: 1467-1441

Social change impacts not just upon voting behaviour and party identity but also the formulation of policy. But how do social changes and political developments interact? Which shapes which? Reflecting a belief that social and political structures cannot be understood either in isolation from each other or from the historical processes which form them, this series will examine the forces that have shaped British society. Cross-disciplinary approaches will be encouraged. In the process, the series will aim to make a contribution to existing fields, such as politics, sociology and media studies, as well as opening out new and hitherto-neglected fields.

Peter Catterall (ed.), *The Making of Channel 4*

Brock Millman, *Managing Domestic Dissent in First World War Britain*

Peter Catterall, Wolfram Kaiser and Ulrike Walton-Jordan (eds), *Reforming the Constitution: Debates in Twenty-first Century Britain*

Brock Millman, *Pessimism and British War Policy, 1916–1918*

Adrian Smith and Dilwyn Porter (eds), *Amateurs and Professionals in Post-war British Sport*

Archie Hunter, *A Life of Sir John Eldon Gorst: Disraeli's Awkward Disciple*

Harry Defries, *Conservative Party Attitudes to Jews, 1900–1950*

Virginia Berridge and Stuart Blume (eds), *Poor Health: Social Inequality before and after the Black Report*

Stuart Ball and Ian Holliday (eds), *Mass Conservatism: The Conservatives and the Public since the 1880s*

Rieko Karatani, *Defining British Citizenship: Empire, Commonwealth and Modern Britain*

Des Freedman, *Television Policies of the Labour Party, 1951–2001*

Marvin Rintala, *Creating the National Health Service: Aneurin Bevan and the Medical Lords*

CREATING THE NATIONAL HEALTH SERVICE

Aneurin Bevan and the Medical Lords

MARVIN RINTALA

Boston College

Foreword by

THE RT. HON. LORD OWEN

FRANK CASS
LONDON • PORTLAND, OR

First published in 2003 in Great Britain by
FRANK CASS PUBLISHERS
Crown House, 47 Chase Side
London N14 5BP

and in the United States of America by
FRANK CASS PUBLISHERS
c/o ISBS, 920 NE 58th Avenue, Suite 300
Portland, Oregon, 97213-3786

Website: www.frankcass.com

British Library Cataloguing in Publication Data

Rintala, Marvin
　Creating the National Health Service: Aneurin Bevan and
　the medical lords. – (Cass series. British politics and society)
　1. Bevan, Aneurin, 1897–1960   2. Moran, Charles McMoran
　Wilson, Baron   3. Horder, Thomas Jeeves Horder, Baron,
　1871–1955   4. National Health Service (Great Britain) –
　History   5. Medical policy – Great Britain – History – 20th century
　I. Title
　362.1'0941'09044

ISBN 0-7146-5506-6 (cloth)
ISBN 0-7146-8404-X (paper)
ISSN 1467-1441

Library of Congress Cataloging-in-Publication Data

Rintala, Marvin.
　Creating the National Health Service: Aneurin Bevan and the
　medical lords / Marvin Rintala.
　　p.　cm. – (Cass series – British politics and society, ISSN 1467-1441)
　Includes bibliographical references and index.
　ISBN 0-7146-5506-6 (cloth) – ISBN 0-7146-8404-X (paper)
　1. National health services – Great Britain – History.　2. Bevan, Aneurin,
　1897–1960.　3. Great Britain – Politics and government – 20th century.
　I. Title. II. Series

RA412.5.G7R566 2003
　362.1'0941–dc21

2003046149

Typeset 11/12.5 Palatino by Cambridge Photosetting Services
Printed in Great Britain by MPG Books, Bodmin, Cornwall

Remembering Liisa

Contents

Foreword by Lord Owen   viii

Series Editor's Preface   xi

PART I: POLITICIANS PRESCRIBE   1

1. Introduction   3
2. Conservatives   8
3. Liberals: Past and Present   14
4. Cabinet Colleagues   36
5. The Minister   58

PART II: DOCTORS DIFFER   67

6. Introduction   69
7. A Royal Physician   75
8. A Royal College   84
9. A Royal Speech   91
10. At the Café Royal   98
11. Away from the Café Royal   111
12. A Battle Royal   118

PART III: DISCIPLES DECIDE   129

13. Disciples Decide   131

Bibliography   143

Index   159

Foreword

Creating the National Health Service covers Britain's greatest piece of twentieth-century social legislation, and is a fascinating account. Every judgement is carefully referenced, which gives academic weight to the book, but it nevertheless reads more like a novel. In seeking to highlight the clash in personality and policy between the two medical prima donnas, Lords Moran and Horder, the book captures the real battle over the nationalization of the hospitals, which was not in Parliament but within the medical profession.

The way Aneurin Bevan outmanoeuvred those who wanted local government control of some hospitals to continue, like Herbert Morrison, is well covered here. Morrison, who made his reputation as Chairman of the LCC (London County Council), personally felt the loss of 32,000 employees in 98 institutions as a result of the nationalization of municipal hospitals. In Cabinet, Morrison lost mainly because Bevan was supported by Christopher Addison, a distinguished physician and former professor of anatomy who in 1919 was appointed by Lloyd George as the first Minister of Health. Addison, now in the Labour Party, was widely respected and was Attlee's closest friend and confidant. Hugh Dalton, the Chancellor, also supported Bevan.

How Bevan played off the differences in the medical profession over the nationalization of the hospitals provides the real stuff of history. Bevan's relationship with Moran, respectively the 'Bollinger Bolshevik' and 'Corkscrew Charlie', gives the flavour of the compromise set in the then fashionable restaurant, Pruniers. This book, taken with the wisdom of the official history of the NHS by Charles Webster, particularly his most recent volume[1] covering resource allocation, and Professor Enthoven's writings on the internal market,[2] could give the Prime Minister and Secretary of State for Health as well as health commentators much food for thought in the present controversy over foundation hospitals.

Looking back today, some find it all too easy to attribute the idea of nationalizing the hospitals to dogmatic left-wing socialism, whereas in fact it was not only strongly advocated by Lord Moran, Churchill's personal physician, but was fully supported by Sir John Hawton, Bevan's key adviser in the Civil Service. The reason Bevan chose this course owed far more to pragmatism and rationality than ideology. The hospital proposals in his predecessor's wartime coalition plan simply would not have worked. The variation in standards of care across the nation's hospitals by 1946 were immense. The good consultants were all crowded together in the large cities and teaching hospitals. It was essential that consultants were attracted to practise in unfashionable and below-standard hospitals and they would only have contemplated doing this if they were confident that standards would be improved by substantial investment from central government. They also needed to be sure that their salaries would not be dependent on a large private practice and that merit would be rewarded, not just in teaching hospitals. To his great credit, Bevan understood that human nature needed such a non-doctrinaire package, and it has withstood the passage of time surprisingly well.

Sadly, the national allocation of resources in the NHS has not achieved the fairer distribution of capital and revenue allocation that it theoretically should have done. The disparities in provision by 1958 had only diminished to a very limited extent. According to any objective criteria, the four London regional health authorities emerged most favourably and the regions in the North and Midlands came off worst. The Resource Allocation Working Party, which I championed as Minister of Health from 1974, produced a formula which could have redressed this imbalance, but successive Ministers in different administrations, facing political flak, particularly from London, relaxed the criteria and took refuge in endless reorganization, whereas steadily applying improved management techniques to fulfil the founding purpose of fairly distributing health resources across the nation could have achieved far more. Scotland and Wales have gained from a higher percentage financial allocation per head of population than in England from the inception to the present day.

The NHS at the start of the twenty-first century is now receiving the boost to its overall spending that it has needed since 1948. But there is abundant evidence that we were able over that period to develop our NHS, despite lower spending than in other countries, because of the in-built efficiencies of having a national service. We need to be very careful today in focusing on decentralization, which is certainly needed, and the new Labour government's welcome second-term conversion to the virtues of the internal market, that the creation of foundation hospitals does not lead us back into the inequality of provision that was the hallmark of a fragmented hospital service prior to the creation of the NHS.

The Rt Hon. Lord Owen
May 2003

NOTES

1. C. Webster, *The Health Service since the War*, Vol. II: *Government and Health Care, the British National Health Service 1958–79*, Stationery Office, 1986.
2. A. Enthoven, *Reflections on the Management of the NHS*, Nuffield Provincial Hospitals Trust, 1984.

Series Editor's Preface

It is axiomatic that the creation of the National Health Service (NHS) was a towering achievement of Clement Attlee's postwar government, even though Attlee himself seems to have been much more impressed by the giving of independence to India. In the public mind, however, the advent of the NHS in 1948 remains one of those events which is, in the language of 1066 and all that, unquestionably 'a good thing'. Indeed, Nigel Lawson was later to describe it as 'the nearest thing the English have to a religion'.

Of course, all this might merely reflect the remarkable success not of the creation of the NHS, but of the propaganda campaign that accompanied it. Ironically, much of that campaign was aimed at the middle classes, those who had hitherto subscribed to various private insurance and, now spared such additional expenses, were to prove amongst the prime beneficiaries of the NHS. Continuing social inequalities in health care were not, however, to receive much attention until the Black Report in the 1970s, and even that, as a recent book in this series has pointed out,[1] achieved little. Such reorganizations as did occur were aimed instead at the management structures of the NHS. An organization that has only one client – the government, which buys health care wholesale for the great British public out of its tax revenues – can only seek to become more efficient through changing its managerial systems, at first periodically and then increasingly frenetically since the mid-1990s. Such changes, however, have had, as yet but little effect on some of the central managerial decisions on which the NHS itself was founded.

For instance, the decision to take health care out of the remit of local government, in the face of considerable opposition within the Labour Cabinet, not only reduced democratic accountability but also, more importantly in terms of health outcomes, the role of public health within the new system. The privileged position of the teaching hospitals preserved regional inequalities in health care. The fiscal arrangements marked a shift away from the principle of social insurance – a path which continued to be pursued on the Continent – to what has become, instead, a unique reliance on general taxation. And the contractual arrangements with senior doctors meant that in some ways the NHS was not so much a national system as a series of cottage industries under a range of powerful consultants, one by-product of which is the increasingly remarked 'NHS by postcode' phenomenon. This has served to vitiate the efficiencies Bevan thought he was achieving through his determination on a national system.

There have been numerous books which have sought to explain how the NHS was created, usually by way of careful analysis of what changes were wrought from the pre-1948 system. However, this book is not a technical history of how the various decisions which produced the NHS were made and implemented, but rather a cultural history of why. In seeking to answer this central question Marvin Rintala skirts long-familiar battlegrounds, such as the stand-off between the British Medical Association (BMA) and Nye Bevan. Instead, he introduces us to the much less well-known conflict between two medical peers, Lords Horder and Moran. By the time the BMA was squaring up to Bevan the battle-lines had already been drawn and the crucial decisions on the shape of the future NHS had already been taken. These decisions, Rintala argues, though taken by Bevan, were structured and informed by Moran's victory over his rival physician. And without Moran's advice, the NHS that came into being might have differed in a number of important respects.

Instead, the NHS that emerged in 1948 was the outcome from a number of conflicts. Bevan's chapel-flavoured rhetoric may have given his creation a religious glow which has remained ever since. But, as Marvin Rintala skilfully shows, behind that front much of the shape of the new NHS was determined rather by medical politics and power, and particularly by Moran. Whilst the rhetoric proved extremely successful in selling the idea of an NHS, Moran's machinations have proved equally enduring in shaping the rather more obscure realities of how the NHS actually works in practice.

Peter Catterall
London

NOTE

1. Virginia Berridge and Stuart Blume, *Poor Health: Social Inequality before and after the Black Report* (London, Frank Cass, 2003).

Part I:

Politicians Prescribe

'I can always see a vision on the horizon which sustains me. I can see now the humble homes of the people with the dark clouds of anxiety, disease, distress, privation hanging heavily over them. And I can see, again, another vision. I can see the Old Age Pension Act, the National Insurance Act and many another Act in their trail descending, like breezes from the hills of my native land, sweeping into the mist-laden valleys, and clearing the gloom away until the rays of God's sun have pierced the narrowest window.'

David Lloyd George,
speaking at Kennington Theatre,
13 July 1912

— 1 —

Introduction

By one interpretation the National Health Service (NHS) was created by a national consensus within Britain. In a political system dominated by parties this view assumes that at least both of the two major British parties, Labour and Conservative, and possibly also the now minor Liberal Party, were in agreement on the essential elements of the NHS.[1] Since only the Labour Party was in governmental office during that creation, it is assumed to have been internally united behind the NHS bill introduced in 1946 by the minister of health. The opposition Conservative Party is, further, assumed to have shared in some significant way(s) in that creation. The latter argument was repeatedly and explicitly made in 1948, as the NHS was coming into operation, by the leader of the Conservative Party. Winston Churchill's speeches then argued that the 'main principles' of the NHS had been 'hammered out' by his wartime Coalition Government before its dissolution in the spring of 1945.[2] Sometimes Churchill went even further, asserting that the 'actual measure' creating the NHS, the National Health Service Act of 1946, 'is of course the product of the National Coalition Government of which I was the head'.[3] This claim was reiterated by Churchill over the next several years.[4] A less sweeping variation of this theme was articulated later by the Earl of Woolton, chosen by Churchill in 1946 to become chairman of the Conservative Party organization.[5] Woolton conceded that a White Paper on health policy published in February 1944 by the Coalition Government 'was a halfway house to the system of a nationalized service, but it was, indeed, a comprehensive one'.[6] This more modest assertion is helpful because it links Churchill's sweeping claim to specific events before 1945. Neither Churchill nor Woolton stressed involvement by the Conservative Party, or its leader, in the legislative process which produced the National Health Service Act of 1946.

Much more important as possible evidence for the consensual interpretation than the 1944 White Paper is the publication in late 1942 of what came to be known as the Beveridge Report on the operation of the British welfare state. That the creation of the NHS implemented part of the Beveridge Report was, and is, widely believed to be true. Since the Beveridge Report and its most important legislative predecessor, the National Insurance Act of 1911, were both Liberal documents, the now-faded Liberal Party could also share in a national consensus, in this case through time. The most important Conservative advocate of the British welfare state later sympathetically described the task of the Labour minister of health beginning in 1945 as 'the initiation of the Health Service', based upon the Beveridge Report.[7] Harold Macmillan's biographer, following his subject, repeated this argument.[8] The assumption that in creating the NHS the Labour Cabinet and Parliament merely implemented the Beveridge Report is not confined to Conservatives. It was accepted in some of the most intellectually sophisticated circles of the Labour Party.[9] Nor is this assumption confined to politicians. It is articulated in recent serious scholarly literature. The Act of 1946 is described as based on the 'Beveridge model',[10] which the Labour Party 'set about implementing',[11] and as incorporating 'the principles of the Beveridge Report',[12] which was 'put into effect'[13] by the NHS Act. The Labour Cabinet 'enacted'[14] the Beveridge Report.

Perhaps revealingly, a possible alternative interpretation, that creation of the NHS flowed naturally from a long-standing explicit policy commitment of the Labour Party, appears seldom in the relevant scholarly literature. There are occasional suggestions that one or another specific aspect of the NHS had been a 'principle of official Socialist policy' or 'the Labour Party's declared policy'.[15] That Labour or Conservative party members, or voters, expected, eagerly or otherwise, the Labour minister of health to introduce his radically innovative NHS bill in 1946 is, at the least, not widely argued. If that minister had merely been expressing either a national or a Labour Party consensus (or conceivably both), his bill might have been effectively representative, but hardly creative, introducing 'little that was new'.[16]

As it is, the second major alternative interpretation of creation of the NHS sees the Labour minister of health, Aneurin Bevan, as the creator, working essentially alone as well as *de novo*, following neither a national consensus nor an established party line. Bevan himself referred to 'my' Health Service,[17] and many others have agreed. Whether the child is seen as healthy or deformed, Bevan is in this second interpretation seen as the sole parent, responsible for 'the inauguration of a free national health service'.[18] 'It was he who made the fundamental decisions';[19] he was 'the founder'[20] of the NHS, which was his 'creation'.[21] He was the 'architect',[22] who did 'construct one of the great British institutions of the twentieth century – the NHS'.[23] That institution is seen as the Emersonian lengthened shadow of one man. As long as that institution exists, it will, according to this interpretation, be associated with Bevan's name,[24] and his name will be associated with his creation, which is seen variously as his memorial, his monument, or his legacy.[25] That creation 'is synonymous with Bevan'.[26] Because of the importance of that creation, the result of Bevan's 'personal intervention',[27] Bevan was 'the chief architect of Britain's welfare state',[28] which assumes there was no British welfare state before 1945. That last assumption is certainly common enough.[29] One future Labour prime minister saw Bevan, personally, as 'the great innovator in health' who also 'triumphantly carried through Cabinet and Parliament a bold and imaginative' bill.[30] The Labour Party might here be seen as an obstacle, not as an originator. To another future Labour prime minister the creation of the NHS was 'brokered by' Bevan's 'imagination' and 'skill'.[31]

Not all perceptions of Bevan were so favourable. In the same speeches in which he claimed credit as the true parent of the NHS, Winston Churchill blamed 'the party and personal malignancy of Mr Bevan' for having 'plunged health policy into its present confusion'.[32] Since the National Health Service Act was then being implemented, Churchill's intent, if not his logic, was clear: he wished to blame Bevan while taking credit for any popular acceptance of Bevan's act. A few days after the NHS came into operation, and also a few days after the minister of health had referred to the Conservative Party which had earlier implemented the means test for welfare benefits as 'lower than vermin',[33] Churchill tried to do more than blame Bevan. This time his intent was to kill:[34]

> We speak of the minister of health, but ought we not rather to say the Minister of Disease, for is not morbid hatred a form of mental disease, moral disease, and indeed a highly infectious form? Indeed, I can think of no better step to signalize the inauguration of the National Health Service than that a person who so obviously needs psychiatrical attention should be among the first of its patients.[35]

Even though Churchill may himself here have been demonstrating 'morbid hatred',[36] Bevan, like all those who exercise power, needs to be understood, so that his act can be understood. This need exists even if a much-used textbook[37] is correct in arguing that the NHS 'did not spring, like Athene fully armed, from the head of Aneurin Bevan but was a point of rapid change in continuing growth'. A significant such point the NHS at the very least surely was. Even a hostile critic of Bevan's significance, who saw him as merely 'the end ... of a series of earlier plans', conceded that he was 'the important and conclusive end'.[38]

Evaluating the evidence for each of the two major interpretations of the creation of the NHS should illuminate that creation. Some aspects of each of these interpretations may have more validity than other aspects. Seeing even the less persuasive aspects may be useful, since the intellectual validity of a political belief is no measure of the tenacity with which it may be held. Myths about the past are often important motivations for political behaviour. Evaluating the evidence for both major interpretations may also clarify whether the third possible interpretation, that creation of the NHS was a long-standing explicit policy commitment of the Labour Party, deserves more credence than it has yet received. It was, after all, a Labour Cabinet and Parliament which approved the National Health Service bill.

NOTES

1. D. Kavanagh, 'The Postwar Consensus', *Twentieth Century British History*, 3, 2 (1992), p. 179.
2. R. James (ed.), *Winston S. Churchill: His Complete Speeches*, vol. 7 (New York: Chelsea House, 1974), pp. 7,629 and 7,674.
3. Ibid., p. 7,679.
4. Ibid., p. 7,822; R. James (ed.), *Winston S. Churchill: His Complete Speeches*, vol. 8 (New York: Chelsea House, 1974), pp. 7,993 and 8,106.
5. J. Hoffman, *The Conservative Party in Opposition 1945–51* (London: Macgibbon & Kee, 1964), p. 81.
6. Earl of Woolton, *The Memoirs of the Rt Hon. The Earl of Woolton* (London: Cassell, 1959), p. 281.
7. H. Macmillan, *Tides of Fortune 1945–1955* (London: Macmillan, 1969), p. 66.
8. A. Horne, *Macmillan: 1894–1956* (London: Macmillan, 1990), p. 297.
9. K. Martin, *Harold Laski (1893–1950): A Biographical Memoir* (New York: Viking, 1953), p. 150n; W. Rodgers and B. Donoughue, *The People into Parliament: A Concise History of the Labour Movement in Britain* (New York: Viking, 1966), p. 145.
10. M. Harrop (ed.), *Power and Policies in Liberal Democracies* (Cambridge: Cambridge University Press, 1992), p. 151.
11. R. Porter, *The Greatest Benefit to Mankind: A Medical History of Humanity* (New York: W. W. Norton, 1998), p. 652.
12. P. Hatcher, 'The Health System of the United Kingdom', in M. Raffel (ed.), *Health Care and Reform in Industrialized Countries* (University Park, PA: Pennsylvania State University Press, 1997), p. 229.

13. L. Freedman, *Politics and Policy in Britain* (White Plains, NY: Longman, 1996), p. 250.
14. S. Steinmo, K. Thelen and F. Longstreth (eds), *Structuring Politics: Historical Institutionalism in Comparative Analysis* (Cambridge: Cambridge University Press, 1997), p. 217.
15. R. Lovell, *Churchill's Doctor: A Biography of Lord Moran* (London: Royal Society of Medical Services, 1992), p. 294.
16. A. Willcocks, *The Creation of the National Health Service: A Study of Pressure Groups and a Major Social Policy Decision* (London: Routledge & Kegan Paul, 1967), p. 28.
17. P. Hollis, *Jennie Lee: A Life* (Oxford: Oxford University Press, 1997), p. 168.
18. G. Foote, *The Labour Party's Political Thought: A History*, 2nd edn (London: Croom Helm, 1986), p. 191.
19. A. Sked and C. Cook, *Post-war Britain: A Political History*, 2nd edn (Harmondsworth: Penguin, 1984), p. 42.
20. J. Campbell, *Lloyd George: The Goat in the Wilderness* (London: Jonathan Cape, 1977), p. 165.
21. P. Clarke, *Hope and Glory: Britain 1900–1990* (London: Penguin, 1997), p. 239; K. Morgan, *Rebirth of a Nation: Wales 1880–1980* (Oxford: Oxford University Press, 1987), p. 345.
22. D. Widgery, *Health in Danger: The Crisis in the National Health Service* (Hamden, CT: Archon, 1979), p. 25.
23. G. Goodman (ed.), *The State of the Nation: The Political Legacy of Aneurin Bevan* (London: Victor Gollancz, 1997), p. 226.
24. Ibid., p. 106.
25. Ibid., pp. 11, 64, 182, 231; K. Morgan, *Labour in Power 1945–1951* (Oxford: Oxford University Press, 1985), p. 163.
26. P. Hennessy, *Never Again: Britain 1945–1951* (London: Vintage, 1993), p. 133.
27. Goodman, *State of the Nation*, p. 124.
28. Sked and Cook, *Post-war Britain*, p. 48.
29. Clarke, *Hope and Glory*, p. 302; A. King (ed.), *Britain at the Polls, 2001* (New York: Chatham House, 2002), p. 20; A. Rowse, *Glimpses of the Great* (Lanham, MD: University Press of America, 1985), p. 70; J. Stevenson, *British Society 1914–45* (Harmondsworth: Penguin, 1984), p. 296; H. Wilson, *A Prime Minister on Prime Ministers* (New York: Summit Books, 1977), p. 278.
30. J. Callaghan, *Time and Change* (London: Fontana, 1988), pp. 68, 94.
31. Goodman, *State of the Nation*, p. 12.
32. James, *Winston S. Churchill*, vol. 7, pp. 7,629 and 7,674.
33. M. Foot, *Aneurin Bevan: A Biography*, vol. 2 (New York: Atheneum, 1974), p. 238.
34. Ibid., p. 243; Goodman, *State of the Nation*, p. 98.
35. James, *Winston S. Churchill*, vol. 7, p. 7,679.
36. Goodman, *State of the Nation*, p. 100.
37. O. Keidan, 'The Health Services', in A. Forder (ed.), *Penelope Hall's Social Services of England and Wales* (New York: Routledge & Kegan Paul, 1969), p. 137.
38. Willcocks, *Creation of National Health Service*, p. 104.

2

Conservatives

In evaluating the argument that there was a national consensus in 1945–48 supporting the creation of the National Health Service, the simplest (but not necessarily excessively simple) matter may be the legislative behaviour of the Conservative Party. Its leader, Winston Churchill, stated in 1948 that 'we supported in principle' Bevan's NHS bill.[1] If so, Conservative practice did not coincide with Conservative principle. At all its procedural stages in the House of Commons the NHS bill was opposed by Conservatives. Even before the third, final, reading of the bill, often a formality, Churchill mobilized his troops into opposition.[2] Whatever words may be used to describe creation of the NHS, 'consensus' should not be among them.[3] Bevan encountered 'dogged obstruction'[4] and 'virulent opposition'[5] from Conservative Members of Parliament. To argue that 'the whole Tory party' fought a long campaign against the NHS[6] is, however, excessive. So is a playwright's claim that the NHS was forced 'through in the teeth of the Conservative Party'.[7] The Conservative Party's response to Bevan's bill was in fact 'fudged'.[8] A Conservative whip was not applied in the House of Lords consideration of a crucial part of Bevan's bill, that nationalizing all British hospitals.[9] This particular issue had substantial potential for electorally effective Conservative partisanship, because many voluntary hospitals had long been closely affiliated with Conservative pillars of local communities.[10] A defeat for Bevan's bill in the House of Lords, where Conservatives were in the majority, could easily have been accomplished. Such a defeat would not have killed Bevan's bill, but it would have been at least politically embarrassing for its author. Such a delay would have sent a strong Conservative Party message of support to and for its local notables. Party leadership had never been Churchill's strength, and it was not so now.

Even in the House of Commons, Conservative speeches critical of Bevan's bill lacked both focus and political effectiveness. The Opposition's reaction there could fairly be termed clumsy. Richard Law (later Lord Coleraine), speaking for the Opposition, was unhelpfully caught in a falsehood by Bevan. Lesser lights such as Law were speaking for that Opposition because its leader remained mute in Commons debate on the creation of the NHS.[11] Churchill apparently chose not to challenge Bevan directly over health policy in the minister's presence, although he so freely criticized Bevan in other, extraparliamentary, surroundings in his absence. This situational silence may have resulted from prudence. If Conservatives generally underestimated Bevan,[12] their leader did not. Churchill respected, admired, and perhaps feared Bevan's parliamentary debating skills. These skills had been developed while Bevan was at best a recovering stammerer who also lisped.[13] These were, of course, the same speech defects with which Churchill had so long struggled.[14] Bevan's extemporaneous maiden speech in the House of Commons, in 1929, had been an incisive attack on David Lloyd George and Winston Churchill.[15] Churchill had afterwards been one of the few privately to congratulate the maiden speaker: 'It is so seldom that we hear a real debating speech nowadays.'[16] A few years later Churchill presented Bevan a copy of his *Marlborough* inscribed 'To Aneurin Bevan with every good wish for a lifetime's happiness'.[17]

This expression of fraternal sentiment did not silence its recipient. Throughout the Second World War, Bevan was the most energetic and effective parliamentary critic of the prime minister,[18] whose leadership after 1940 he feared would cause Britain to lose the war.[19] The claim that during the Second World War 'there was room in the leadership for'[20] Bevan could not be less accurate. Since there was no wartime official Opposition in Parliament there was no leader of the Opposition, which may later have confused some scholars. Bevan in effect played that role,[21] sparing few supporters of the government. In August 1940 he characterized Ernest Thurtle, a Labour Member of Parliament who had, Bevan thought, too robustly defended the prime minister, as a 'pimp'. The Speaker of the House of Commons, generally vigilant against unparliamentary language, did not insist on a retraction. The Speaker's tolerance in this case may have been apt, for Thurtle was eventually to receive office under Churchill as a junior information minister.[22] Thurtle was certainly flexible. He had earlier served as a lieutenant to his pacifist father-in-law, George Lansbury, in the latter's rise to leader of the Labour Party. Bevan may have been the only wartime Member of Parliament who 'could stand up to Churchill in debate and at the same time get across to the man on the street'.[23] One of his postwar Cabinet colleagues described Bevan as 'the greatest natural orator in the Party and he also had tremendous political sex appeal'.[24] Bevan not only held his own against Churchill, he may have been the most formidable debater in the House of Commons.[25] When, in 1951, he told the Commons he was resigning from the Labour Cabinet because he could not accept even proposed minor charges for NHS patients, Churchill told an assistant: 'I wish we had someone on *our* side who could speak like this.'[26] Churchill was not alone among Bevan's political opponents in admiring his speaking skills. Charles (later Lord) Hill, Secretary of the British Medical Association (BMA) during the creation of the NHS, and later Conservative Member of Parliament, conceded that Bevan was 'without doubt the best parliamentary speaker of his generation'.[27]

If Churchill remained silent in Commons debate over the NHS to avoid direct confrontation with Bevan, he nevertheless, or perhaps therefore, could have privately approached, directly or indirectly, Bevan to suggest particular changes in the NHS bill. In speaking for the Opposition, Richard Law pointedly criticized Bevan for having 'cast aside the opportunity to introduce a measure approved on all sides'.[28] The creation of the NHS contradicts the argument that in the British political system every Cabinet 'will tend to seek a compromise with' the Opposition.[29] If Bevan seemed unwilling to come to an agreement with Conservatives, the leader of the latter appears not to have attempted or approved any constructive initiative over the NHS. On another medical policy matter Churchill did indirectly approach Bevan on a Cabinet bill for which Bevan was responsible. That bill would have banned manufacture in Britain of heroin. After Robert Boothby, Churchill's faithful lieutenant, introduced a motion to reject this bill, Churchill told Boothby he would vote, and possibly speak, against the bill. Churchill asked Boothby to carry this message to Bevan. The message was received, and Bevan withdrew the bill.[30] On the much more important matter of the NHS, Churchill does not seem to have stirred himself. He was generally an unenthusiastic leader of the Opposition. When he did speak in Commons debate in that role he often sounded as if he were speaking as an individual rather than for his party.[31] Perhaps he was. In the case of the NHS, he neither spoke nor acted.

Health policy did not often much interest Churchill. He displayed as little general enthusiasm for it as for visiting other people's sickbeds. He was soon bored by even brief friendly discussion of the most basic aspects of health policy.[32] When, during the Second World War, minister of health Ernest Brown submitted a memorandum to the prime minister, Brown got it back with only one set of annotations, by the prime minister's personal physician.[33] Brown's health policy preferences would, in any event, have said nothing about any Conservative Party commitment, because Brown was a National Liberal, an orphaned offshoot of a fading third party. Brown's successor as minister of health was Henry Willink, a barrister who identified himself as a National Conservative, not quite a Conservative just as Brown was not quite a Liberal. Willink's ministerial appointment at Health, until July 1945, was his first and last ministerial position. It would probably be fair to judge both Brown and Willink as 'rather second-rate Ministers',[34] but Willink at least left behind the 1944 White Paper cited by the Earl of Woolton as evidence of a Conservative commitment to the goal of a national health service. That White Paper had, however, been written by John Hawton, a civil servant at the Ministry of Health, and Willink's commitment to his own White Paper may have been minimal.[35] Churchill's only involvement with the Willink White Paper seems to have been to ask, at Cabinet, a few questions about its content, questions clearly inspired by his personal physician.[36] Willink later opposed Bevan's bill on the grounds that it did not follow his own White Paper. This objection was certainly based on fact. In writing his bill Bevan had ignored the Willink White Paper, which he discarded as soon as he became minister of health.[37] That discarding was dramatically literal. He had taken Willink's recommendations home to read over a weekend. On his return he threw the document into his ministry wastebasket, describing it to his civil servants as 'no good'.[38] If Ernest Brown had left any health policy recommendations, they would doubtless have suffered the same fate at Bevan's hands. The latter had a long-standing contempt for Brown flowing from what seemed to him Brown's reactionary policies as minister of labour in the great depression of the 1930s. It had been while protesting against Brown's policies that in 1937 Bevan was briefly suspended from the privileges of House of Commons membership.[39] Of Brown's work at Health there was not much evidence. The most significant social policy event to take place while Brown was there was publication in late 1942 of the Beveridge Report, which Brown had nothing to do with.

NOTES

1. James, *Winston S. Churchill*, vol. 7, p. 7,715.
2. Foot, *Aneurin Bevan*, vol. 2, pp. 156, 158; Goodman, *State of the Nation*, p. 92; N. Goodman, *Wilson Jameson: Architect of National Health* (London: George Allen & Unwin, 1970), p. 122; D. Owen, *In Sickness and In Health: The Politics of Medicine* (London: Quartet Books, 1976), p. 1; Sked and Cook, *Post-war Britain*, pp. 40–1.
3. H. Glennester, *British Social Policy since 1945* (Oxford: Blackwell, 1995), p. 52.
4. G. Goodman, *State of the Nation*, p. 90.
5. I. Bulmer-Thomas, *The Growth of the British Party System*, vol. 2 (London: John Baker, 1965), p. 176.
6. M. Foot, *Aneurin Bevan*, vol. 1 (London: Granada, 1982), p. 409.
7. A. Bennett, *Forty Years On, Getting On, Habeas Corpus, and Enjoy* (London: Faber & Faber, 1991), p. 156.
8. R. Rose, *Do Parties Make a Difference?*, 2nd edn (Chatham, NJ: Chatham House, 1984), p. 154.
9. S. Grimes, *The British National Health Service: State Intervention in the Medical Marketplace, 1911–1948* (New York: Garland, 1991), p. 168.
10. Widgery, *Health in Danger*, p. 27.
11. P. Addison, *Churchill on the Home Front 1900–1955* (London: Pimlico, 1993), p. 390; T. Burridge, *Clement Attlee: A Political Biography* (London: Jonathan Cape, 1985), p. 195; H. Dalton, *High Tide and After: Memoirs 1945–1960* (London: Frederick Muller, 1962), p. 362; Foot, *Aneurin Bevan*, vol. 2, pp. 147, 254; F. Gray, 'How GPs Came to Heel in NHS', *Pulse*, 41, 48 (1981), p. 14; D. Howell, *British Social Democracy: A Study on Development and Decay* (London: Croom Helm, 1976), p. 152; Sked and Cook, *Post-war Britain*, pp. 44–5.
12. Sked and Cook, *Post-war Britain*, p. 41.
13. Foot, *Aneurin Bevan*, vol. 1, pp. 19–20, 29, 39, 42, 97; G. Goodman, *State of the Nation*, pp. 77, 86, 92, 120, 233; P. Howarth, *George VI: A New Biography* (London: Hutchinson, 1987), p. 191; J. Wheeler-Bennett, *King George VI: His Life and Reign* (London: Macmillan, 1958), p. 652.
14. M. Rintala, *Lloyd George and Churchill: How Friendship Changed Politics* (Lanham, MD: Madison Books, 1995), p. 634.
15. Campbell, *Lloyd George*, pp. 258–9; G. Goodman, *State of the Nation*, pp. 84–5; J. Grigg, *The Young Lloyd George* (London: Eyre Methuen, 1973), p. 100.
16. Foot, *Aneurin Bevan*, vol. 1, p. 108.
17. Ibid., p. 242n.
18. V. Brittain, *Diary 1939–1945: Wartime Chronicle*, A. Bishop and Y. Bennett (eds), (London: Victor Gollancz, 1989), p. 159; Bulmer-Thomas, *Growth of British Party System*, vol. 1, p. 146; W. Churchill Jr, *His Father's Son: The Life of Randolph Churchill* (London: Phoenix, 1997), pp. 224–5; Clarke, *Hope and Glory*, p. 222; W. and A. Eden Green (eds), *Testament of a Peace Lover: Letters from Vera Brittain* (London: Virago, 1988), p. 232; Foot, *Aneurin Bevan*, vol. 2, p. 32; G. Goodman, *State of the Nation*, pp. 51–2, 189–92; Hollis, *Jennie Lee*, pp. 109–11; T. Lindsay and M. Harrington, *The Conservative Party 1918–1970* (New York: St Martin's, 1974), p. 135; Morgan, *Rebirth of a Nation*, p. 297; H. Nicolson, *Diaries and Letters 1939–1945* (New York: Atheneum, 1967), p. 231.
19. Nicolson, *Diaries and Letters 1939–1945*, p. 244.
20. C. Parkinson, *Left Luggage: A Caustic History of British Socialism from Marx to Wilson* (Boston, MA: Houghton Mifflin, 1967), p. 172.
21. T. Driberg, *Ruling Passions* (New York: Stein & Day, 1979), p. 193; H. Pelling, *A Short History of the Labour Party*, 5th edn (New York: St Martin's, 1976), p. 90; Rodgers and Donoughue, *People into Parliament*, p. 139.
22. A. Roberts, *Eminent Churchillians* (New York: Simon & Schuster, 1994), pp. 176, 208.
23. C. King, *With Malice toward None: A War Diary* (London: Sidgwick & Jackson, 1970), p. 306.
24. Dalton, *High Tide*, p. 363.
25. Freedman, *Politics and Policy*, p. 136; G. Goodman, *State of the Nation*, pp. 189, 193; Hollis, *Jennie Lee*, p. 111.

26. M. Gilbert, *Winston S. Churchill*, vol. 8 (London: Minerva, 1990), p. 707n.
27. Lord Hill of Luton, *Both Sides of the Hill* (London: Heinemann, 1964), p. 92.
28. Foot, *Aneurin Bevan*, vol. 2, p. 147.
29. M. Rintala, 'The Two Faces of Compromise', *Western Political Quarterly*, 22 (1969), p. 327.
30. R. James, *Robert Boothby: A Portrait of Churchill's Ally* (New York: Viking, 1991), p. 339.
31. Hoffman, *Conservative Party in Opposition*, p. 268; Rintala, *Lloyd George and Churchill*, p. 147.
32. A. Boyle, *Poor Dear Brendan: The Quest for Brendan Bracken* (London: Hutchinson, 1974), p. 345; Lovell, *Churchill's Doctor*, pp. 266–7.
33. King, *With Malice toward None*, p. 253.
34. W. Mackenzie, *Power and Responsibility in Health Care: The National Health Service as a Political Institution* (Oxford: Oxford University Press, 1979), p. 155.
35. G. Goodman, *State of the Nation*, p. 113; Hennessy, *Never Again*, p. 135.
36. J. Pater, *The Making of the National Health Service* (London: King Edward's Hospital Fund for London, 1981), pp. 73–4.
37. Foot, *Aneurin Bevan*, vol. 2, pp. 118, 133, 147.
38. N. Goodman, *Wilson Jameson*, p. 121.
39. Foot, *Aneurin Bevan*, vol. 1, pp. 241, 256–7, 284.

3

Liberals: Past and Present

In view of the widespread belief that Bevan's National Health Service bill followed the health policy recommendations of the Beveridge Report, the latter needs clarification. Officially it was the Report of the Interdepartmental Committee on Social Insurance and Allied Services, which committee of civil servants existed even before Sir William (later Lord) Beveridge became its chairman. In 1941 Arthur Greenwood, who had been Labour minister of health in 1929–31, and was now minister without portfolio in the Coalition government, asked his party and Cabinet colleague Ernest Bevin, minister of labour and national service, to suggest a chairman for this interdepartmental committee. Bevin, eager to rid himself of what he saw as an irritatingly officious Beveridge, who was serving as Bevin's expert adviser on manpower,[1] called Greenwood with 'just the man for you. I'm sending Beveridge round in the morning'.[2] Beveridge was so sent, and appointed chairman by Greenwood.[3] The assertion that Beveridge was recruited by Conservatives[4] is without foundation. So is the claim[5] that the Coalition government asked Beveridge to recommend changes in the welfare system. The breadth of Beveridge's prescriptive intentions became apparent only after he began working on the committee when they were first noticed by his fellow civil servants on the committee. Those more cautious committee colleagues either chose, or were told by their civil service superiors, to reduce their committee participation. In the end, the Beveridge Report was Beveridge's report, as he proudly if imprudently proclaimed in public while campaigning for its approval by the Coalition government, as well as later.[6]

Bevin's motives in pushing Beveridge on Greenwood may have been impure, but his words were apt. Beveridge had long been acknowledged, including by himself, as one of Britain's most distinguished experts on social policy. He had held senior civil service and academic appointments. His civil service career had effectively begun when, in 1908, the Liberal president of the Board of Trade, Winston Churchill, had, at the urging of the prominent social reformers Beatrice and Sidney Webb, recruited Beveridge to the staff of the Board of Trade.[7] One of Beveridge's first actions at the Board of Trade had been to submit to his minister a lengthy memorandum on the need for unemployment insurance, with which recommendation Churchill soon agreed.[8] Beveridge's academic career had peaked as director of the London School of Economics and Political Science, 1919–37, during which time he was narrowly elected[9] to serve as vice-chancellor of the University of London, 1926–28. He knew, and was known by, many of the most senior members of the British political elite. He was not, however, always able to use those personal relationships to influence policy. At no stage was he personally involved in policy discussions of either the wartime Coalition or the postwar Labour Cabinets.[10] His aggressive manner of speaking was unhelpful,[11] contributing to the impression that he was 'an incompetent and self-advertising old humbug'.[12] Beveridge's most serious personal weakness, however, was his acute sense of superiority.[13] He may have been omnipresent but not omnipotent precisely because he considered himself omniscient. He did not hide his contempt for particular any more than all politicians. In January 1945 he described Churchill as a querulous old man no longer of any political importance.[14] During the Second World War, at the same time as he was aggravating Ernest Bevin, he was annoying two other senior Labourites, Lord Privy Seal and deputy prime minister Clement Attlee and minister for economic affairs Hugh Dalton, by treating them as if he were still director of the London School and they were still junior faculty members there, Attlee as lecturer (1913–23) and Dalton as reader (1920–35). As director he had been especially arrogant towards faculty members identified with the Labour Party.[15] This patronizing treatment was even less helpful when the NHS was being created, for now Attlee was prime minister and Dalton chancellor of the exchequer. Beveridge was not much better at cultivating younger rising political stars. The only reference to Aneurin Bevan in his published memoirs, which end effectively with the general election of 1945, is an icy mention of Bevan's criticism of Beveridge's chairmanship of the interwar Unemployment Insurance Statutory Committee. Even though Beveridge saw the world from an intensely personal perspective, in which a tooth infection was reported as a medical crisis, he omitted in his memoirs mention of the fact that Bevan may have been the most adamant wartime political supporter of the Beveridge Report.[16]

The claim that the Beveridge Report 'caught the imagination of Mr Churchill and some of his colleagues'[17] is far from the truth. Even further removed is the assertion that 'all parties were committed'[18] to the Beveridge Report. In 1943 the Coalition government refused to commit itself to implementation of the policy recommendations of the Beveridge Report. Neither the prime minister, leader of the Conservative Party, nor the deputy prime minister, leader of the Labour Party, was enthusiastic about the report.[19] Since both disliked its author,[20] this was perhaps predictable. Creation of a Social Security League to mobilize popular support for implementation of Beveridge's proposals[21] may not have reduced that dislike. Prime Minister Churchill did his best to smother the report when it was published. He made a stinging attack on it in a personal memorandum to his Cabinet colleagues, and his formal statement to them made it clear that he would not allow implementation of the report before the next general election.[22]

This coldness to the Beveridge Report is unsurprising. The Cabinet was, after all, dominated by Conservatives and Labourites, and Beveridge was neither. He was a non-socialist collectivist,[23] aptly described by Bevan in 1942 as 'a social evangelist of the old Liberal School'. This was by no means a fatal flaw in Bevan's eyes. He commended the Beveridge Report for describing 'the conditions in which the tears might be taken out of capitalism'. Bevan's continuation was intended to be even more generous, although Beveridge would hardly have been pleased: 'We should not be surprised, therefore, if all unconsciously by so doing he threatens capitalism itself.'[24]

Beveridge's heart had always been Liberal, and in 1944 he finally joined the Liberal Party in order to stand, successfully, as its candidate in a wartime parliamentary by-election.[25] A year earlier he had accepted the advice of a sitting Liberal Member of Parliament not to stand as an opposition candidate in a by-election that year, to avoid aggravating the prime minister, who might still eventually accept the recommendations of the Beveridge Report. That sitting Liberal had not himself practised such passivity, instead actively aiding many backbench Labour and a few Liberal members of the House of Commons to push for implementation of Beveridge's recommendations. That sitting Liberal had also voted with those backbenchers against the Cabinet's decision not to implement the report.[26] That sitting

Liberal was David Lloyd George, casting what turned out to be his last House of Commons vote after 53 uninterrupted years as a Member of Parliament. Immediately after some, if not nearly enough, backbenchers had voted for his plan and against the government, Beveridge revealed: 'I am having the fun of my life' because his report might yet 'bring down a Government'.[27] Although defeated for re-election to the House of Commons in the 1945 general election, Beveridge remained an eminent Liberal. After the death of Lloyd George in early 1945, Beveridge may well have been Britain's pre-eminent Liberal. His report served his party as not only a valuable policy document, but as an election manifesto in 1945. Indeed, the Beveridge Report may have been in effect the only manifesto the Liberal Party offered voters in that election.[28]

Lloyd George's support, and the ensuing centrality for the Liberal Party of the Beveridge Report, were both appropriate because it was a solidly Liberal document, a direct descendant of pre-1914 Liberal social reform.[29] Even shortly before the First World War, however, it would not have been an example of the most advanced Liberal social policy. The essence of Liberal social policy after the party's landslide 1906 general election victory was willingness to tax the rich to give to the poor.[30] That willingness was most dramatically expressed in Chancellor Lloyd George's controversial 1909 Budget, which taxed landowners to help pay for old age pensions.[31] Since that year, but only then, the Budget has been used to redistribute income from the rich to the poor by every left-of-centre British government.[32] Beveridge was no Lloyd George. In 1942 he told the other members of his committee that poverty 'could be abolished by a re-distribution of income within the working classes, without touching any of the wealthier classes at all'.[33] This meant that better-paid employed workers would financially support their less fortunate, including unemployed, colleagues. Capitalism was, or at least the capitalists were, safe.

Beveridge's own summary of his report described it as 'based on the contributory principle of giving benefits as of right in return for contributions rather than free allowances from the State'.[34] This principle of insurance was a reversion to the Liberal past, not a signpost to the Labour future. Bevan eliminated rather than expanded insurance coverage under the 1911 National Insurance Act, as natural growth of that Act would have suggested.[35] To describe the Beveridge Report as 'designed to establish basic rights'[36] is, at best, one-sided. Beveridge was in fact embarrassed to be identified as father of the British 'welfare state', which term he disliked, preferring 'social service state', which to him implied that citizens had duties as well as rights. He was even more embarrassed to be identified as creator of the National Health Service, on the grounds that Bevan was such. The NHS was not his child. In 1942 he had declined to embrace a complete takeover of medical services by the state.[37]

Beveridge could not have claimed paternity of the NHS even if he had wanted to. The assertion that the Beveridge Report included 'proposals for a national health service'[38] is misleading. The assertion that Beveridge had 'always advocated'[39] creation of a national health service is doubly misleading. His report merely assumed there would be such a service. Beveridge's own summary of his report also assumed there would be some kind of national health service without revealing its nature or how it would be implemented. In contrast to the plethora of detail on other forms of social insurance, the text of the report essentially ignored medical insurance.[40] In a radio speech shortly after its publication, Beveridge argued that, if his report were implemented, 'everyone will be insured' for, among other human needs, 'medical treatment', by 'a single weekly contribution paid through one insurance stamp'.[41]

Few Britons read Beveridge's report. Many listened to his radio speech. Perhaps more of his radio audience might have listened more closely to what he recalled of the British past:

> The plan, as I have set it out briefly, is a completion of what was begun a little more than thirty years ago when Mr Lloyd George introduced National Health Insurance, and Mr Winston Churchill, then President of the Board of Trade, introduced Unemployment Insurance. The man who led us to victory in the last war was the Minister responsible for Health Insurance. The Minister who more than thirty years ago had the courage and imagination to father the scheme of Unemployment Insurance, a thing then unknown outside Britain, is the man who is leading us to victory in this war.[42]

Beveridge's history was a bit rusty, but the core of his message was truthful. By the time the National Insurance bill of 1911, Part II of which created unemployment insurance, had been introduced into the House of Commons, Churchill was no longer president of the Board of Trade, where his successor, Sydney Buxton, played little role in writing or passing that bill. Churchill had at the Board of Trade already done most of the preparatory work for Part II,[43] so he properly deserved credit from Beveridge.

In contrast to his unjustified claim to credit for the National Health Service Act of 1946, Churchill had earlier modestly described himself as involved 'only in a minor way' in the National Insurance Act of 1911, giving instead the credit to 'one man' who was 'a man of genius – a man of courage, armed with power'.[44] Three decades later, Churchill repeated that he had shared in a minor way 'in making the Act of 1911'[45] for which Lloyd George was responsible. David Lloyd George was in 1911 not reluctant to take such credit, for 'I have devoted three years of labour, research, consultation, and continuous thought to that proposal'.[46] That statement was not much of an exaggeration. Like the People's Budget of 1909, national insurance was very much Lloyd George's personal project.[47] At the end of a 1911 speech in Birmingham, he elaborated on this personal commitment to his bill:

> This year, this Session I have joined the Red Cross. I am in the ambulance corps. I am engaged to drive a wagon through the twistings and turnings and ruts of the Parliamentary road. There are men who tell me I overloaded that wagon. I have taken three years to pack it carefully. I cannot spare a single parcel, for the suffering is very great. There are those who say that my wagon is half-empty. I say it is as much as I can carry. Now there are some who say I am in a great hurry. I am rather in a hurry, for I can hear the moanings of the wounded, and I want to carry relief to them, in the alleys, the homes where they lie stricken.[48]

Even though Churchill had not been driving the ambulance wagon, he enthusiastically embraced all, not merely Part II, of the 1911 Act. Churchill informed George V that the Act 'is far more important to the prosperity contentment & security of Your Majesty's Kingdom, than any other measure of our times'.[49] That might well have been true. It might well also be true that, lesser than Lloyd George's as it was, Churchill's role in the 1911 Act may have been the most important legislative achievement of his long political career.

Beveridge's assertion that unemployment insurance had been invented in Britain was much further off the mark than his acknowledgement of Churchill's 1911 role. The first welfare state had been created in Imperial Germany several decades before 1911, by Chancellor Otto von Bismarck. The Iron Chancellor proudly saw his system of social insurance as 'the finest work of our government which has been so clearly blessed by God'.[50]

Churchill's claim to George V had referred only to an earthly kingdom. Bismarck's claim, involving a heavenly kingdom as well, was made in a political system where the divine right of kings, and their chancellors, was still articulated without shame. Although Bismarck eventually contemplated including unemployment insurance,[51] that aspect was still missing from the German welfare state when his ministerial career ended in 1890. By 1911, Luxembourg, Norway and Serbia, among other European states, had already followed in Germany's social policy footsteps, and Belgium had created an unemployment insurance system. Since old-age pensions had already been initiated in Britain by Lloyd George, the 1911 Act was not even the first legislation to move towards a British welfare state. The British pension system was, however, not insurance, since it was financed from taxation, not participants' contributions.

Lloyd George had been much impressed by Bismarck's welfare state during a 1908 visit, early in his chancellorship of the exchequer, to Germany. The contributory aspect especially caught his observant eye.[52] Two years later he sent W. J. Braithwaite, one of his senior civil servants, to investigate in further detail the German health insurance system. Lloyd George used the German system as his model for much of the National Insurance bill.[53] Already in 1908 he had urged Prime Minister H. H. Asquith to 'thrust a big slice of Bismarkianism [*sic*] over the whole underside of our industrial system'.[54] It is therefore not surprising that Lloyd George privately described the 1911 bill as being 'on German lines'[55] or that in 1911, equally privately, Churchill saw Lloyd George as having 'imported' social insurance from Germany.[56] The panel system, in which local insurance committees drew up lists of participating doctors from which patients could choose their own doctors, was borrowed from Germany. Even the German practice of stamped insurance cards, which aroused much initial hostility in Britain, was imported.[57] Churchill had no objection to such borrowing. Perhaps more surprising was Lloyd George's explicit public praise[58] for details of the German health insurance system and Churchill's public praise, while First Lord of the Admiralty, for the 1911 Act for being 'as great as anything which Bismarck ever did for the social life of Germany'.[59] This British act was, in turn, seen favourably in advanced German social policy circles before 1914.[60]

The German roots of the British welfare state were hardly likely to be stressed, or even acknowledged, by Beveridge, Lloyd George, Churchill or perhaps anyone else in Britain during the

Second World War. Those roots nevertheless existed. To refer, however, to Lloyd George's 'conversion to social reform during his visit to Germany in the summer of 1908'[61] is seriously misleading. Lloyd George needed no such conversion. His commitment to social reform was of much longer standing.[62] He knew without visiting Germany that ambulance wagons were needed in Britain. 1908 was undeniably an important year in Lloyd George's creation of a welfare state in Britain. In 1912, Churchill recalled visiting Lloyd George four years earlier at the latter's home in north Wales, 'and in two days very memorable to me hearing him outline and unfold the whole of the vast project of the Budget of 1909 and the national insurance scheme against sickness and unemployment'.[63] Lloyd George had on that occasion recently returned from Germany. He went there in 1908 not seeking a political cause but because as the new chancellor of the exchequer he was finally in a position to implement his vision of social justice. He had been preaching that vision long enough. His persistent advocacy of non-contributory old-age pensions, for instance, went back at least as far as 1892.[64]

As his ambulance wagon speech acknowledged, Lloyd George was fully aware that the health insurance system he created in 1911 was imperfect. Along with a relatively small (about one-sixth) contribution from the Treasury, that system was financed essentially by contributions, not general tax revenues.[65] It was therefore based on insurance, not on the entitlement of every British person. Most people were uncovered. Except for a modest maternity benefit, the 1911 Act covered only employed persons, not their dependents. Women and children were mostly excluded. If they were to visit a physician, therefore, most male workers' wives and all their children had to go as private patients. Even for employed workers the most expensive medical problems were not covered. Insurance payments could be made only for out-patient visits to participating general practitioners, not to specialized consultant doctors or to hospitals, as provided for in the German system. Lloyd George's ambulance wagon did not go to hospitals. So major surgery as well as most complicated diagnostic procedures were not covered.[66] These various gaps in coverage, Beveridge was to argue in his 1942 radio address, needed to be filled but, as he acknowledged, everything about 'how' that would be accomplished was 'left open' in his report 'for further enquiry'.[67] Even if Churchill's Coalition government had agreed to implement the Beveridge Report little that was new would have happened in health policy.

In 1911, Lloyd George had no expectation that his Act would prove permanent. He noted to R. G. Hawtrey, his private secretary: 'Insurance necessarily temporary expedient. At no distant date hope State will acknowledge full responsibility in the matter of making provision for sickness breakdown and unemployment ... Insurance will then be unnecessary.'[68] Lloyd George's 1911 hope remained long unrealized. In interwar Britain few members of the British establishment shared that hope. Even a social reformer like William Temple, future Archbishop of Canterbury, could not envisage such entitlement.[69] The health insurance system created by Lloyd George lasted for 35 years.

Even with its inadequacies, the 1911 health insurance system worked, and on the whole, worked well. For the first time, most British workers had ready and regular access to a general practitioner of their choice for medical advice and treatment. Ten million people who had no previous medical insurance were now insured. All this was accomplished in an actuarially sound manner.[70] Implementation was quick. The first contributions were received in July 1912 and the first payments were made in January 1913.[71] The Act was amended in 1913, 1918, 1920, 1922, 1924, 1928, 1932, 1934 and 1936, in relatively minor ways. The chief consequence of these legislative changes was gradually to expand coverage from approximately one-third to more than one-half of the British population.[72] The administrative structure Lloyd George created in 1911 was still essentially intact in 1948 when the National Health Service Act replaced the National Insurance Act.[73]

That a structure intended by its architect[74] to be temporary served usefully so long suggests that its architect had designed well. Perhaps no other British politician could have pushed the National Insurance bill through Cabinet and Parliament in 1911.[75] Certainly no other senior British politician had before him tried to do such a thing. Since the late nineteenth century, when the Poor Law Board had been merged with the Local Government Board, the latter ministry had responsibility for what national health policy Britain had.[76] Lloyd George's own Cabinet colleague, John Burns, the president of the Local Government Board, had done nothing about health insurance even when so urged by his expert advisers. Considering the general lack of enthusiasm for social reform among these advisers,[77] Burns' indolence is especially notable. As chancellor of the exchequer, Lloyd George had behind him no established specialized ministry of health to create, or to implement, his system.[78] Such a specialized ministry of health, first urged in 1820 by Jeremy Bentham, was not created until, as prime minister, Lloyd George pushed enabling legislation through Parliament in 1918. The 1911 Act had, however, already created the National Research Committee, later incorporated as the Medical Research Council.[79] Wilmot Herringham, a senior physician at St Bartholomew's Hospital, London, and vice-chancellor of the University of London, saw in 1919 this creation as 'a momentous event' for medical research in Britain, adding: 'It is worthy of note that neither of the two [*sic*] official parties moved a finger in this direction. What has been accomplished we owe to the insight of a single individual, Mr Lloyd George.'[80]

Lloyd George wanted in 1911 not only to push the National Insurance bill through Parliament, but he wanted to do so with the support of as many Members of Parliament as possible. He therefore went considerably out of his way to be friendly to likely opponents. Now, as on many other occasions,[81] he attempted to straddle all parties. For him parties had only instrumental, not inherent, value.[82] The inherent value was for him policies, not parties.[83] Coalitions were his preferred strategy. He would have been happy to see political allegiance transferred from party to nation.[84] This bill was therefore intentionally named. To Lloyd George the National Insurance Act would increase a common sense of British nationhood by requiring contributions by employers and taxpayers as well as the larger contributions by employees. The compulsory nature of these contributions alienated many traditionally individualistic Liberals, but such contributions appealed to those Conservatives who favoured an organic theory of the state. The bitterly partisan F. E. Smith (later Earl of Birkenhead) acknowledged this when he told his fellow Conservatives that Lloyd George's bill bound 'the employer, the State, and the employee in a common bond, and it recognized the solidarity of the nation'.[85]

Lloyd George never accepted for himself the primacy of party loyalty, but he fully understood its significance for most Members of Parliament. So, introducing his bill in the Commons, he appealed to 'all parties ... to help the Government not merely to carry this bill through but to fashion it; to strengthen it where it is weak, to improve it where it is faulty'.[86] He asserted later that this offer had been unprecedented.[87] This may well have been a valid assertion. Lloyd George's offer was not only novel, it was taken seriously by him and by many others. To characterize the legislative progress of the National Insurance bill as 'almost miraculously free from opposition'[88] is an overstatement, but, considering the level of partisan acrimony over the simultaneous consideration of the Parliament bill, which in stripping the House of Lords of its legislative power had enraged the Conservative Opposition, Lloyd George succeeded surprisingly well in muting party disagreements over the National Insurance bill. Although he was also the chief political architect of the Parliament bill,[89] he let his Cabinet colleagues, especially Churchill, manage the Commons debate over the Parliament bill.[90] For Lloyd George social reform was far more important than the constitutional question. The National Insurance bill was his bill, not the Liberal Party's bill. Many Liberals, in Cabinet and Parliament, were unenthusiastic about social reform.[91] Lloyd George's personal priority helped pacify Conservatives over the National Insurance bill, the first two readings of which were carried without a division of the House of Commons. The second reading overlapped especially closely with final Commons consideration of the Parliament bill.[92] H. W. Forster, speaking for the Conservative Opposition, had praised Lloyd George's handling of an early draft of his bill as that of a 'master of the art of conciliation, and no one could pilot a difficult bill through the House with more success'.[93] Privately, Austen Chamberlain, a senior Conservative, recorded his first impressions of the health insurance part of the 1911 bill as 'bold, sound and comprehensive and in many respects original. This is Lloyd George's part.' Soon, equally privately, Chamberlain also recorded the ultimate compliment from a politician about a successful political opponent: 'His Sickness scheme *is* a good one and he is on the right lines this time. I must say I envy him the opportunity and I must admit that he has made good use of it.'[94] While Conservatives did not support the bill on its third, final, reading in the House of Commons, some of them did take up Lloyd George's offer to participate in framing the bill's final version. One of them, Leo Amery, much later happily recalled Lloyd George's 'imaginative, constructive radicalism'[95] and his own 1911 experiences as the newest Member of Parliament, co-operating with other backbench Conservatives: 'We worked indefatigably and, I think, very much surprised Lloyd George by our mastery of the subject when the bill reached Committee. We certainly played a useful part in improving the Bill.'[96]

Lloyd George not only listened respectfully to individual Members of Parliament, however junior, of all parties. He carefully crafted and revised his bill in specific ways to achieve as broad support among all three parties – Liberal, Conservative and Labour – as possible. A young barrister, Wilfrid (later Lord) Greene, recruited to translate Lloyd George's decisions into statutory language, was often kept busy making overnight revisions.[97] Lloyd George's chief means of achieving consensus across parties was by expanding the list of approved societies to whom state medical benefits might be paid.[98] Originally he had contemplated only existing friendly societies as eligible to serve as such approved societies. Friendly societies were private nonprofit benevolent organizations whose members banded together for mutual insurance purposes, including receiving medical care from a panel of affiliated doctors. These members were typically either among the better-paid and/or more prudent members of the working classes or the least prosperous and therefore even more prudent members of the middle classes. They were, not surprisingly, likely to be at least potential Liberal Party voters. By 1911, many friendly societies were in financial difficulties. Their financial well-being would be buttressed by their selection as approved societies. This improvement was welcomed not only by members of financially distressed friendly societies, but also by those many Liberal members of Cabinet and Commons whose principled enthusiasm for social reform was less than Lloyd George's.

To attract Conservative support, or at least to blunt Conservative opposition, Lloyd George added commercial insurance companies, closely connected to the Conservative Party, to the list of potential approved societies. Lloyd George also faced determined opposition from many Labourites. Beatrice and Sidney Webb and their followers disapproved of insurance payments, which did not require character improvements in the recipients.[99] Such principled puritanism met with indifference from Lloyd George, but he did set out to appease those workers who resented the prospect of bearing the heaviest financial burden in the form of compulsory contributions.[100] Lloyd George further expanded the list of potential approved societies to include trade unions, giving workers another important reason to become and remain trade union members. When even this inducement to the trade union base of the Labour Party seemed inadequate, Lloyd George appealed successfully to the material interest of present and prospective Labour Members of Parliament. The first Labour members had introduced into the House of Commons during the previous decade a new phenomenon: substantial numbers of professional politicians who had no independent unearned income. Britain had long been a plutocracy, ruled by those who did not need parliamentary salaries. Unlike most Liberal and Conservative Members of Parliament, most Labour Members needed, if they were to have significant parliamentary careers, as

Max Weber would put it, to live off as well as for politics.[101] Lloyd George understood this problem. Before he began earning a ministerial salary in 1905, he had served 15 unpaid years as a Member of Parliament. Only his younger brother's energy in their joint law practice had kept Lloyd George solvent. By agreeing to introduce salaries for all Members of Parliament Lloyd George not only opened the possibility of parliamentary careers for non-rentier Liberals and Conservatives, but he also assured the support of Labour Members of Parliament for the National Insurance bill.[102] There were doubtless some less wealthy sitting Liberals and Conservatives who with their families also silently blessed the benevolent chancellor of the exchequer, however modest his initial gift.

Friendly societies, commercial insurance companies and trade unions were all material-interest-based pressure groups with a particular connection to a particular party. There was one further material-interest group, less connected to a particular party, which was a much sharper thorn in Lloyd George's side in 1911. That was the doctors; more precisely, the general practitioners who, the National Insurance bill assumed, would join a panel of doctors affiliated with a particular approved society. Since specialist and hospital doctors, mostly if not entirely overlapping groups in Britain then, would not be paid by approved societies, such doctors, and their representative organizations, did not lobby Lloyd George about his bill. Their absence made Lloyd George's task in 1911 much simpler, although not necessarily easier than Aneurin Bevan's task in creating the National Health Service during 1945–48. For all practical purposes the only relevant medical lobbying in 1911 was done by the British Medical Association (BMA), whose primary concern was the material interest of general practitioners. Faced with the National Insurance bill the BMA acted as a bourgeois trade union,[103] with, according to George Bernard Shaw, 'skill and ruthlessness impossible to our less instructed and more sentimental unions of labourers and mechanics. It was this union that, by the threat of a general strike, brought Mr Lloyd George to his knees over the Insurance Act.'[104] Shaw's criticism of the BMA's activity in 1911 has been echoed in scholarly judgements that the BMA 'played a shameful and obstructive role',[105] 'not one of which the Association has any cause to be proud'.[106] The BMA did little to improve medical aspects of the bill before it was enacted, making no effort, for instance, to rectify the bill's disconnection from existing public health services.[107] During the legislative process, Lloyd George, however, consulted the BMA as little as possible, on the privately expressed ground that 'A Deputation of Doctors is almost always a Deputation of swell Doctors: it is impossible to get a Deputation of poor Doctors or slum Doctors.'[108] This statement might have been more apt if specialist hospital physicians had been involved. Even if his rationalization had been true, Lloyd George's bill presupposed the willingness of a great many general practitioners to contract with the state to provide a service for workers outside slum areas. BMA members might well have had as much right to bargain collectively for their conditions of employment as labourers and mechanics, Shaw notwithstanding.

Instead of dealing with the BMA, in 1911 Lloyd George relied heavily on advice and assistance from a handful of doctors personally known to him. Especially active in this respect was Christopher (later Lord) Addison, a distinguished physician and eminent professor of anatomy with extensive experience in the East End of London, who had recently been elected a Liberal Member of Parliament.[109] Lloyd George organized a Liberal Insurance Committee, under Addison, to propagandize for the National Insurance bill.[110] Equally important, Addison conducted his own private canvass of doctors, finding, as he reported to Lloyd George, that enough general practitioners would enlist in panels of doctors even if the panel system were boycotted, as threatened, by the BMA. Addison's assistance was vital in Lloyd George's conflict of wills with the BMA.[111]

Shaw's statement that Lloyd George had been brought to his knees in 1911 by the BMA was far from the truth. The attempt at enforced genuflection was certainly made,[112] but it was unsuccessful. When Lloyd George eventually broke down and met with doctors' delegations he found it 'Most useful. I am in the saddle ... & I mean to ride hard over hurdles & ditches – & win.'[113] He did win, by the simple expedient of raising the per capita payment for each patient to each participating panel doctor to a level higher than the prevailing average annual income of British general practitioners. He thereby attracted younger and less prosperous doctors, glad to have the higher wages and security of a panel practice.[114] The 'swell Doctors' who could afford to talk of professional independence were left high and dry. Not for nothing had the chancellor of the exchequer, earlier president of the Board of Trade, settled or prevented many a strike. Lloyd George got his doctors, and his knees remained unbent.

Since Lloyd George was not only unbent but unbroken, the BMA was without a friend in a court that mattered even more to it now that Britain had a degree of state medicine. For many years the political influence of the BMA was weakened by its unsuccessful hard line in 1911. By contrast, after 1911 Addison became ever closer to both Lloyd George and Churchill.[115] During the First World War, Lloyd George established the first British governmental fund for medical research. In 1919, Addison was named by Prime Minister Lloyd George to be Britain's first minister of health.[116] At this point, the prime minister made a serious strategic error. Probably because Addison was being moved from the ministerial post of president of the Local Government Board, where his responsibilities had included housing policy, the new Ministry of Health was now assigned housing policy along with health policy.[117] Understandably responding to an urgent need for new housing immediately after the end of the First World War, Addison's preoccupation at his new ministry became housing policy. When more conservative (not necessarily all Conservative) members of Lloyd George's postwar coalition Cabinet objected to Addison's enthusiasm for encouraging the building of new housing by governmental subsidies, he was ungraciously sacked by the prime minister,[118] eager for a continued coalition between Liberals and Conservatives. In making Addison the scapegoat for Conservative criticism of his own housing policies, Lloyd George was far from his finest hour.[119] His prime ministership survived Addison's fall, but Addison's housing policies eventually survived even longer.

Those policies soon resurfaced. The heavy involvement of the British government in building homes began, but did not end, with Addison. He had made housing a social service.[120] His construction subsidies soon became the bone over which the animals were snarling.[121] When he became minister of health two years after Addison left, Neville Chamberlain, who had thought Addison's subsidies a good idea, restored as much of them as he could over opposition from many of his fellow Conservatives.[122] Chamberlain's return to construction subsidies was understandable, since in fact Addison's policy had built much new housing, and of a higher, more healthful quality than earlier construction.[123] Addison also survived, moving eventually to the Labour Party, where he had parliamentary and ministerial careers as distinguished as his earlier medical career had been.[124] The respect in which he was held in all parties and in both Houses of Parliament was evident when in April 1945 he was chosen, as a member of the House of Lords, to lead the British parliamentary delegation to visit Buchenwald, newly liberated.[125]

Lloyd George's unfortunate coupling of health and housing policies also long survived Addison's ministry. The idiosyncrasies of Addison's ministerial progress became enshrined in British governmental structure. Housing problems distracted interwar health ministers.[126] This lack of functional clarity still existed when Aneurin Bevan became minister of health in 1945. If unsatisfied need for more, and more adequate, housing was an important policy problem in Britain after the First World War, it was even more crucial after the damage done to Britain's housing stock by German bombs in the Second World War. Then one in three houses had been destroyed or damaged, and almost none built.[127] Britain had no minister of housing until 1951, when Prime Minister Churchill chose Harold Macmillan as such. A few months earlier, Prime Minister Attlee had finally removed housing policy from the Ministry of Health, assigning it to a resurrected Ministry of Local Government and Planning. Macmillan claimed, probably correctly, that he had chosen the name for the new Ministry of Housing.[128] He also, later, saw Bevan as having 'failed over his housing policy for the simple reason that the Ministry over which he presided was too wide in its responsibilities'.[129] Prime Minister Attlee certainly made a great administrative error by continuing with health and housing policies in the same ministry.[130] Bevan's housing policy was unpopular, and he himself does not seem to have regarded it as a success.[131] He had earlier spoken with enthusiasm on housing policy in the Commons,[132] but as minister of health he was preoccupied with other health matters.[133] He did, however, pay more attention to the quality of housing constructed than did Hugh Dalton, who eventually inherited housing policy later in Attlee's prime ministership.[134] Bevan's concern for the quality of public housing was of long standing.[135] After a solid start the quantity of housing construction under Bevan did decline, and as minister of health he was doubtless less successful in dealing with housing than health matters.[136] The unpopularity of his housing policy may have been inevitable. Public opinion polls in 1945 showed that for Britons new housing was their highest policy priority, ranking above even jobs.[137] Attlee's government nevertheless reversed this order, placing industrial reconstruction before new housing construction.[138]

Even though as leader of the Opposition he never attacked Bevan's health policy in the House of Commons, Churchill did, briefly, there refer to Bevan's housing policy in 1946:

But it is maddening for the people who need the homes and houses merely to see the right hon. Gentleman working out his little party spites, as well as personal and class spites which in the great position he now occupies he ought to have outlived. I have heard him described as a new Lloyd George. Good gracious me, it was certainly not by this kind of contribution that this former great Welshman made his name a household word which will long endure and be remembered in the homes of Britain.[139]

This was not in fact an attack on Bevan's housing policy, which may well have merited critical parliamentary discussion, but an attack on Aneurin Bevan for not being David Lloyd George. Campaigning in Wales in 1950, Churchill returned, a bit more coyly, to this theme: 'There can be no greater insult to his memory than to suggest that today Wales has a second Lloyd George. Oh, I think it much better not to mention names.'[140] To Churchill, no one could match Lloyd George, who was 'without a rival'.[141] Churchill's praise of his friend and leader may well have been justified, but if he was suggesting that Bevan's housing policy was inferior to Lloyd George's housing policy immediately after the First World War, his memory had failed him. No member of Lloyd George's Coalition Cabinet had defended Addison so strongly as Churchill when Lloyd George threw Addison to the Conservative wolves.[142] Churchill's favourite, Lloyd George, had not been the stifler of housing construction in 1921, but the architect of the twin peaks of the 1909 Budget and the National Insurance Act of 1911. Then Lloyd George had been 'the champion of the weak and the poor. Those were great days.'[143] That architect remained Churchill's benchmark for political leadership. In May 1945, while still prime minister, he had warned his personal physician: 'The doctors aren't going to dictate to the country, they tried to do that with Lloyd George.'[144]

NOTES

1. A. Bullock, *The Life and Times of Ernest Bevin*, vol. 2 (London: Heinemann, 1967), p. 225; Burridge, *Clement Attlee*, p. 150; K. Harris, *Attlee* (London: Weidenfeld & Nicolson, 1984), pp. 219, 236; Hennessy, *Never Again*, p. 72; H. Oxbury, *Great Britons: Twentieth-century Lives* (Oxford: Oxford University Press, 1985), p. 35; F. Williams, *A Prime Minister Remembers: The War and Post-war Memoirs of the Rt Hon. Earl Attlee* (London: Heinemann, 1961), p. 56.
2. K. Jeffreys, *The Churchill Coalition and Wartime Politics, 1940–1945* (Manchester: Manchester University Press, 1995), pp. 117–18.

3. Bulmer-Thomas, *Growth of British Party System*, vol. 2, p. 143; Pelling, *Short History*, p. 96.
4. Parkinson, *Left Luggage*, p. 126.
5. Freedman, *Politics and Policy*, p. 245.
6. W. Beveridge, *The Price of Peace* (New York: W. W. Norton, 1945), pp. 8, 11; Bulmer-Thomas, *Growth of British Party System*, vol. 2, p. 148; M. Cole, *The Life of G. D. H. Cole* (London: Macmillan, 1971), pp. 247–8; Stevenson, *British Society*, p. 454.
7. J. Grigg, *Lloyd George: The People's Champion 1902–1911* (Berkeley, CA: University of California Press, 1978), p. 314; J. Harris, *Unemployment and Politics: A Study in English Social Policy 1886–1914* (Oxford: Oxford University Press, 1972), pp. 207, 284–5.
8. R. Churchill, *Winston S. Churchill*, vol. 2, companion part 2 (London: Heinemann, 1969), pp. 852–3, 883–4; D. Cregier, *Bounder from Wales: Lloyd George's Career before the First World War* (Columbia, MO: University of Missouri Press, 1976), p. 164.
9. W. Beveridge, *Power and Influence* (New York: Beechhurst, 1955), pp. 193, 209.
10. Burridge, *Clement Attlee*, p. 150; J. Harris, *William Beveridge: A Biography* (Oxford: Clarendon, 1977), p. 448.
11. T. Jones, *A Diary with Letters 1931–1950* (London: Oxford University Press, 1954), p. 488.
12. R. Soloway, *Demography and Degeneration: Eugenics and the Declining Birthrate in Twentieth-century Britain* (Chapel Hill, NC: University of North Carolina Press, 1995), p. 313.
13. Burridge, *Clement Attlee*, p. 150; R. Lowe, *The Welfare State in Britain since 1945*, 2nd edn (London: Macmillan, 1999), p. 134.
14. King, *With Malice toward None*, p. 287.
15. J. Harris, *William Beveridge*, p. 369; I. Kramnick and B. Sherman, *Harold Laski: A Life on the Left* (New York: Allen Lane Penguin, 1993), pp. 323–6, 330; Martin, *Harold Laski*, pp. 63, 88–91; A. Taylor, *Politicians, Socialism and Historians* (New York: Stein & Day, 1982), pp. 174, 178.
16. Beveridge, *Power and Influence*, pp. 225, 266; Nicolson, *Diaries and Letters 1939–1945*, p. 281.
17. F. Williams, *Press, Parliament and People* (London: William Heinemann, 1946), p. 82.
18. Wilson, *A Prime Minister on Prime Ministers*, pp. 289–90.
19. Bullock, *Life and Times of Ernest Bevin*, vol. 2, pp. 226–7; Hollis, *Jennie Lee*, p. 105; Morgan, *Rebirth of a Nation*, p. 297; Pelling, *Short History*, p. 92.
20. Burridge, *Clement Attlee*, p. 150; F. Williams, *A Prime Minister Remembers*, p. 57.
21. M. Cole, *Life of G. D. H. Cole*, p. 241n.
22. W. Churchill, *The Hinge of Fate* (New York: Bantam, 1974), pp. 838–9; M. Green, *Children of the Sun: A Narrative of 'Decadence' in England after 1918* (New York: Basic Books, 1976), p. 312.
23. K. Morgan, *Consensus and Disunity: The Lloyd George Coalition Government 1918–1922* (Oxford: Clarendon, 1986), p. 21.
24. D. Hill (ed.), *Tribune 40: The First Forty Years of a Socialist Newspaper* (London: Quartet Books, 1977), pp. 4, 46.
25. Bulmer-Thomas, *Growth of British Party System*, vol. 2, p. 143; G. DeGroot, *Liberal Crusader: The Age of Sir Archibald Sinclair* (London: Hurst, 1993), p. 216; T. Jarman, *Socialism in Britain: From the Industrial Revolution to the Present Day* (New York: Taplinger, 1972), p. 177.
26. Beveridge, *Power and Influence*, pp. 324–5; Bullock, *Life and Times of Ernest Bevin*, vol. 2, p. 231; Bulmer-Thomas, *Growth of British Party System*, vol. 2, p. 148; Hennessy, *Never Again*, p. 76; Hollis, *Jennie Lee*, p. 112; R. McKenzie, *British Political Parties: The Distribution of Power within the Conservative and Labour Parties*, 2nd edn (New York: Frederick A. Praeger, 1963), p. 327; K. Morgan, *Labour People: Leaders and Lieutenants, Hardie to Kinnock* (Oxford: Oxford University Press, 1987), p. 199; Morgan, *Rebirth of a Nation*, p. 297; M. Pugh, *Lloyd George* (London: Longman, 1993), p. 180; Rodgers and Donoughue, *People into Parliament*, p. 141; P. Rowland, *Lloyd George* (London: Barrie & Jenkins, 1975), p. 789.
27. Nicolson, *Diaries and Letters 1939–1945*, p. 282.
28. Bulmer-Thomas, *Growth of British Party System*, vol. 2, p. 43; Clarke, *Hope and Glory*, p. 215; G. Goodman, *State of the Nation*, p. 52; M. Sissons and P. French (eds), *Age of Austerity 1945–51* (Harmondsworth: Penguin, 1964), p. 16.

29. DeGroot, p. 212; A. Heidenheimer, H. Heclo and C. Adams, *Comparative Public Policy: The Politics of Social Choice in America, Europe, and Japan* (New York: St Martin's, 1990), p. 239; Stevenson, *British Society*, pp. 455–6.
30. Pugh, *Lloyd George*, p. 47.
31. Rintala, *Lloyd George and Churchill*, p. 88.
32. Sissons and French, *Age of Austerity*, p. 190.
33. Beveridge, *Power and Influence*, p. 306.
34. W. Beveridge, *The Pillars of Security: And Other War-time Essays and Addresses* (New York: Macmillan, 1943), pp. 74–5.
35. Hollis, *Jennie Lee*, p. 105; J. Jewkes and S. Jewkes, *The Genesis of the British National Health Service*, 2nd edn (Oxford: Basil Blackwell, 1962), pp. 1–2; Stevenson, *British Society*, pp. 455–6.
36. Steinmo, Thelen and Longstreth, *Structuring Politics*, p. 217.
37. J. Harris, *William Beveridge*, pp. 448, 459; Nicolson, *Diaries and Letters 1939–1945*, p. 239.
38. C. Ham, *Health Policy in Britain: The Politics and Organisation of the National Health Service*, 2nd edn (London: Macmillan, 1985), p. 15.
39. G. Goodman, *State of the Nation*, p. 54.
40. Beveridge, *Pillars of Security*, pp. 69, 73; Clarke, *Hope and Glory*, pp. 213–14, 222; Grimes, *British National Health Service*, pp. 85–6; D. Hill, *Both Sides*, p. 834; Jeffreys, *Churchill Coalition*, p. 118; Morgan, *Labour in Power*, p. 154; Pater, *Making of National Health Service*, p. 47; R. Pearce, *Attlee* (London: Longman, 1997), p. 153.
41. Beveridge, *Pillars of Security*, p. 62.
42. Ibid., p. 66.
43. R. Churchill, *Winston S. Churchill*, vol. 2, p. 286; Pugh, *Lloyd George*, p. 54.
44. R. James (ed.), *Winston S. Churchill: His Complete Speeches*, vol. 2 (New York: Chelsea House, 1974), p. 2,014.
45. James, *Winston S. Churchill*, vol. 7, p. 7,137.
46. H. du Parcq, *Life of David Lloyd George*, vol. 4 (London: Caxton, 1913), p. 776.
47. Cregier, *Bounder from Wales*, p. 165.
48. Du Parcq, *Life of David Lloyd George*, vol. 4, p. 788.
49. R. Churchill, *Winston S. Churchill*, vol. 2, companion part 2, p. 1,064.
50. A. Taylor, *Bismarck: The Man and the Statesman* (New York: Vintage, 1967), p. 202.
51. Ibid., p. 204.
52. Cregier, *Bounder from Wales*, p. 116; Grigg, *Lloyd George: People's Champion*, p. 314; T. Jones, *Lloyd George* (London: Oxford University Press, 1951), p. 36; C. Wrigley, *David Lloyd George and the British Labour Movement: Peace and War* (Hassocks: Harvester, 1976), p. 38.
53. Grigg, *Lloyd George: People's Champion*, p. 322; Heidenheimer, Heclo and Adams, *Comparative Public Policy*, p. 58; Hennessy, *Never Again*, p. 121; Pugh, *Lloyd George*, p. 56.
54. R. Churchill, *Winston S. Churchill*, vol. 2, companion part 2, p. 863.
55. O. Carey Evans, *Lloyd George was My Father* (Llandysul: Gomer, 1985), p. 53.
56. G. Riddell, *More Pages from My Diary 1908–1914* (London: Country Life, 1934), p. 19.
57. Cregier, *Bounder from Wales*, p. 180; Grigg, *Lloyd George: People's Champion*, p. 332; Jones, *Lloyd George*, p. 41.
58. Du Parcq, *Life of David Lloyd George*, vol. 4, p. 783.
59. James, *Winston S. Churchill*, vol. 2, p. 2,014.
60. Cregier, *Bounder from Wales*, p. 184; M. Green, *The von Richthofen Sisters: The Triumphant and the Tragic Modes of Love* (London: Weidenfeld & Nicolson, 1974), p. 28.
61. K. Morgan (ed.), *Lloyd George: Family Letters 1885–1936* (Cardiff: University of Wales Press and Oxford: Oxford University Press, 1973), p. 8.
62. Grigg, *Lloyd George: People's Champion*, p. 313; Pugh, *Lloyd George*, p. 40.
63. James, *Winston S. Churchill*, vol. 2, p. 2,014.
64. H. du Parcq, *Life of David Lloyd George*, vol. 1 (London: Caxton, 1912), p. 168; *Life of David Lloyd George*, vol. 2 (London: Caxton, 1912), pp. 214–15; Pugh, *Lloyd George*, p. 40; Wrigley, *David Lloyd George*, p. 33.
65. H. Clegg, *Medicine in Britain*, 4th edn (London: Longmans, Green, 1951), p. 30.
66. P. Addison, *Now the War is Over: A Social History of Britain 1945–51* (London: British Broadcasting Corporation, 1985), p. 89; R. Numbers, *Almost Persuaded: American*

Physicians and Compulsory Health Insurance 1912–1920 (Baltimore, MD: Johns Hopkins University Press, 1978), p. 12; M. Pugh, *State and Society: British Political and Social History 1870–1992* (London: Edward Arnold, 1994), p. 112; R. Stevens, *In Sickness and in Wealth: American Hospitals in the Twentieth Century* (New York: Basic Books, 1989), pp. 86, 190.

67. Beveridge, *Pillars of Security*, p. 65.
68. Cregier, *Bounder from Wales*, p. 165; Grigg, *Lloyd George: People's Champion*, pp. 350–1.
69. J. Kent, *William Temple: Church, State and Society in Britain, 1880–1950* (Cambridge: Cambridge University Press, 1992), p. 128.
70. Clegg, *Medicine in Britain*, p. 27; J. Hollingsworth, J. Hage and R. Hanneman, *State Intervention in Medical Care: Consequences for Britain, France, Sweden, and the United States, 1890–1970* (Ithaca, NY: Cornell University Press, 1990), p. 158; A. MacNalty, *The History of State Medicine in England* (London: Royal Institute of Public Health and Hygiene, 1948), p. 69; Pelling, *Short History*, p. 27.
71. Pugh, *Lloyd George*, p. 57.
72. Addison, *Now the War is Over*, p. 96; Keidan, 'Health Services', p. 145; MacNalty, *History of State Medicine*, p. 69.
73. W. Beveridge, *Social Insurance and Allied Services: Presented to Parliament by Command of His Majesty, November 1942* (New York: Agathon, 1969), p. 25; Lord Brain, *The Doctor's Place in Society* (London: London School of Economics and Political Science, 1963), p. 4.
74. J. Brand, *Doctors and the State: The British Medical Profession and Government Action in Public Health, 1879–1912* (Baltimore, MD: Johns Hopkins University Press, 1965), p. 210.
75. F. Honigsbaum, *The Division in British Medicine: A History of the Separation of General Practice from Hospital Care 1911–1968* (London: Kogan Page, 1979), p. 332.
76. I. Jennings, *Cabinet Government*, 3rd edn (Cambridge: Cambridge University Press, 1959), pp. 95, 317.
77. J. Mackintosh, *The British Cabinet*, 3rd edn (London: Stevens, 1977), p. 287; MacNalty, *History of State Medicine*, pp. 68–70.
78. Grimes, *British National Health Service*, p. v.
79. Grigg, *Lloyd George: People's Champion*, p. 349; F. Honigsbaum, *The Struggle for the Ministry of Health 1914–1919* (London: G. Bell, 1970), p. 50; MacNalty, *History of State Medicine*, p. 80.
80. W. Herringham, *A Physician in France* (London: Edward Arnold, 1919), p. 149.
81. Lord Beaverbrook, *Men and Power 1917–1918* (London: Hutchinson, 1956), p. xvii; Grigg, *Lloyd George: People's Champion*, pp. 323–4.
82. Campbell, *Lloyd George*, pp. 55, 280. The classic statement of the distinction between inherent and instrumental value is by C. Friedrich, *Man and His Government: An Empirical Theory of Politics* (New York: McGraw-Hill, 1963), pp. 54–5.
83. A. Taylor (ed.), *Lloyd George: Twelve Essays* (New York: Atheneum, 1971), p. 80.
84. R. Scally, *The Origins of the Lloyd George Coalition: The Politics of Social Imperialism, 1900–1918* (Princeton, NJ: Princeton University Press, 1975), p. 221.
85. Du Parcq, *Life of David Lloyd George* (London: Caxton), vol. 3, p. 577.
86. Grigg, *Lloyd George: People's Champion*, p. 330.
87. Ibid., p. 344.
88. Scally, *Origins of Lloyd George Coalition*, p. 215.
89. Rintala, *Lloyd George and Churchill*, pp. 87–105.
90. Taylor, *Lloyd George*, p. 80.
91. J. Buchan, *The King's Grace 1910–1935* (London: Hodder & Stoughton, 1935), p. 31; M. Thomson, *David Lloyd George: The Official Biography* (London: Hutchinson, 1948), p. 210.
92. Du Parcq, *Life of David Lloyd George*, vol. 3, p. 577; Scally, *Origins of Lloyd George Coalition*, p. 227.
93. Du Parcq, *Life of David Lloyd George*, vol. 3, p. 579.
94. A. Chamberlain, *Politics from Inside: An Epistolary Chronicle 1906–1914* (New Haven, CT: Yale University Press, 1937), pp. 336, 338.
95. J. Marchant (ed.), *Winston Spencer Churchill: Servant of Crown and Commonwealth* (London: Cassell, 1954), p. 56.
96. Grigg, *Lloyd George: People's Champion*, p. 336.

97. Jones, *Lloyd George*, p. 40.
98. Pugh, *Lloyd George*, pp. 55–7.
99. G. Searle, *The Quest for National Efficiency: A Study in British Politics and Political Thought, 1899–1914* (Berkeley, CA: University of California Press, 1971), p. 254.
100. Cregier, *Bounder from Wales*, pp. 164–5; du Parcq, *Life of David Lloyd George*, vol. 3, p. 580; R. Shannon, *The Crisis of Imperialism 1865–1915* (London: Granada, 1974), p. 407.
101. H. Gerth and C. Mills (eds), *From Max Weber: Essays in Sociology* (New York: Oxford University Press, 1972), pp. 84–128.
102. I. Bulmer-Thomas, *The Growth of the British Party System*, vol. 1 (London: John Baker, 1965), p. 214; Cregier, *Bounder from Wales*, p. 183; K. Morgan, *The Age of Lloyd George* (London: George Allen & Unwin, 1971), p. 45; F. Owen, *Tempestuous Journey: Lloyd George, His Life and Times* (London: Hutchinson, 1954), pp. 207–8; Pugh, *Lloyd George*, p. 57; Wrigley, *David Lloyd George*, p. 39.
103. E. Halévy, *The Rule of Democracy 1905–1914 (Book II)*, 2nd edn, E. I. Watkins, trans. (New York: Peter Smith, 1952), p. 478; Mackenzie, *Power and Responsibility*, p. 72.
104. B. Shaw, *Doctors' Delusions, Crude Criminology, and Sham Education* (London: Constable, 1950), p. 44.
105. Pugh, *State and Society*, p. 241.
106. A. Carr-Saunders and P. Wilson, *The Professions* (Oxford: Clarendon, 1933), p. 95.
107. Brand, *Doctors and State*, p. 235.
108. Cregier, *Bounder from Wales*, p. 180.
109. Brand, *Doctors and State*, pp. 230, 235–6; Morgan, *Consensus and Disunity*, p. 82; Morgan, *Labour People*, p. 190.
110. Cregier, *Bounder from Wales*, p. 186.
111. Ibid., p. 180; Brand, *Doctors and State*, p. 230; J. Grigg, *Lloyd George: From Peace to War 1912–1916* (Berkeley, CA: University of California Press, 1985), p. 258.
112. Clarke, *Hope and Glory*, p. 216.
113. Grigg, *Lloyd George: People's Champion*, p. 341; Morgan, *Lloyd George*, p. 160.
114. D. Fraser, *The Evolution of the British Welfare State: A History of Social Policy since the Industrial Revolution* (London: Macmillan, 1973), p. 218; Pugh, *Lloyd George*, pp. 56–7.
115. Grigg, *Lloyd George: From Peace to War*, pp. 258–9, 262, 273, 476, 481, 491; Jones, *Lloyd George*, p. 156; Morgan, *Consensus and Disunity*, pp. 27, 82–3; Taylor, *Lloyd George*, p. 230; A. Taylor, *Essays in English History* (Harmondsworth: Penguin, 1982), pp. 225, 240–2, 254, 259, 272.
116. *British Medical Journal*, 2 May 1936, p. 15; MacNalty, *History of State Medicine*, p. 87; Oxbury, *Great Britons*, p. 2.
117. K. Feiling, *The Life of Neville Chamberlain* (Hamden, CT: Archon, 1970), p. 127; Jennings, *Cabinet Government*, p. 318; Pugh, *Lloyd George*, p. 140.
118. D. Dutton, *Austen Chamberlain: Gentleman in Politics* (Bolton: Ross Anderson, 1985), p. 162; Morgan, *Consensus and Disunity*, pp. 90, 98; Taylor, *Lloyd George*, p. 241.
119. Clarke, *Hope and Glory*, p. 156; Taylor, *Essays in English History*, p. 259.
120. Freedman, *Politics and Policy*, p. 253; Stevenson, *British Society*, p. 222; Taylor, *Lloyd George*, p. 240.
121. D. Dilks, *Neville Chamberlain*, vol. 1 (Cambridge: Cambridge University Press, 1984), pp. 274–5.
122. Ibid., p. 310; Feiling, *Life of Neville Chamberlain*, pp. 89, 103.
123. Pugh, *Lloyd George*, p. 140; Stevenson, *British Society*, pp. 222–3, 225.
124. C. Attlee, *As It Happened* (New York: Viking, 1954), pp. 215, 297–8.
125. Driberg, *Ruling Passions*, pp. 210, 212.
126. Mackenzie, *Power and Responsibility*, p. 155.
127. Clarke, *Hope and Glory*, p. 240; S. Fielding, P. Thompson and N. Tiratsoo, *'England Arise!': The Labour Party and Popular Politics in 1940s Britain* (Manchester: Manchester University Press, 1995), pp. 62, 102–3; D. Fox, *Health Policies, Health Politics: The British and American Experience 1911–1965* (Princeton, NJ: Princeton University Press, 1986), p. 136n; Horne, *Macmillan*, p. 343; H. Pelling, 'The 1945 General Election Reconsidered', *Historical Journal*, 23, 2 (1980), p. 413.
128. Macmillan, *Tides of Fortune*, pp. 375–6. His success at that ministry, in turn, made Macmillan's name famous. Morgan, *Labour in Power*, p. 163.

129. Macmillan, *Tides of Fortune*, p. 66.
130. Morgan, *Labour in Power*, p. 163.
131. Fielding, Thompson and Tiratsoo, *'England Arise'*, p. 172; J. Lee, *My Life with Nye* (London: Jonathan Cape, 1980), p. 158.
132. Foot, *Aneurin Bevan*, vol. 1, p 283n.
133. Clarke, *Hope and Glory*, p. 241; Sked and Cook, *Post-war Britain*, p. 46.
134. Morgan, *Labour People*, p. 129.
135. G. Goodman, *State of the Nation*, p. 81.
136. Clarke, *Hope and Glory*, p. 241; Pelling, *Short History*, p. 99.
137. Hollis, *Jennie Lee*, p. 124.
138. Clarke, *Hope and Glory*, p. 241.
139. James, *Winston S. Churchill*, vol. 7, p. 7,407.
140. James, *Winston S. Churchill*, vol. 8, p. 7,926.
141. James, *Winston S. Churchill*, vol. 7, p. 7,138.
142. Morgan, *Consensus and Disunity*, pp. 100, 102–4.
143. James, *Winston S. Churchill*, vol. 7, p. 7,136.
144. Lord Moran, *Churchill: Taken from the Diaries of Lord Moran: The Struggle for Survival 1940–1965* (Boston, MA: Houghton Mifflin, 1966), p. 270.

Cabinet Colleagues

If Churchill's Commons assault on Bevan had intellectual substance it was to accuse the minister of health of being excessively partisan. This was a surprising charge against Bevan, who was, as Harold Macmillan put it, 'at heart and in character a supreme individualist'.[1] This was so in almost all social contexts,[2] including his party membership. He was either the firebrand or the stormy petrel of the Labour Party.[3] Even a hostile critic conceded that Bevan was 'the conscience of the Labour left'.[4] Party loyalty meant little to him. When told he needed to become a team player if he wished to lead the Labour Party, he suggested the price was too high for him to pay.[5] In the spring of 1939 he had been expelled from the Labour Party, not to be let back in for the rest of that year, for supporting Sir Stafford Cripps' attempt to organize a British Popular Front against fascism.[6] Such an argument was still heresy at the highest levels of both the Labour and Conservative parties. Only Archibald Sinclair, leader of the Liberal Party, broke ranks on this matter.[7]

Sharp as it was, Bevan's parliamentary criticism of Churchill's leadership during the Second World War was much less brutal than his parliamentary criticism of Labour members of Churchill's Coalition Cabinet. Minister of Labour Ernest Bevin was prominent among those members.[8] Such criticism, especially when justified, did not endear him to his party's leaders. Nor did his defence, that it was 'better that Ministers should be embarrassed than that Parliament should die'.[9] His wartime criticism of Bevin placed him in danger of another expulsion from the Labour Party.[10] When Bevin heard Bevan described as his own worst enemy, Bevin observed: 'Not while I'm alive, he ain't.'[11] This response was much enjoyed by Clement Attlee, leader of the Labour Party.[12]

Bevin was far from alone among leading Labourites in feeling the barb of Bevan's sharp tongue. Even though the wartime

Labour home secretary, Herbert Morrison, was, typically for him, more enthusiastic about the Beveridge Report than either Attlee or Bevin, Morrison got little respect from Bevan, perhaps because Morrison, also typically for him, loyally accepted the eventual Cabinet line.[13] Bevan's wartime attacks on Morrison, whose vast official kingdom included the police establishment, were especially incisive.[14] When Morrison tried, with varying success, to suppress newspaper articles, and even newspapers, critical of Cabinet policy, Bevan, in a Commons speech, described Morrison as 'the witch-finder of the Labour Party, the smeller out of evil spirits'.[15] To Morrison those spirits had long been leftists. At a mass meeting held in London to defend freedom of the press many unpleasant things were said about the home secretary.[16] Perhaps the unkindest cut of all may have been Bevan's reference to Morrison as 'a little Cockney'.[17] In another wartime quarrel, over public ownership of industry, Bevan characterized Morrison as 'a fifth-rate Tammany hall boss'.[18] For some reason many people, including Morrison himself and Morrison's biographers, came to believe that Bevan had elevated Morrison to a 'third-rate' Tammany boss. When asked later by Harold Wilson whether he had actually so characterized Morrison, Bevan proudly repeated 'fifth-rate'.[19]

Bevan's allusion should have been to a 'first-rate' boss. Morrison was an exceedingly astute machine politician who ran a most successful party machine. He was for many years the unchallenged boss of the Labour Party organization in greater London. No party leader ever so dominated local politics and government in London as Morrison did.[20] Few national political leaders in Britain have also been municipal bosses. Morrison was the most important twentieth-century example of this distinctive combination. His role as 'the great personality'[21] of the London County Council (LCC) paralleled the nineteenth-century domination of Birmingham by Joseph Chamberlain, first as a Liberal and then as a Liberal Unionist (for which one can fairly read: Conservative).[22] Chamberlain's rule of Birmingham was perhaps less noteworthy because government did fewer things in his time, because Birmingham was not London and, most importantly, because Chamberlain had broader policy interests than Morrison, whose main concern was patronage. The London County Council provided many social services, and many opportunities for partisan preference. In the medical field alone, in 1940 it owned about 40,000 general hospital beds and about 35,000 mental hospital beds, making the LCC the world's largest hospital authority at that time.[23] It may also have been the best municipal health service in the world.[24] Many municipal hospitals outside London were experiencing more modest improvement.[25] Many municipal hospital jobs were relatively secure and, therefore, much valued, especially during the great depression of the 1930s. Morrison had in 1939 yearned for municipal takeover of London's private voluntary hospitals as well.[26] Local councillors throughout Britain, including London, were also able to arrange preferential admission to municipal hospitals. The abuse of managerial power depicted in his novels by A. J. Cronin, a doctor himself, could be painfully close to the truth. Since in many urban areas those councillors were predominantly Labour, Morrison was far from alone in his party.[27] Nor was preference for local governmental control of hospitals unknown in other parties. Neville Chamberlain had preferred local governmental control over medical services to a medical monopoly.[28]

It is therefore hardly surprising that during 1945–48 Bevan's desire to nationalize all, including municipal, hospitals was bitterly opposed by Morrison.[29] To say that Morrison was 'dismayed'[30] by Bevan's desire would be an understatement. It is no longer necessary, as it once was for the former secretary of the BMA, to 'only guess what'[31] Morrison thought of Bevan and his national-ization proposal. There was, as Harold Wilson later put it, 'a classical confrontation'[32] within the Cabinet between Morrison and Bevan over whether municipal hospitals would remain under the control of local government or be placed under the control of specialized regional administration levels of a national health service. In this confrontation Bevan had few advantages. Within the Cabinet he was not generally one of its most influential members.[33] He was not, as has been claimed,[34] a senior member of the Cabinet, but politically the junior member of that body.[35] He had not been significantly involved in making Labour Party policy, including health policy, before or during the Second World War.[36] His appointment as minister of health had been something of a surprise. That appointment violated hierarchical expectations among many members of the Parliamentary Labour Party. Many powerful, and power-seeking, eyebrows were raised.[37] Those eyebrows went even higher when it was learned that the prime minister, who sought to keep his Cabinet as small as possible,[38] would give the minister of health Cabinet rank, which had not been, and would not be, always the case.[39] Even Cabinet rank could not always save a minister of health from failure.[40] In Attlee's Cabinet, Bevan certainly stood out. He was not only politically but biologically the junior Cabinet member. At 47 he was in a group whose average age was over 60.[41] Attlee's Cabinet was one of the most experienced ever to take office in Britain.[42] In addition to Attlee, Ernest Bevin, Stafford Cripps, Hugh Dalton and Herbert Morrison were all of prime ministerial stature,[43] although inclusion of Arthur Greenwood and William Lord Jowitt among Attlee's most important ministers[44] is unintelligible. In 1941, Greenwood had been minister without portfolio, assigned to find a chairman for the interdepartmental committee which resulted in the Beveridge Report. Already, Greenwood's addiction to alcohol excluded him from major ministerial responsibility.[45]

In contrast to Bevan's lack of seniority, Morrison as Lord President of the Council and leader of the House of Commons was also deputy prime minister. As such, he substituted for the prime minister whenever the latter was, for any reason, absent from Cabinet. When Attlee was present, Morrison sat next to him, and was always called upon first to speak.[46] He seldom declined that opportunity. He was for Bevan a formidable opponent. He was also Bevan's enemy.[47] While his Cabinet colleague, Morrison described Bevan to a journalist: 'Power, that's all he wants, power for himself and he doesn't care what happens to the party as long as he gets it.'[48] Morrison saw Bevan as possessed of 'a feeling of hatred for me'.[49] This perception revealed little about Bevan, who was, as Harold Macmillan observed, not a hater.[50] Morrison may have been revealing himself rather than describing Bevan's psyche. Macmillan wrote in his diary that Morrison was 'the meanest man I know ... utterly incapable of magnanimity'.[51] When, in Cabinet meetings in late 1945, Morrison made his assault, carefully crafted in speech and writing, on Bevan's intention to nationalize all of Britain's hospitals, the minister of health was in deep trouble.[52] Few of the other members of the Cabinet could be expected to leap to Bevan's assistance. Most of them could remember all too well the difficulties he had long created for his own party's leadership.

Probably, besides Morrison, Bevan's most serious potential problem in the Cabinet was Ernest Bevin. The foreign secretary had not forgotten Bevan's wartime criticisms. He almost always took criticism personally and was apt to be vindictive. For him principled disagreements became personal feuds. He was suspicious of the motives of his fellow politicians, for whom he cared little and by whom he was not loved.[53] In spite of the fact that, although he claimed he never read books,[54] and he may have been one himself, Bevin had a particular distaste for intellectuals, among whom he counted Bevan. For him intellectuals were unreliable and irresponsible. That perception may have been strengthened by the disrespect shown Bevin, an authentic British worker in his origins, in the 1930s by middle-class intellectuals in the Labour Party, but it had existed even earlier.[55]

Bevan was fortunate that he was not the only Cabinet colleague despised by Bevin. He was even more fortunate that he was not the Cabinet colleague most passionately hated by Bevin. He was most fortunate that Bevin hated most passionately his own opponent and enemy, Morrison. Bevin and Morrison hated each other.[56] As one of their Cabinet colleagues put it, for Morrison Bevin felt 'a strong, almost pathological dislike and distrust'.[57] To the end of his life the mere mention of Morrison's name would set off Bevin's anger. That was literally so. Before his death, Bevin's last political wish may have been to subvert what he saw as yet another Morrisonian machination.[58] Their earliest conflicts may have been those of a powerful party organization boss opposed by a powerful trade union boss (Bevin's fiefdom was the Transport and General Workers' Union),[59] but those origins had long since been outgrown. Their feud had been literally ongoing since at least as early as 1931.[60] At meetings of the wartime Coalition Cabinet, Bevin would audibly make asides attacking Morrison's parentage and proposals. The attacks on Morrison's parentage were especially noteworthy in view of Bevan's own illegitimate birth. He never learned the identity of his father.[61] No suggestion coming from Morrison was likely to rouse Bevin's enthusiasm, or even receive a fair hearing, because he never approved of its author.[62] In July 1945, Attlee had appointed Bevin foreign secretary, a job Bevin did not want, to avoid the confrontations inevitable if both Bevin and Morrison had ministerial responsibility for domestic policy.[63]

Now in the emerging cold war, Bevin had his ministerial plate full with foreign policy. He also mustered up enough prudence not to force a rupture with Bevan over a matter in the latter's domain, let alone to Morrison's benefit. Bevin and Bevan never became friends, but their relationship did become civil,[64] especially when Bevin learned, 'Me and him can do business.'[65] Faced with the need to choose between Bevan and Morrison, Bevin had no qualms in aiding the defeat of his worst enemy. In 1951, the dying Bevin was sacked as foreign secretary, a job he had grown to love after an initial lack of enthusiasm, by Attlee, to whom he had been uniquely faithful. Insult was added to injury when Morrison was named as his successor. Bevin's preference would have been Bevan.[66] Bevin lamented: 'I'd sooner have had Nye than 'Erbert.

He might have turned out quite good.'[67] Morrison was a failure at the Foreign Office.[68] This was hardly surprising. He was an assertive advocate, not a diplomatic negotiator, and provincial rather than cosmopolitan. Loving London, he knew, and cared, less about even the rest of Britain, let alone the rest of the world. In a reflective moment, while seeking to supplant Attlee as prime minister, Morrison said he sometimes longed to go back to the London County Council. That had been a quiet, decent, useful life.[69] It had also been an environment in which his power was unchallenged. Appropriately he was to be memorialized by Herbert Morrison House in Walworth, meeting place of the Greater London Regional Council of the Labour Party.

While Bevin's hatred of Morrison was the extreme example, none of Attlee's senior Cabinet colleagues even liked any of the others.[70] Carl Schmitt, the German political scientist who saw the basis of politics as distinguishing between friend and foe, would have recognized their mutual enmities.[71] To speak of the 'cohesion of the Labour Ministers'[72] is to miss the mark completely. If Attlee's Cabinet was experienced and talented, it was also fractious. Bevan, Bevin, Cripps, Dalton and Morrison were the lead horses, but they were, to use Harold Wilson's term, 'five head-strong horses'.[73] How, for instance, Stafford Cripps would orient himself in the confrontation between Bevan and Morrison was less predictable than with Bevin. The relationship between Bevan and Cripps was, and is, often assumed to be close, with Bevan seen as one of Cripps' supporters.[74] After the possible fact, Attlee claimed that to assure the independent-minded Bevan's fidelity to Cabinet policy, Cripps had been assigned to be Bevan's watchdog.[75] This claim has been accepted by at least one distinguished scholar.[76] Attlee's assertion seems unlikely. Cripps would have been a most improbable guardian of group loyalty. Bevan never acknowledged a political mentor,[77] including Cripps, and it is hard to see Bevan as anyone's follower. He and Cripps had co-operated closely for several years shortly before the Second World War.[78] Assuming that one of them dominated the other is, however, unrealistic. Although eight years younger, Bevan was Cripps' senior in House of Commons membership. After a financially lucrative career at the bar, Cripps had entered politics only at 40. Whether his aunt, Beatrice Webb, had not bothered to recruit him earlier or had been unsuccessful in so doing, apparently is unknown. When he did enter politics, it was at a relatively senior level. Cripps had a powerful patron. That patron was Herbert Morrison, who recommended hiring Cripps to represent in legal matters the London County Council.[79] When urged by Morrison to join the Labour Party, Cripps initially responded: 'I am more interested in the church.'[80] Eventually he accepted the offer from Morrison, who arranged a parliamentary nomination for a safe Labour district with an upcoming by-election for his new recruit.[81] When, late in Attlee's prime ministership, Cripps was forced to leave the Treasury, he urged Attlee not to promote Bevan to the chancellorship. Bevan did not get the Treasury, but Cripps' urging was probably not a significant factor. Neither Attlee nor Cripps had much influence with the other.[82] Perhaps because he could not decide whether he disliked Morrison, who had once been his powerful patron, or Bevan, who had once been his Popular Front campaign colleague, more, Cripps played little direct role in the Cabinet dispute over nationalizing hospitals.

Bevan was probably without a friend in the Cabinet, but he did have at least two principled supporters, neither among the most powerful of his colleagues, on his NHS plans. One of these supporters, minister of education Ellen Wilkinson,[83] may have been a surprise to Bevan. Wilkinson had long been a significant figure on the left wing of the Labour Party. She had supported a prewar Popular Front, and when Cripps had been expelled from the Labour Party over that issue she served as his intermediary with the party.[84] She and Jennie Lee, before the latter's marriage to Aneurin Bevan, had been parliamentary allies and also friends, but this connection dwindled when Wilkinson became close to Herbert Morrison.[85] She campaigned almost ceaselessly for replacement of Attlee as leader of the Labour Party by Morrison. Since this campaigning continued throughout the last few months before the 1945 general election victory of the Labour Party, there was some surprise when Attlee chose her for his Cabinet.[86] In addition to being Morrison's loyal lieutenant, Wilkinson was also his mistress.[87] Bevan may not have been alone in his surprise over support from Wilkinson. That she was serious in that support is clear. She always took all of her responsibilities seriously, perhaps too seriously. In early 1947, Ellen Wilkinson took her own life.

Bevan's other principled supporter in the Cabinet was perhaps less of a surprise, but even more of an asset than Wilkinson. It was Christopher, now Lord, Addison, who had given Lloyd George crucial assistance with the National Insurance bill of 1911. Addison now gave Bevan crucial assistance in the Cabinet.[88] With Lloyd George dead, Churchill mute, and Beveridge irrelevant on health policy, Addison was the human link between the National

Insurance Act and the National Health Service Act. All four had been Liberals in 1911. As the Labour leader in a hostile House of Lords, and also secretary of state for the dominions in a world, and for a party, hostile to imperialism, Addison, now well into his seventies, could not give Bevan much practical daily assistance. He could not do for Bevan what he did for Lloyd George. The oldest member of the Cabinet could nevertheless help his youngest colleague achieve Lloyd George's ultimate goal from 1911, health care available to all Britons, not merely those who were insured.

Within the Cabinet, Addison helped Bevan in three important ways. First, as not only the oldest but also the most experienced member of the Cabinet, widely and deeply respected if probably not feared within the Cabinet room, his blessing gave Bevan's radical proposal respectability with some of the more conventional members of the Cabinet. Second, as a distinguished physician who had served as Britain's first minister of health, Addison's support gave Bevan's plan valuable medical respectability within the Cabinet. Third, and probably most importantly in this situation, Addison had been on close personal terms with Attlee since 1931, when both had served as Labour ministers. Addison was Attlee's model for ministerial behaviour, and Addison returned that professional admiration. Addison was also one of Attlee's few friends, and certainly the only one in the Cabinet. He was also unique in the Cabinet as the prime minister's confidant.[89]

Given the Cabinet's constellation of mutually antagonistic voices, the deciding voice in the confrontation between Bevan and Morrison would be Attlee's. Like many of his senior Cabinet colleagues the prime minister appears to have had no strong policy preference in this confrontation. Two valuable comprehensive biographies of Attlee barely mention the creation of the National Health Service.[90] This relative silence is appropriate because Attlee was so little involved. Even if within the Labour Party his heart was left-of-centre,[91] and within the House of Commons the party had moved leftward with the 1945 general election,[92] whether hospitals should be owned by national or local governments was not a clearly ideological issue. That Morrison may generally have been 'the arch-Right-winger' in Attlee's Cabinet[93] was therefore irrelevant on this issue. The prime minister probably saw no persuasive reason to deviate in this case from his customary manner of handling Cabinet meetings, with their frequent disputes. This was hardly the only bitter confrontation within his Cabinet.

After Morrison made his case in Cabinet for continued municipal ownership of hospitals, Attlee tried to defuse the controversy, saying that the differences between Bevan and Morrison were probably less fundamental than they appeared. This was wide of the mark, but Attlee did not see his task as making an intellectual, let alone a moral, judgement. Further calming the waters, but stretching the truth even further, Attlee suggested the same persons would run the hospitals, and the major expenditure would fall on the Treasury, under either approach.[94] The former suggestion ignored the specialized regional hospital authorities under Bevan's proposal, as well as the contribution made to municipal finances by local ratepayers. Neither Attlee, Bevan nor any other Cabinet member seems to have noticed that centralized Treasury responsibility for medical expenditures would enable, far more effectively than had been the case in Britain or would be the case elsewhere, centralized control of the national level of medical expenditures.[95] Costs could be controlled if there was a political will so to do.

Attlee's Cabinet intervention did open the door for participation by the chancellor of the exchequer, Hugh Dalton. Morrison had already appealed in effect to the greater cost to the national Treasury of Bevan's plan.[96] The claim that as Chancellor Dalton was hostile to Bevan[97] is the reverse of the truth. Dalton was distinctive as chancellor in willingly providing, and even encouraging, financial support for social reform.[98] So was his successor at the Treasury, Cripps.[99] In that respect, both resembled Lloyd George's pioneering performance as chancellor. Further, Dalton had long admired and liked Bevan, as he often did dynamic younger potential colleagues.[100] Finally, Dalton liked to humiliate senior colleagues whom he disliked. Morrison was prominent among such.[101] Morrison returned the favour.[102] So Dalton gladly supported Bevan.[103]

If, as in this confrontation, Attlee acted at Cabinet meetings as a distant arbiter, not a passionate player, he was far from powerless. Even an aloof arbiter's presiding hand can be firm.[104] Attlee, furthermore, may have appeared detached, but he had feelings, often far from benevolent, towards many of his Cabinet colleagues, although he was both judicious and agile enough to keep many of those feelings invisible from those beheld. Perhaps that is why among so many gifted colleagues and ambitious rivals who openly articulated their mutual animosities, he survived two decades as leader of the Labour Party. He certainly had personal perceptions of both present combatants, Bevan and Morrison.

Before 1945, Attlee had minimal possible contact with Bevan. With Morrison, Attlee had voted in 1939 to expel Bevan from the Labour Party for the latter's support of a popular front against fascism.[105] Like his wartime Labour ministerial colleagues, Attlee had then felt the sting of Bevan's tongue and pen.[106] The deputy prime minister therefore favoured, this time unsuccessfully, again expelling Bevan from the Labour Party.[107] The incoming prime minister nevertheless in 1945 appointed Bevan a Cabinet-level minister of health. Attlee later recalled: 'For Health I chose Aneurin Bevan, whose abilities had up to now been displayed only in opposition, but I felt that he had it in him to do good service.'[108] This clinical language carried a mixed message. One possible reading is that Bevan's abilities had been unrecognized until Attlee, in 1945, revealed them. Another possible reading is that prior to 1945 Bevan's political role, including in his own party, had been entirely negative, only to be turned around under Attlee's leadership. Both readings emphasize, and properly so, Attlee's significance in Bevan's career. Without Attlee's initiative, Bevan would not have been appointed minister of health, let alone with Cabinet rank. That initiative was surely magnanimous on Attlee's part.[109] Attlee may well also have felt that it was less dangerous to have Bevan inside the Cabinet than outside. Many of his other Cabinet appointees, furthermore, had done much more damage to Attlee personally than Bevan, so much their junior, had been able yet to achieve.

Among those others was Morrison. Attlee had his own reasons for distrusting Morrison.[110] When, shortly before the 1935 general election, George Lansbury resigned as leader of the Labour Party, there were relatively few sitting Labour Members of Parliament who would choose the new leader from among themselves. The party's representation, including many of its former frontbenchers, had been decimated in the 1931 general election. Among those defeated in 1931 was Morrison, who otherwise might well have succeeded Lansbury.[111] After Attlee was chosen leader, Labour lost the 1935 general election, but Morrison regained a parliamentary seat. Morrison now challenged Attlee for the leadership, but lost.[112] Attlee fought back against Morrison with indirect actions, not angry confrontations. Sometimes, indeed, studied inaction was his chosen weapon. In 1944, for instance, he let an important memorandum from Morrison die of neglect, seriously weakening Morrison's credibility.[113] Attlee acted as if he were paying no attention when, immediately after the Labour Party victory in the 1945 general election, Morrison tried to supplant Attlee as its leader, and hence become the incoming prime minister.[114] Even after Attlee was firmly installed at 10 Downing Street Morrison continued his efforts to replace him.[115] In these efforts he was repeatedly frustrated not only by Attlee's quietly shrewd judgement but also by Bevin's passionately determined hostility.[116] Even after Bevin's death Attlee, now in opposition, would not leave the leadership until it was clear Morrison would not become his successor.[117]

At the crucial Cabinet meeting on the NHS bill, the prime minister summed up the discussion in Bevan's favour.[118] The prime minister preferred Bevan to Morrison.[119] Bevan had won the Cabinet battle.[120] Attlee's summing up was the decisive moment[121] in the creation of the National Health Service. All of Britain's hospitals would be nationalized.[122]

Even after Attlee's decision, Morrison did not give up. He was a tenacious as well as formidable opponent.[123] Defeated in one arena, he moved to another. He now set his party machine to work. Past and present officials of the London County Council wrote letters to *The Times*, and formed delegations to Ministry of Health officials, protesting against nationalization of municipal hospitals.[124] Even in London, however, some of Morrison's hopes were frustrated. When Bevan appeared personally before the London Labour Party Executive Committee, he converted his sceptical audience. The London County Council eventually caved in as well,[125] but Morrison persisted in personally aggravating Bevan and relished the hostility Bevan encountered from general practitioners in the British Medical Association.[126] In 1950, Morrison opposed Bevan's promotion to a more powerful ministry on the grounds that Bevan had made a mess of the Ministry of Health, and should be made to stay there to clean it up.[127] Long after the National Health Service had been created, and after Aneurin Bevan had died, Morrison skilfully used the language of thoughtful detachment to reveal: 'I am not too happy about the working of the hospital scheme under the National Health [*sic*] Act. Responsibility is difficult to apportion and define ... I incline to the view that the local management at the hospitals could be the responsibility of elected local authorities suitable for the purpose.'[128] Bevan had already, in his own writings, drawn his own conclusion from his NHS battle with Morrison: 'Local authorities are notoriously unwilling to delegate any of their functions or responsibilities to others.'[129]

Morrison did gain a partial victory with his persistence even after Attlee's summing up. Local government authorities were permitted by the National Health Service Act of 1946 to implement a range of public health programmes.[130] The London County Council, for instance, needed 4,843 employees to perform these functions. At the same time, because of nationalization of its previously municipal hospitals, the LCC lost 32,000 employees in 98 institutions.[131] Smaller-scale versions of this substantial net loss of local governmental power occurred throughout Britain. The NHS Act may well have given the Ministry of Health greater direct control of more health subsystems than has been achieved by any other democratic government.[132] Nationalization of all hospitals may have been the most decisive governmental action regarding hospitals ever taken in a Western nation.[133] Nationalization of municipal hospitals may not have increased the total amount of governmental power, but it undeniably centralized that power. The inescapable fact was that under the NHS Act local governments lost all their medical powers except in public health matters. Leaving the latter with local governments did not serve the national health, especially given increasing financial restraints on local governments.[134] The net loss of local governmental power was probably much more significant than the total amount of power voluntary hospitals, also nationalized, had collectively possessed.[135] The judgement that it took a pragmatic Labour minister, Bevan, to remove the last vestige of local governmental control over medicine[136] is slightly exaggerated but hardly misleading.

That judgement is also essentially correct in describing Bevan as pragmatic. In nationalizing municipal hospitals, Bevan was not acting as a loyal partisan. In defending municipal hospitals, Morrison *was* so acting. Fidelity to party meant much to Morrison, and little to Bevan. Within the Cabinet, Morrison argued that nationalization of hospitals was outside the Labour Party's 1945 general election manifesto. Bevan apparently accepted the validity of Morrison's argument, but countered that nationalizing hospitals would be in accordance with the spirit, if not the letter, of that manifesto.[137] Morrison was correct about the manifesto's provisions. No mention was made of nationalizing any hospitals, municipal or voluntary. The scholarly argument that the manifesto added 'such old Labour themes as a national health service' to the newer themes of the Beveridge Report, by mentioning if playing down 'the possible nationalization of the hospital service',[138] is seriously misleading. The only health policy provisions of that manifesto were meaninglessly bland, even for a campaign document:

HEALTH OF THE NATION AND ITS CHILDREN

By good food and good homes, much avoidable ill-health can be prevented. In addition the best health services should be available for all. Money must no longer be the passport to the best treatment.

In the new National Health Service there should be health centres where the people may get the best that modern science can offer, more and better hospitals, and proper conditions for our doctors and nurses. More research is required into the causes of disease and the ways to prevent and cure it.

Labour will work specially for the care of Britain's mothers and their Children – children's allowances and school medical and feeding services, better maternity and child welfare services. A healthy family life must be fully ensured and parenthood must not be penalized if the population of Britain is to be prevented from dwindling.[139]

There was, in 1945, no Labour Party blueprint for a universal free health service.[140] There had been a proposal, made by the Socialist Medical Association, a small pressure group, to the 1945 Labour Party conference, that a salaried municipal service should be administered by local government.[141] When he became minister of health, Bevan told his civil servants to draft a legislative proposal for a tax-funded health service free to every Briton. After receiving a draft proposal based on physicians becoming salaried employees of local governments, Bevan burst out laughing, adding: 'You cannot do this to me. Go away and think again.'[142] Bevan did not want a salaried medical service, let alone one run by local governments. The Socialist Medical Association would be disappointed by Bevan's NHS.[143]

There was, further, no 'old Labour theme' of a national health service. Health policy had not been a high priority for the Labour Party during the interwar decades.[144] The 1935 Labour Party election manifesto, before the last prewar general election, promised only to 'vigorously develop the health services' and to deal with maternal mortality.[145] *Labour's Immediate Programme* (1937) was precise about desirable industrial and employment policies, but vague on the idea of a state medical service.[146] This relative silence on health policy was even true of the leading Fabian intellectuals who wrote so much about their personal visions of a more socially just Britain. Sidney and Beatrice Webb, in their pioneering *The State and the Doctor* (1910), did not mention the desirability or the possibility of a governmental (whether local or national) takeover of voluntary hospitals, whose continuance they saw as a given. The poor, to the Webbs, would continue to be the only recipients of governmental medicine. They would receive medical treatment, but from the least prestigious doctors. George Bernard Shaw, whose eyes looked higher, urged in 1911 that London's most prestigious specialized hospital physicians should become civil servants: 'Municipalize Harley Street.'[147] Bevan, even more creative, nationalized Harley Street. The most prestigious specialized hospital physicians became accessible to those in greatest medical need.

In 1942, the year of the Beveridge Report, G. D. H. Cole published his hopes for *Great Britain in the Post-war World*, which included medical treatment 'open to everyone in the community without any charge'.[148] Serious socialist that he was, Cole listed many British institutions which in his view ought to be nationalized. No mention was made by him in this context of any medical institutions, including hospitals or private medical practices.[149]

Also in 1942, a more audible voice was raised at the annual Labour Party conference. James Griffiths, a Member of Parliament powerful both among Welsh coalminers and within the national Labour Party organization, who would become minister of national insurance in 1945, introduced a resolution calling for a national health service. Griffiths' motion resulted in preparation of a report, *National Service for Health*, published in 1943 by the Labour Party. Unlike the Beveridge Report, this document discussed health policy seriously, thoughtfully and in detail. It was, by far, the most impressive Labour Party statement about health policy before 1945. Unlike the Beveridge Report, *National Service for Health* appears to have been virtually ignored by all of its possible audiences, including within the Labour Party. As minister of health Bevan seems to have taken no notice of *National Service for Health*, which urged a very different national health service from that which Bevan created. The report emphasized that a state medical service needed to be preventive as well as curative.[150] Bevan's NHS was almost entirely diagnostic and curative and very little preventive.[151] As in 1911, public health was assigned a low priority,[152] and its segregation in local government discouraged its integration with diagnostic and curative medical services.[153] Even though one goal of the NHS Act was 'to secure improvement in the physical and mental health of the people',[154] the concept of health was nowhere defined in the act.[155] The other goal of the act, to secure improvement in 'the prevention, diagnosis and treatment of illness',[156] was incompletely realized. Diagnosis and treatment overwhelmed prevention. *National Service for Health* saw only a full-time, salaried, pensionable medical service,[157] which Bevan would not create, as financially free to emphasize prevention, rather than treatment, of illness. Voluntary hospitals, according to the same 1943 document, should be subsidized by local governments, which would receive seats on the governing bodies of voluntary hospitals in proportion to local governmental subsidies of those hospitals' budgets.[158] This meant there would be no nationalization of voluntary, or, for that matter, municipal hospitals. Instead: 'Wide powers must be left to Local Authorities, it is they who must be responsible for the detailed administration of the service.'[159] This all sounded later like Morrison, not Bevan.

Bevan's bill not only upset but also surprised local government authorities, including Labour-dominated municipal councils. Indeed, Bevan's proposal to nationalize hospitals took all of Britain by surprise.[160] Among those most surprised by Bevan's bill as a whole, and certainly even more agitated than local government authorities, were members of a group essentially detached from hospitals: general practitioners predominantly organized in the British Medical Association. The greatest anger among general practitioners was aroused by Bevan's intention to ban sale of private medical practices by doctors who were retiring from practice or by estates of doctors who had died while still practising medicine. General practitioners were most often in individual rather than group private practices. British medicine had therefore acquired a competitive character.[161] Entrepreneurship was required for professional success. As capitalists British general practitioners needed to invest considerable sums of money. Not only was medical training expensive, but establishing oneself in private practice required substantial capital to buy an existing practice or create a new one. This need for capital closed medical careers for many gifted potential doctors who were not already financially privileged.[162] An entirely new practice would become profitable, if at all, only after considerable passage of time. The only alternative was to purchase the assets, including professional goodwill, of a successful practice that had just ended or was soon to end. The purchase price was generally one and one-half years' gross income of the medical practice involved. Sometimes what was offered for sale, often in a locality previously unknown to prospective purchasers, was a sad remnant of a once-successful, even distinguished, medical career.[163] Frequently sale of even a successful practice was urgently needed for retirement or for support of surviving spouses and/or children.

Bevan saw medicine, at least as it was structured in Britain, as a profession in which individual commercialism ran counter to the most appropriate social values.[164] To him the NHS would be 'opposed to the hedonism of capitalist society'.[165] His determined opposition to the custom of purchasing and selling patient goodwill originated in his firm belief that the custom was inherently evil.[166] Patients as well as doctors were dehumanized. He saw it 'as being inconsistent with a civilized community and with a reasonable health service for patients to be bought and sold over their heads'.[167] This belief was distinctive, and perhaps even unique, among the British political elite in 1945. If any other powerful member of that elite, including within the Labour Party, found such commercial transactions within medicine to be morally objectionable, the feeling appears not to have been expressed. For Bevan abolition of the sale of patient goodwill was the single detailed provision of his bill which mattered the most.[168]

More surprising than the lack of ethical concern on this matter among other politicians was the defence by the British Medical Association of the sale and purchase of private practices. In 1946 the BMA representative body voted 229 to 13 for the retention of such commerce.[169] This result was strikingly different from results of a 1944 poll of British doctors by the British Institute of Public Opinion, in which only one-third of the respondents had favoured retention of this custom.[170] In spite of the earlier poll results, this was the issue which aroused the greatest fear within the BMA.[171] Bevan still would not budge.[172] The NHS Act of 1946 therefore provided that any doctor who joined the NHS could not lawfully 'sell the goodwill, or any part of the goodwill of the medical practice' of that doctor.[173] This provision gave the NHS Act Bevan's personal stamp. He did recognize that many doctors then practising had earlier invested substantial sums to purchase their practices. When they retired or died, there would be financial compensation to them or their estates. That compensation when eventually made may have been far above the market price.[174] Such generosity would not have offended Bevan, who wanted to end the practice, not harm the practitioner. Those doctors who chose to remain in private practice without joining the NHS were, of course, free to continue to buy and sell patient goodwill. So, long after 1948, when the NHS Act became operative, some private practices were advertised for sale.[175] The BMA, even in

1948, was still insisting on freedom for all doctors, including those within the NHS, to buy and sell their practices.[176] The leader of the BMA's effort later conceded it had continued 'long after it was clear there was no public or political support for its view'.[177] Not until 1954 did the BMA representative body apparently, and in 1956, more explicitly, decide to abandon this issue.[178] The minister of health had altered long-standing behaviour, and perhaps also the ethical perspectives, of the British medical profession. It may be no accident, given Bevan's inherent values, that the National Health Service may be the closest Britain has come to institutionalizing altruism.[179]

NOTES

1. Macmillan, *Tides of Fortune*, p. 66.
2. Foot, *Aneurin Bevan*, vol. 1, pp. 71, 89–92; G. Goodman, *State of the Nation*, p. 42.
3. E. Estorick, *Stafford Cripps: Master Statesman* (New York: John Day, 1949), p. 147; Fraser, *Evolution of British Welfare State*, p. 215; Morgan, *Labour People*, p. 125.
4. Roberts, *Eminent Churchillians*, p. 78.
5. K. Morgan, *The Red Dragon and the Red Flag: The Cases of James Griffiths and Aneurin Bevan* (Aberystwyth: National Library of Wales, 1989), p. 6.
6. Foot, *Aneurin Bevan*, vol. 1, pp. 286–300, 310; G. Goodman, *State of the Nation*, pp. 50, 187–8; Hollis, *Jennie Lee*, pp. 87–108; R. Jenkins, *Mr Attlee: An Interim Biography* (London: William Heinemann, 1948), pp. 205–6; R. Jenkins, *Nine Men of Power* (New York: British Book Centre, 1974), p. 92; Morgan, *Red Dragon*, p. 6; Sissons and French, *Age of Austerity*, pp. 179–81.
7. Foot, *Aneurin Bevan*, vol. 1, p. 289; Jenkins, *Nine Men*, p. 93.
8. A. Bevan, *In Place of Fear* (New York: Simon & Schuster, 1953), p. 32; Bullock, *Life and Times of Ernest Bevin*, vol. 2, pp. 165, 191, 233, 238, 303–9, 321; A. Bullock, *Ernest Bevin: Foreign Secretary* (New York: W. W. Norton, 1983), p. 77; G. Goodman, *State of the Nation*, p. 189; K. Harris, *Attlee*, pp. 229–30, 244–5; Hollis, *Jennie Lee*, pp. 110, 113; Jenkins, *Mr Attlee*, p. 233; Morgan, *Red Dragon*, p. 6.
9. Foot, *Aneurin Bevan*, vol. 1, p. 330.
10. Oxbury, *Great Britons*, p. 34.
11. Jenkins, *Nine Men*, p. 72.
12. Bullock, *Ernest Bevin*, p. 77.
13. G. Goodman, *State of the Nation*, p. 53; King, *With Malice toward None*, pp. 211–13.
14. Driberg, *Ruling Passions*, p. 93; Hollis, *Jennie Lee*, p. 110; King, *With Malice toward None*, pp. 166, 171.
15. Foot, *Aneurin Bevan*, vol. 1, p. 355.
16. Brittain, *Diary*, p. 140.
17. Foot, *Aneurin Bevan*, vol. 1, p. 356.
18. Ibid., p. 494; Morgan, *Labour People*, p. 176.
19. B. Donoughue and G. Jones, *Herbert Morrison: Portrait of a Politician* (London: Weidenfeld & Nicolson, 1973), pp. 390, 477; H. Morrison, *Herbert Morrison: An Autobiography* (London: Odhams, 1960), p. 263.
20. Clarke, *Hope and Glory*, p. 179; Hennessy, *Never Again*, p. 139; B. Inglis, *Abdication* (New York: Macmillan, 1966), p. 252; Morgan, *Labour People*, pp. 176, 178; Morgan, *Rebirth of a Nation*, p. 30; C. Ponting, *1940: Myth and Reality* (Chicago, IL: Ivan R. Dee, 1993), p. 6; A. Sampson, *The Changing Anatomy of Britain* (New York: Vintage, 1984), p. 203; F. Williams, *Ernest Bevin: Portrait of a Great Englishman* (London: Hutchinson, 1952), p. 184.

21. Willcocks, *Creation of National Health Service*, p. 99.
22. Rintala, *Lloyd George and Churchill*, pp. 50–3; Sampson, *Changing Anatomy of Britain*, p. 199.
23. G. Rivett, *The Development of the London Hospital System 1823–1982* (London: King Edward's Hospital Fund for London, 1986), p. 268.
24. S. Inwood, *A History of London* (New York: Carroll & Graf, 1998), p. 308.
25. M. Powell, 'An Expanding Service: Municipal Acute Medicine in the 1930s', *Twentieth Century British History*, 8, 3 (1997), pp. 334–57.
26. C. Webster, 'Conflict and Consensus: Explaining the British Health Service', *Twentieth Century British History*, 1, 2 (1990), p. 144.
27. *British Medical Journal*, 1 July 1978, pp. 28–9; A. Cronin, *Shannon's Way* (Boston, MA: Little, Brown, 1983), pp. 152–9; Lowe, *Welfare State in Britain since 1945*, p. 175.
28. R. Self (ed.), *The Neville Chamberlain Diary Letters*, vol. 1 (Aldershot: Ashgate, 2000), p. 395.
29. Fraser, *Evolution of British Welfare State*, p. 215; Glennester, *British Social Policy since 1945*, p. 50; G. Goodman, *State of the Nation*, p. 56; N. Goodman, *Wilson Jameson*, p. 122; Grimes, *British National Health Service*, p. 126; Rivett, *Development of London Hospital System*, p. 264; Widgery, *Health in Danger*, p. 30.
30. Lowe, *Welfare State*, p. 374, n10.
31. C. Hill, *Both Sides*, p. 99.
32. H. Wilson, *A Personal Record: The Labour Government 1964–1970* (Boston, MA: Little, Brown, 1971), p. 765.
33. Dalton, *High Tide*, p. 362.
34. G. Forsyth, *Doctors and State Medicine: A Study of the British Health Service* (London: Pitman Medical Publishing, 1966), p. 19.
35. J. Campbell, *Aneurin Bevan and the Mirage of British Socialism* (New York: W. W. Norton, 1987), p. 169.
36. G. Goodman, *State of the Nation*, p. 1; Hollis, *Jennie Lee*, p. 112; Morgan, *Labour in Power*, p. 151.
37. H. Dalton, *The Fateful Years: Memoirs 1931–1945* (London: Frederick Muller, 1957), p. 470; Foot, *Aneurin Bevan*, vol. 2, p. 26; Morgan, *Labour in Power*, p. 151; Rodgers and Donoughue, *People into Parliament*, p. 145.
38. Burridge, *Clement Attlee*, p. 187.
39. Lowe, *Welfare State*, pp. 183, 376, n32.
40. M. Burch, 'Prime Minister and Whitehall', in D. Shell and R. Hodder-Williams (eds), *Churchill to Major: The British Prime Ministership since 1945* (Armonk, NY: M. E. Sharpe, 1995), pp. 113, 125; R. Crossman, *The Diaries of a Cabinet Minister*, vol. 3 (London: Hamish Hamilton and Jonathan Cape, 1977), p. 330; M. Thatcher, *The Downing Street Years* (New York: Harper Collins, 1993), pp. 589, 607–14; H. Young, *The Iron Lady: A Biography of Margaret Thatcher* (New York: Noonday Press, 1989), pp. 548–9.
41. Burridge, *Clement Attlee*, p. 190; Foot, *Aneurin Bevan*, vol. 2, pp. 20, 25; Hollis, *Jennie Lee*, pp. 123–4; Sissons and French, *Age of Austerity*, p. 21.
42. Clarke, *Hope and Glory*, p. 216; G. Goodman, *State of the Nation*, p. 182; Rodgers and Donoughue, *People into Parliament*, p. 144.
43. Freedman, *Politics and Policy*, p. 136.
44. Sissons and French, *Age of Austerity*, p. 20.
45. Ponting, *1940*, pp. 5–6.
46. Burridge, *Clement Attlee*, p. 186; Campbell, *Aneurin Bevan*, p. 169.
47. R. James, *Anthony Eden* (New York: McGraw-Hill, 1987), p. 336; Pearce, *Attlee*, p. 154.
48. Donoughue and Jones, *Herbert Morrison*, p. 465.
49. Morrison, *Herbert Morrison*, p. 263.
50. Macmillan, *Tides of Fortune*, pp. 65–6.
51. Horne, *Macmillan*, p. 339.
52. Fox, *Health Policies*, pp. 135–6, 139; G. Goodman, *State of the Nation*, pp. 108, 122–3; Grimes, *British National Health Service*, p. 137; Ham, *Health Policy*, p. 16; Hennessy, *Never Again*, p. 139; Morgan, *Labour in Power*, pp. 154–6; Pater, *Making of National Health Service*, p. 109.
53. A. Bullock, *The Life and Times of Ernest Bevin*, vol. 1 (London: Heinemann, 1960), p. 571; Bullock, *Ernest Bevin*, p. 56; Hollis, *Jennie Lee*, p. 79; Jenkins, *Nine Men*, p. 72; Rowse, *Glimpses*, pp. 42, 46, 52; Taylor, *Politicians*, pp. 26–7; F. Williams, *Ernest Bevin*, p. 211.

54. Taylor, *Politicians*, p. 125.
55. Bullock, *Life and Times of Ernest Bevin*, vol. 1, pp. 531, 553; M. Cole, *Life of G. D. H. Cole*, p. 193; Jenkins, *Nine Men*, p. 66; Rowse, *Glimpses*, pp. 36, 42, 350.
56. Bullock, *Life and Times of Ernest Bevin*, vol. 2, p. 337; Bullock, *Ernest Bevin*, p. 76; Jenkins, *Nine Men*, p. 74; Mackenzie, *Power and Responsibility*, p. 362; Morgan, *Labour People*, pp. 152, 177; Oxbury, *Great Britons*, p. 253; Rowse, *Glimpses*, pp. 56, 71; Taylor, *Politicians*, p. 128; F. Williams, *Ernest Bevin*, pp. 183–7.
57. Dalton, *High Tide*, p. 243.
58. Bullock, *Life and Times of Ernest Bevin*, vol. 2, p. 5; Bullock, *Ernest Bevin*, p. 90; Dalton, *High Tide*, p. 158; Morgan, *Labour People*, p. 151; Wilson, *A Prime Minister on Prime Ministers*, p. 298.
59. T. Evans, *Bevin of Britain* (New York: W. W. Norton, 1946), pp. 186–7; Jenkins, *Nine Men*, p. 64; Rowse, *Glimpses*, pp. 46, 56.
60. Bullock, *Life and Times of Ernest Bevin*, vol. 1, pp. 459, 510, 514; Bullock, *Life and Times of Ernest Bevin*, vol. 2, pp. 286–7; K. Harris, *Attlee*, p. 228; Morgan, *Labour People*, p. 151.
61. Bullock, *Life and Times of Ernest Bevin*, vol. 2, p. 117; Oxbury, *Great Britons*, p. 35.
62. Bullock, *Life and Times of Ernest Bevin*, vol. 2, p. 337; Jenkins, *Nine Men*, p. 71; Rowse, *Glimpses*, p. 50.
63. Bulmer-Thomas, *Growth of British Party System*, vol. 2, pp. 161, 198, n13; Clarke, *Hope and Glory*, p. 216; P. Giddings, 'Prime Minister and Cabinet', in Shell and Hodder-Williams, *Churchill to Major*, p. 33; K. Harris, *Attlee*, p. 264; Morgan, *Labour People*, p. 126; Rowse, *Glimpses*, p. 71.
64. Bullock, *Ernest Bevin*, p. 77; Foot, *Aneurin Bevin*, vol. 2, p. 31.
65. Foot, *Aneurin Bevan*, vol. 2, p. 32.
66. Pearce, *Attlee*, p. 136.
67. Bullock, *Ernest Bevin*, p. 834.
68. G. Brown, *In My Way* (New York: St Martin's, 1971), p. 246; Clarke, *Hope and Glory*, p. 246; Dalton, *High Tide*, p. 245; G. Goodman, *State of the Nation*, pp. 58, 197–8; D. Healey, *The Time of My Life* (New York: W. W. Norton, 1990), p. 126; Oxbury, *Great Britons*, p. 253; Rowse, *Glimpses*, pp. 51, 70; Wilson, *A Prime Minister on Prime Ministers*, pp. 291, 298.
69. Dalton, *High Tide*, p. 243.
70. Brown, *In My Way*, p. 247.
71. C. Schmitt, *The Concept of the Political*, G. Schwab, trans. (New Brunswick, NJ: Rutgers University Press, 1976), p. 26.
72. R. Butler, *The Art of the Possible: The Memoirs of Lord Butler* (Harmondsworth: Penguin, 1973), p. 134.
73. Freedman, *Politics and Policy*, p. 137; Wilson, *A Prime Minister on Prime Ministers*, p. 291.
74. Jenkins, *Nine Men*, p. 90.
75. F. Williams, *A Prime Minister Remembers*, pp. 248–9.
76. Morgan, *Red Dragon*, p. 13.
77. Foot, *Aneurin Bevan*, vol. 2, p. 39.
78. C. Cooke, *The Life of Richard Stafford Cripps* (London: Hodder & Stoughton, 1957), pp. 188–9, 193, 236–7.
79. P. Strauss, *Cripps: Advocate Extraordinary* (New York: Duell, Sloan & Pearce, 1942), p. 59.
80. Donoughue and Jones, *Herbert Morrison*, p. 123.
81. Estorick, *Stafford Cripps*, pp. 68–71; Jenkins, *Nine Men*, p. 86; Strauss, *Cripps*, p. 59.
82. Jenkins, *Nine Men*, p. 88; F. Williams, *A Prime Minister Remembers*, p. 245.
83. G. Goodman, *State of the Nation*, p. 124.
84. P. Brookes, *Women at Westminster: An Account of Women in the British Parliament 1918–1966* (London: Peter Davies, 1967), pp. 118–19; Morgan, *Labour People*, p. 179.
85. Hollis, *Jennie Lee*, p. 152; Morgan, *Labour People*, p. 102; F. Williams, *A Prime Minister Remembers*, p. 3.
86. Brooks, *Women at Westminster*, pp. 125, 142–3, 165; Sissons and French, *Age of Austerity*, p. 22.
87. Morgan, *Labour People*, p. 178.
88. Ibid., p. 191; K. Morgan, *The People's Peace: British History 1945–1950* (Oxford: Oxford University Press, 1992), p. 38.

89. Burridge, *Clement Attlee*, p. 189; K. Harris, *Attlee*, p. 87; Morgan, *Labour People*, pp. 138, 146–7, 191.
90. Burridge, *Clement Attlee*; K. Harris, *Attlee*.
91. Burridge, *Clement Attlee*, p. 296; Healey, *Time of My Life*, p. 153; Morgan, *Labour People*, p. 147.
92. Foot, *Aneurin Bevan*, vol. 2, p. 26.
93. Ibid., p. 225.
94. Burridge, *Clement Attlee*, p. 355, n87.
95. Glennester, *British Social Policy*, p. 51.
96. Pearce, *Attlee*, p. 153.
97. G. Goodman, *State of the Nation*, p. 47.
98. Foot, *Aneurin Bevan*, vol. 2, p. 36; Morgan, *Labour People*, pp. 120, 126.
99. D. Hill, *Tribune 40*, p. 81; Morgan, *Labour People*, p. 173.
100. Foot, *Aneurin Bevan*, vol. 2, p. 226; Rowse, *Glimpses*, p. 52.
101. Dalton, *High Tide*, p. 141; Foot, *Aneurin Bevan*, vol. 2, p. 226; Morgan, *Labour People*, p. 178.
102. Morgan, *Labour People*, pp. 119–20.
103. G. Goodman, *State of the Nation*, p. 123; B. Pimlott (ed.), *The Political Diary of Hugh Dalton: 1918–40, 1945–60* (London: Jonathan Cape, 1986), p. 602.
104. Freedman, *Policy and Politics in Britain*, p. 136; Pearce, *Attlee*, p. 136.
105. R. Jackson, *Rebels and Whips: An Analysis of Dissension, Discipline and Cohesion in British Political Parties* (London: Macmillan, 1968), pp. 130n–131n.
106. K. Harris, *Attlee*, pp. 204–5, 244–5.
107. Ibid., p. 229.
108. Attlee, *As It Happened*, p. 215.
109. Foot, *Aneurin Bevan*, vol. 2, p. 27.
110. Bullock, *Ernest Bevin*, p. 76.
111. Bullock, *Life and Times of Ernest Bevin*, vol. 1, pp. 571–2.
112. Attlee, *As It Happened*, p. 116; McKenzie, *British Political Parties*, p. 361; Rowse, *Glimpses*, p. 58; Strauss, *Cripps*, p. 144.
113. Morgan, *Labour People*, p. 139.
114. Bullock, *Life and Times of Ernest Bevin*, vol. 2, pp. 391–2; K. Harris, *Attlee*, pp. 262–5; F. Williams, *Ernest Bevin*, pp. 238–9; F. Williams, *A Prime Minister Remembers*, pp. 3–8.
115. Bullock, *Ernest Bevin*, p. 455; Dalton, *High Tide*, p. 242.
116. Bullock, *Life and Times of Ernest Bevin*, vol. 2, p. 118; K. Harris, *Attlee*, p. 347.
117. G. Goodman, *State of the Nation*, p. 207; P. Gordon Walker, 'Attlee', in Lord Longford and J. Wheeler-Bennett (eds), *The History Makers* (New York: St Martin's, 1973), p. 303; Healey, *Time of My Life*, p. 153; Morgan, *Labour People*, pp. 144, 179; Wilson, *A Prime Minister on Prime Ministers*, pp. 279, 299.
118. Pearce, *Attlee*, p. 154.
119. Rowse, *Glimpses*, pp. 50, 67.
120. Morgan, *Labour People*, p. 208.
121. Ibid., p. 140.
122. Addison, *Now the War is Over*, p. 99; G. Godber, *The Health Service: Past, Present and Future* (London: Athlone, 1975), p. 16.
123. Campbell, *Aneurin Bevan*, p. 170; Pearce, *Attlee*, p. 154.
124. Foot, *Health Policies*, p. 137; Honingsbaum, *Division in British Medicine*, pp. 212, 290.
125. J. Parker, *Father of the House: Fifty Years in Politics* (London: Routledge & Kegan Paul, 1982), p. 84; Pater, *Making of National Health Service*, p. 118.
126. Campbell, *Aneurin Bevan*, p. 175; Lee, *My Life with Nye*, p. 157.
127. Dalton, *High Tide*, p. 350.
128. H. Morrison, *Government and Parliament: A Survey from the Inside*, 3rd edn (London: Oxford University Press, 1964), pp. 293–4.
129. Bevan, *In Place of Fear*, p. 199.
130. R. Brain, *Medicine and Government* (London: Tavistock Publications, 1967), p. 4; Willcocks, *Creation of National Health Service*, p. 94.
131. Fox, *Health Policies*, p. 139n.
132. Heidenheimer, Heclo and Adams, *Comparative Public Policy*, p. 61.
133. Porter, *Greatest Benefit to Mankind*, p. 653.

134. Brain, *Doctor's Place in Society*, p. 5; Fielding, Thompson and Tiratsoo, *'England Arise!'*, p. 105.
135. Godber, *Health Service*, pp. 17–18; N. Goodman, *Wilson Jameson*, p. 111; Willcocks, *Creation of National Health Service*, pp. 99, 107.
136. F. Honigsbaum, 'The Evolution of the NHS', *British Medical Journal*, 301, 6, 754 (1990), p. 698.
137. Hennessy, *Never Again*, p. 139; Pater, *Making of National Health Service*, pp. 110–11.
138. Morgan, *Labour in Power*, p. 143.
139. F. Craig (ed.), *British General Election Manifestos 1900–1974* (London: Macmillan, 1975), p. 129.
140. Jewkes and Jewkes, *Genesis of British National Health Service*, p. 2.
141. Fox, *Health Policies*, p. 133; Grimes, *British National Health Service*, pp. 136–7.
142. *British Medical Journal*, 2 July 1988, p. 14.
143. Kavanagh, 'Postwar Consensus', p. 184; Morgan, *People's Peace*, p. 64; Morgan, *Red Dragon*, p. 9.
144. Campbell, *Aneurin Bevan*, p. 166.
145. Craig, *British General Election Manifestos*, p. 109.
146. Morgan, *Labour in Power*, p. 143.
147. B. Shaw, *The Doctor's Dilemma: A Tragedy* (London: Penguin, 1987), p. 86.
148. G. Cole, *Great Britain in the Post-war World* (London: Victor Gollancz, 1942), p. 140.
149. Ibid., pp. 82–91.
150. Labour Party, *National Service for Health* (London: Labour Party, 1943), p. 13; Sked and Cook, *Post-war Britain*, p. 38.
151. Hollis, *Jennie Lee*; Lowe, *Welfare State*, p. 178.
152. Widgery, *Health in Danger*, p. 32.
153. Brain, *Doctor's Place in Society*, p. 5.
154. *National Health Service Act, 1946*: 9 & 10 Geo. 6. Ch. 81 (London: Her Majesty's Stationery Office, no date), A3.
155. Keidan, 'Health Services', p. 135.
156. *NHS Act 1946*, A3.
157. Labour Party, *National Service for Health*, pp. 8, 12, 14, 18.
158. Ibid., p. 16.
159. Ibid., p. 12.
160. Grimes, *British National Health Service*, p. 136.
161. A. J. Cronin, *The Citadel* (New York: Bantam Books, 1962), p. 270; A. Lindsey, *Socialized Medicine in England and Wales: The National Health Service, 1948–1961* (Chapel Hill, NC: University of North Carolina Press, 1962), p. 170; Lowe, *Welfare State*, p. 172.
162. H. Hopkins, *The New Look: A Social History of the Forties and Fifties in Britain* (Boston, MA: Houghton Mifflin, 1964), p. 134.
163. Carr-Saunders and Wilson, *The Professions*, p. 100; Foot, *Aneurin Bevan*, vol. 2, p. 109; P. Gemmill, *Britain's Search for Health: The First Decade of the National Health Service* (Philadelphia, PA: University of Pennsylvania Press, 1960), pp. 117–18; Lowe, *Welfare State*, p. 172; R. Stevenson, *Morell Mackenzie: The Story of a Victorian Tragedy* (London: William Heinemann Medical Books, 1946), p. 17; Widgery, *Health in Danger*, p. 9.
164. Widgery, *Health in Danger*, p. 25.
165. Bevan, *In Place of Fear*, p. 86.
166. Grimes, *British National Health Service*, p. 173.
167. Foot, *Aneurin Bevan*, vol. 2, p. 181.
168. F. Honigsbaum, *Health, Happiness, and Security: The Creation of the National Health Service* (London: Routledge, 1989), p. 150.
169. Gray, 'How GPs Came to Heel', p. 14.
170. Supplement to *British Medical Journal*, 5 August 1944, pp. 28–9; Lindsey, *Socialized Medicine*, pp. 50–1.
171. Grimes, *British National Health Service*, p. 155; C. Hill, *Both Sides*, p. 98.
172. Fraser, *Evolution of British Welfare State*, p. 219.
173. Gemmill, *Britain's Search for Health*, p. 117.
174. Lindsey, *Socialized Medicine*, pp. 42, 51; Lowe, *Welfare State*, p. 375, n14; Widgery, *Health in Danger*, p. 31.
175. Lindsey, *Socialized Medicine*, pp. 157, 205.

176. Campbell, *Aneurin Bevan*, p. 174.
177. Lord Hill of Luton, 'Aneurin Bevan among the Doctors', *British Medical Journal*, 24 November 1973, p. 469.
178. Supplement to *British Medical Journal*, 10 July 1954, p. 44; 21 July 1956, p. 61; Lindsey, *Socialized Medicine*, p. 158.
179. Hennessy, *Never Again*, p. 132.

— 5 —

The Minister

If the creation of the National Health Service was not the result of a consensus across party lines or a consensus within the Labour Party or a natural development of the 1911 National Insurance Act (created by Liberals), the case for Aneurin Bevan as the creator of the NHS is greatly strengthened. Bevan's contribution was surely substantial.[1] Perhaps no other British politician at the time could have revived health policy from the 'parlous state' in which it was left by the Willink White Paper.[2] It is unlikely that a Conservative minister of health would have nationalized municipal hospitals, let alone voluntary hospitals. Even within the Labour Party his vision may have been unique.[3] It is unlikely that any other likely Labour minister of health would have pushed so strongly for nationalization of hospitals. Christopher Lord Addison might have been a committed supporter of Bevan's initiative, but he was more than a few years past his vigorous prime. None of the other frontbench Labourites even thought of hospital nationalization before Bevan asked them to support it. It was his bill, not theirs. The entire bill – not merely the elimination of the sale of professional goodwill by NHS doctors – strongly bore his personal stamp and was his own work.[4] For Bevan, governing was a matter of priorities.[5] The NHS became his highest priority.[6] With the NHS, Bevan demonstrated that passionate devotion to a cause which Max Weber saw[7] as the first need of a charismatic leader, who alone has a genuine vocation for political leadership.

That the NHS became Bevan's cause was not entirely situational. In July 1945, Bevan's first choice of ministerial positions was Health.[8] For most Britons health policy was not then a burning issue.[9] It was so, however, for Bevan. If he failed to focus on housing policy, which was such a burning issue for the public, it was to focus instead on health policy, which became his ministerial preoccupation. As prime minister, Clement Attlee was a delegator of authority to his ministers.[10] In this respect Attlee resembled H. H. Asquith, whose significance as prime minister (1908–16) was not in what he did, but in what he tolerated others doing.[11] Asquith had tolerated Lloyd George's 1909 Budget and the 1911 National Insurance Act. Bevan not only enjoyed but made good use of the freedom Attlee's permissiveness gave his ministers.[12] Within Harold Lasswell's typology of leadership[13] Bevan was very much more of an 'agitator' than an 'administrator'. As minister of health he nevertheless displayed a sure grasp of administrative technique despite his lack of previous ministerial experience.[14] Not only could the agitator act as an administrator, he did so without losing any of his creative dynamism. He established the basis for a radically new system of medical care with remarkable speed and with generous Treasury funding.[15] The creation of the NHS doubled public expenditure on health care.[16] He put the NHS across in Cabinet and Parliament. In and outside Cabinet and Parliament he overcame opposition which would have deterred an administrator seeking consensus.[17] A future Labour prime minister would write admiringly of Bevan as 'a formidable minister who used a combination of moral suasion and personal power to bring opponents into line'.[18] Those opponents were especially determined among general practitioners in the BMA.[19] Most of the opponents were, sooner or later, converted. By March 1948 the British Institute of Public Opinion found that Conservatives supported Bevan's NHS by a margin of two to one.[20]

Converting the BMA was a slower process. While the NHS was being created many of the BMA's notables may well have hated Bevan. Eventually, most of these would recall with respect an impressive display of ministerial competence. When talking with doctors, which he did willingly, unlike Lloyd George in 1911, Bevan always answered their questions himself, without needing to consult his senior civil servants.[21] In so answering, he never equivocated for even a moment. He also immediately spotted weaknesses in his opponents' cases.[22] The most important of those BMA opponents was later to refer to 'the wisdom of Bevan's courageous proposals for hospital unification' and to write that the 'real Bevan was a man of distinction, even greatness'.[23] When Bevan died in 1960, an editorial in the *British Medical Journal*, in whose pages he had been excoriated while minister of health, referred to his 'force of character' and 'powers of debate', which made him 'the most brilliant minister of health this country has ever had'. That editorial ended: 'The medical profession may hope to find in future Ministers of Health men with the imagination and flexibility of mind of Aneurin Bevan.'[24] Because of Bevan's success, those future ministers did enjoy public support in standing up to sectional pressures.[25] They discovered: 'The mantle of Saint Nye Bevan is a strong shield, whichever party is in power.'[26]

Possible canonization aside, the creation of the NHS was for Bevan, by any terms, a success. It was, if not Britain's, at least Bevan's, finest hour.[27] By November 1948, he could announce in the House of Commons that more than 93 per cent of Britain's population was enrolled in the NHS. Caring for them by then were more than 90 per cent of Britain's general practitioners.[28] Given differences within the Cabinet, professional opposition and eternal excuses for backsliding, Bevan's ministerial achievement was prodigious.[29] Even the senior civil servants in his own ministry had tried to obstruct nationalization of hospitals.[30] His appointment by Attlee proved to have been a brilliant stroke.[31] The NHS was the most radically ambitious, and proved to be the most popular, the most cherished and the most enduring achievement of Attlee's prime ministership.[32] It became the permanent jewel in Labour's crown,[33] the most successful initiative by the British left in the twentieth century.[34] A future Labour prime minister saw the NHS as the 'living embodiment of British democratic socialism'.[35] Superlatives flowed. The NHS was seen as 'the greatest single achievement of the postwar "social revolution"',[36] and even 'the most enlightened social reform' in British history.[37] Because it became 'the social institution of which the British would feel most proud',[38] the Labour Party got credit from voters for Bevan's creation for at least the rest of the twentieth century,[39] perhaps even 'for ever more'.[40] After the Conservatives returned to power under Churchill in 1951, they did not attempt to repeal the NHS Act.[41] This eventual Conservative Party acceptance of the NHS apparently surprised Bevan.[42] When a Conservative prime minister, Margaret Thatcher, much later, long after Bevan's death, appeared to threaten the NHS, the most energetic of its many defenders were the general practitioners in the British Medical Association. In a 1990 BMA poll 85 per cent of general practitioners opposed hospitals opting out of NHS control.[43] Not only had doctors as well as patients benefited from the NHS, doctors as well as patients had come to trust the NHS.[44] The 1968 report of the Royal Commission on Medical Education concluded that 'the institution of the National Health Service must rank as one of the greatest social advances in our history'.[45]

That Britain became the first Western society to offer all of its people comprehensive health care free at the point of delivery[46] was certainly noticed abroad. The NHS may have been 'admired throughout the world',[47] at least by many progressives, but the claim that the NHS 'became a model for the world'[48] has yet to be realized, even for the first such emulator. That a half-century later the NHS has not been reproduced elsewhere is especially striking in view of its lasting political popularity in Britain. A careful 1974 cross-national study, of five social policy areas (education, health care, housing, old-age security and employment), as perceived by citizens in four developed democratic nations (Britain, West Germany, the Netherlands and the United States) found the highest single policy satisfaction level to be that of the British for their health care policies.[49] That high satisfaction level was spread across class lines. Similar results were found in an end-of-century poll. When British voters were asked to identify which government achievements had contributed most to British life, 46 per cent (49 per cent of Conservative voters) identified the creation of the NHS.[50] Which social groups, the 1974 study further suggested, are assured health care is the result of specific national political choices, not merely the product of socioeconomic development,[51] which may, of course, be shared across national boundaries. Perhaps no other nation has replicated the National Health Service because no other nation has had Aneurin Bevan making health policy decisions. That he was minister of health may explain the anomaly of a conservative political system producing the 'most radical and comprehensive public health service in the world'.[52]

If the National Health Service was created by Aneurin Bevan, its roots are still not yet adequately explained. How health policy became Bevan's highest priority and, separately, how the specific contours of the NHS came to be his strongly preferred means for achieving his highest priority, are not immediately evident. These two questions have often been confused. The origins of Bevan's inherent and instrumental values have been merged into one question. In the process, the roots of the NHS have been too easily identified with Bevan's personal roots. This confusion has surfaced in serious scholarly studies. The conflict between the BMA and the minister of health has been seen as one between an organization which 'consisted mainly of conservative and middle-class Anglo-Saxons' in England and 'a supremely agile Welsh socialist',[53] who persisted with 'the obstinate determination of a Welshman'.[54] Bevan's 'well-nourished class resentments' had been 'nurtured by that crucible of socialism, the Welsh mining valleys'.[55] Workers in Welsh coalmines were certainly the bedrock of British socialism. Not only was Bevan born and raised in such a Welsh valley, his father and his father's father were coalminers. When he was turning 14, Aneurin Bevan became a coalminer himself, and remained such for the next seven years.[56] He served as a miners' agent, and his entire parliamentary career was spent representing, from 1929 until his death in 1960, the Ebbw Vale division of Monmouthshire, in which division he had been born and raised. His constituents were largely coalminers and their families, many of whom had been part of his daily life and work. He was fighting their battles when he crossed swords during the great depression of the 1930s with less militant trade union leaders such as Ernest Bevin.[57]

In so doing Aneurin Bevan was not merely speaking for his constituents. Their votes were necessary to his parliamentary career but they were also his own people. He spoke for them without hesitation and without apology because he was one of them. His inherent values were their inherent values because he had learned those values from them: 'His strong personal convictions had been forged in South Wales.'[58] The first two decades of his life were spent in the shelter, but also the seclusion, of his home valley. In that valley 'he was cradled'.[59] As a young miner he not only still lived with his parents and siblings, but he worked beside his father and brother and boyhood companions in the same mines. After his father was converted to socialism, so was he. This political transformation occurred not merely in his own family. Welsh miners moved easily from their dominant equalitarian ethic of Protestant nonconformity to the equalitarian ethic of British socialism. Bevan's father was a Baptist, his mother a Methodist who moved to Baptism, and the young Aneurin Bevan was a faithful attendant at Sunday school.[60] When part of a Sunday-school class broke away to form a local branch of the Independent Labour Party, the adolescent Bevan also moved. The social gospel of Welsh nonconformity had found a new home. So had Bevan. That new home, like the former, integrated the personal and the political. The texture of his life shaped his ideas.[61] Personal identity and group consciousness were not in conflict, let alone isolated from each other. When he was a young adult, Bevan's family and community faced the same problems. When his ill father was denied sickness benefits, Bevan fought successfully to have those benefits restored.[62] The father was to die, in his son's arms, of the dreaded coalminers' disease, pneumoconiosis.[63]

David Bevan had been a founding member of the Tredegar Working Men's Medical Aid Society.[64] This local mutual insurance society has been seen as the prototype[65] of 'an embryonic'[66] National Health Service. The society is argued to have 'blossomed' into the NHS as Bevan 'applied to the nation the lessons he had learned'[67] in his youth in Wales.

The NHS bore no significant resemblance to the Tredegar Working Men's Medical Aid Society, worthy as the latter organization surely was. That society was local not national, in its creation private not governmental, restricted not universal, providing insurance not an entitlement. The operation of that society mattered to the youthful Aneurin Bevan[68] and to Tredegar, but it did not serve as his guide for planning the NHS. Some of his local political activities did serve to introduce him to health policy questions, and provided an early practical focus for attempting to implement his equalitarian values. After election in 1922 to his first governmental office, Urban District Councillor Bevan became active on health policy issues, including the medical needs of unemployed workers not covered under the National Insurance Act of 1911. Serving on the council's Hospitals Committee, he learned more about medical care beyond that provided by general practitioners.[69] He now observed at first hand the relative lack of well-equipped modern hospitals, and the resentment of commercialized health care, which characterized south Wales.[70] Such learning experiences would, of course, have been possible in many other parts of Britain, especially outside the largest urban concentrations of prestigious teaching hospitals. What Bevan observed might well have been relatively general. That he learned to give priority to the need for equal access to quality medical treatment was his personal achievement.

Bevan also needed to learn how to reach that goal. He was confident of his diagnosis, but uncertain which treatment would cure. His personal experience and observation taught him what was inadequate in the operation of the National Insurance Act of 1911. That experience and observation could not teach him how to achieve Lloyd George's unattained ultimate goal, which was also now his own goal. No party in Britain, including his own, could provide adequate instruction in implementing his goal. The Beveridge Report was silent on how medical care could be restructured. Civil servants in the Ministry of Health were unused to ministers who asked large questions, especially on health, not housing, policy. Bevan needed expert practical advice. The most likely relevant possible experts were consultant physicians. The largest organization of British doctors, the BMA, did not share his goal, and had bitterly opposed even Lloyd George's partial restructuring of British medicine in 1911. In any event, Bevan was too much an individualist to listen to any institution. What he needed was an expert confidential adviser whom he trusted, or could come to trust. The field was not large. Preoccupied with his official duties, Christopher Lord Addison might have offered an occasional ear, but does not seem to have done even that. Bertrand Lord Dawson, former president of the Royal College of Physicians (London), who had late in life taken part in the Parliamentary Medical Group attempting to influence successive ministers of health,[71] had died a few months earlier. There were in Britain in late 1945 two most likely such medical consultants. Bevan's choice would significantly mould the features of the National Health Service, which may have had in consequence two parents, not only one creator. With his choice the minister acquired not only an adviser, but an ally.

NOTES

1. B. Griffith, S. Iliffe and G. Rayner, *Banking on Sickness: Commercial Medicine in Britain and the USA* (London: Lawrence & Wishart, 1987), p. 26.
2. Honingsbaum, *Division in British Medicine*, p. 324.
3. G. Goodman, *State of the Nation*, p. 34; Pugh, *State and Society*, p. 240.
4. Morgan, *Labour People*, p. 208; Morgan, *Red Dragon*, p. 9.
5. F. Williams, *A Prime Minister Remembers*, p. 89.
6. Morgan, *Labour People*, p. 208.
7. Gerth and Mills, *From Max Weber*, p. 115.
8. Foot, *Aneurin Bevan*, vol. 1, p. 509.
9. *British Medical Journal*, 1 July 1978, p. 29.
10. Burch, 'Prime Minister and Whitehall', p. 111.
11. M. Rintala, 'Taking the Pledge: H. H. Asquith and Drink', *Biography*, 16 (1993), p. 111.
12. Burridge, *Clement Attlee*, p. 190; Foot, *Aneurin Bevan*, vol. 2, pp. 25, 30.
13. H. Lasswell, *Psychopathology and Politics* (New York: Viking, 1960), pp. 2, 8, 78–152, 262; H. Lasswell, *Power and Personality* (New York: Viking, 1969), pp. 59, 63, 88–9.
14. Clarke, *Hope and Glory*, pp. 222–3.
15. Brain, *Doctor's Place in Society*, p. 5; Clegg, *Medicine in Britain*, p. 30; Lowe, *Welfare State*, p. 183; Mackenzie, *Power and Responsibility*, p. 155; I. Richard, *We, the British* (Garden City, NY: Doubleday, 1983), p. 184.
16. Webster, 'Conflict and Consensus', p. 150.
17. Honigsbaum, *Division in British Medicine*, p. 324; C. Howard, '"After This, What?": To 1945 and Beyond', *Historical Journal*, 28, 3 (1985), p. 768.
18. G. Goodman, *State of the Nation*, p. 12.
19. Foote, *Labour Party's Political Thought*, p. 273; Honigsbaum, *Division in British Medicine*, pp. 323–4.
20. Grimes, *British National Health Service*, p. 192.
21. *British Medical Journal*, 1 July 1978, p. 31; Gray, 'How GPs Came to Heel', p. 14.
22. C. Hill, *Both Sides*, p. 94.
23. Ibid., p. 86; C. Hill, 'Aneurin Bevan', p. 469.

24. *British Medical Journal*, 26 July 1960, p. 204.
25. H. Daalder, 'Cabinet Reform since 1914', in V. Herman and J. Alt (eds), *Cabinet Studies: A Reader* (New York: St Martin's, 1975), p. 258.
26. Mackenzie, *Power and Responsibility*, p. 148.
27. K. Laybourn, *The Rise of Labour: The British Labour Party 1890–1979* (London: Edward Arnold, 1988), p. 116.
28. Foot, *Aneurin Bevan*, vol. 2, p. 213; Morgan, *Labour in Power*, p. 160; Sked and Cook, *Post-war Britain*, p. 45.
29. Sked and Cook, *Post-war Britain*, p. 46.
30. Webster, 'Conflict and Consensus', p. 146.
31. Burridge, *Clement Attlee*, p. 190; Hollis, *Jennie Lee*, p. 123.
32. G. Goodman, *State of the Nation*, p. 92; Hollis, *Jennie Lee*, pp. 131, 158; K. Jeffreys, *The Labour Party since 1945* (London: Macmillan, 1993), pp. 18–19, 32; Lowe, *Welfare State*, p. 167; Pearce, *Attlee*, p. 135; Sissons and French, *Age of Austerity*, p. 242.
33. Jeffreys, *Labour Party*, p. 18.
34. G. Goodman, *State of the Nation*, p. 232.
35. Ibid., p. 11.
36. Hopkins, *New Look*, p. 135.
37. D. Owen, *In Sickness*, p. 2.
38. Sked and Cook, *Post-war Britain*, p. 42.
39. Clarke, *Hope and Glory*, p. 24; Griffith, Iliffe and Rayner, *Banking on Sickness*, p. 26; Webster, 'Conflict and Consensus', p. 149.
40. Harrop, *Power and Policy*, p. 168.
41. R. Blake and W. Louis (eds), *Churchill* (New York: W. W. Norton, 1993), p. 8; Jeffreys, *Churchill Coalition*, p. 215; Richard, *We, the British*, p. 184; K. Robbins, *Churchill* (London: Longman, 1992), p. 161.
42. Bevan, *In Place of Fear*, p. 87.
43. G. Goodman, *State of the Nation*, pp. 57, 227; Morgan, *People's Peace*, p. 494; *The Guardian*, 10 October 1990, p. 2.
44. G. Goodman, *State of the Nation*, p. 125; Sked and Cook, *Post-war Britain*, p. 45.
45. N. Goodman, *Wilson Jameson*, p. 124.
46. Pearce, *Attlee*, p. 154.
47. Morgan, *Labour in Power*, p. 162.
48. L. Abse, *Margaret, Daughter of Beatrice: A Politician's Psycho-biography of Margaret Thatcher* (London: Jonathan Cape, 1989), p. 154.
49. Heidenheimer, Heclo and Adams, *Comparative Public Policy*, pp. 354–6.
50. J. Bartle, 'Why Labour Won – Again', in A. King, *Britain at the Polls, 2001*(New York: Chatham House, 2002), p. 180.
51. Heidenheimer, Heclo and Adams, *Comparative Public Policy*, p. 58.
52. Honigsbaum, 'The Evolution of the NHS', p. 694.
53. Addison, *Now the War is Over*, pp. 101–2.
54. Sissons and French, *Age of Austerity*, p. 244.
55. Morgan, *People's Peace*, p. 38.
56. Foot, *Aneurin Bevan*, vol. 1, pp. 13–14, 21, 38.
57. Morgan, *Red Dragon*, pp. 4–5.
58. Lowe, *Welfare State*, p. 178.
59. Abse, *Margaret, Daughter of Beatrice*, p. 153.
60. Foot, *Aneurin Bevan*, vol. 1, pp. 13, 17, 23; S. Koss, *Nonconformity in Modern British Politics* (London: B. T. Batsford, 1975), p. 149.
61. Widgery, *Health in Danger*, p. 25.
62. Foot, *Aneurin Bevan*, vol. 1, p. 48.
63. Bevan, *In Place of Fear*, p. 26.
64. Foot, *Aneurin Bevan*, vol. 1, pp. 14, 70; Sissons and French, *Age of Austerity*, p. 241; Widgery, *Health in Danger*, p. 25.
65. Abse, *Margaret, Daughter of Beatrice*, p. 173.
66. Foot, *Aneurin Bevan*, vol. 1, p. 66.
67. Abse, *Margaret, Daughter of Beatrice*, p. 102.
68. Fox, *Health Policies*, p. 134.
69. Foot, *Aneurin Bevan*, vol. 1, pp. 55, 57, 66–8.

70. Lowe, *Welfare State*, p. 178.
71. H. Morris-Jones, *Doctor in the Whips' Room* (London: Robert Hale, 1955), p. 160.
    Dawson's death was unnoticed by M. Bruce, *The Coming of the Welfare State* (London:
    B. T. Batsford, 1961), p. 284.

Part II:

Doctors Differ

'For all the world, I count it not an inn, but an hospital ...'
Sir Thomas Browne, *Religio Medici*

6

Introduction

The creation of the National Health Service has attracted the attention of a great many authors, scholarly and otherwise. Most of those authors discuss the role of doctors in the creation of the NHS. Some of those authors write of 'the hostility of the medical profession to the government's proposals',[1] whose effect was that 'the representatives of the medical profession opposed'[2] the creation of the NHS. This perception of a profession united in its hostility stresses conflict between minister of health Aneurin Bevan and the British Medical Association. A more consensual variation of this theme sees the BMA as 'the body with which the government negotiated the role of the medical profession in the NHS'.[3]

Such emphasis upon a unified medical profession ignores the fact that British doctors differed in their reactions to the prospective NHS. Some other authors not only recognize those differences, but emphasize divergent reactions by general practitioners and consultants. This emphasis reflects the major social cleavage within the practice of British medicine. Most British doctors were then general practitioners, with primary responsibility for the medical care of most Britons, but without hospital privileges. Hospitals were essentially the domain of consultant physicians and surgeons. Originally, consultants had not been specialists, but merely those relatively few doctors frequently called in to give a second opinion in difficult cases. As possible medical treatments expanded, a consultant not only gave a second diagnostic opinion but, if necessary, carried out a specialized technique or surgical procedure beyond the recognized scope of the general practitioner. Since such specialized diagnostic tools or treatments often needed hospital facilities, consultants gradually became hospital physicians who also maintained separate and individual private practices. Authors stressing this professional cleavage see general practitioners as represented by the BMA and consultants as represented by three royal colleges: Physicians, Surgeons and Obstetricians/Gynaecologists.[4] Consultants are seen as 'pleased by the proposed NHS',[5] having 'got what they wanted' from Bevan[6]. Since general practitioners are seen as 'bitterly opposed',[7] the 'division of interest between the specialist and the general practitioner made possible the introduction of the NHS'.[8]

Common to both emphases is the assumption that doctors, whether they spoke with one voice or with two voices, spoke through one or more organized pressure groups. Policy in this case is seen as influenced by 'the major pressure groups with an interest in health services'.[9] An early influential scholarly study by Harry Eckstein both reflected and encouraged such a focus with its title: *Pressure Group Politics: The Case of the British Medical Association*.[10] This focus was further strengthened by publication of Aneurin Bevan's recollections, which argued: 'No pressure groups are more highly organized in Britain than the professions, and among these the medical professions are the strongest.'[11] During 1945–48, Bevan certainly skilfully exploited the cleavage between consultants and general practitioners,[12] which was for him another example of his broader understanding of politics as 'the arena of interests'.[13] This understanding may explain what has been seen as an anomaly,[14] that the creation of so idealistic an institution was remarkably unaltruistic.

To see consultants differing from general practitioners over the NHS is surely more perceptive than to see British doctors united against the NHS. Illuminating 'the complex nature of intra-medical politics'[15] is a necessary scholarly advance. There is, however, an important similarity, which is not a strength, shared by the two approaches. The 'parts played by individuals'[16] in creating the NHS are often overlooked. The personal influence exerted by particular doctors, not merely particular politicians, is slighted and sometimes ignored. Authors who see doctors united against the NHS would have no reason to search deeply or widely for attitudes and actions of individual doctors. Authors who see the creation of the NHS as involving a corporate struggle between consultants and general practitioners might also fail to search for such individual attitudes and actions. If there was a 'curious combination of anger and accommodation in the medical profession',[17] it may be that, say, individual consultants who were angry should be studied along with individual consultants who were accommodating. That is one important task of the present study.

Individual doctors are visible in the NHS literature mostly when they are wearing some kind of institutional hat. That hat is briefly labelled, but how it was donned, how securely it was on, and how it would be doffed remain unexamined matters. In British medicine at the time, many different institutional hats were worn, not necessarily at different times, by one prestigious doctor. Even in the cases of those with multiple hats little attention has been paid to serious biographical study. Often the face, and even an old medical school tie, remains hidden under the hat. The names of the two doctors dominating the present study do not appear in the index to Eckstein's *Pressure Group Politics*. Aneurin Bevan's published recollections do not mention his private negotiations, which determined at least the fate of hospitals and hospital doctors in the NHS, with one of those two doctors. Perhaps politicians prefer to maintain public silence about the politics of personal influence, but scholars should be more diligent.

Even Bevan occasionally distinguished among consultants, telling British medical students that his NHS bill had the support of 'the best elements on the specialist side of the profession'.[18] The best of the best was for him Charles Wilson, Lord Moran, his chief and constant consultant ally. In the discussions creating the NHS Moran was considered, including by himself, to represent hospital consultant doctors.[19] Not all consultants, however, agreed with Moran, who was president of the Royal College of Physicians (London). The fellows of that college were in fact deeply divided over the NHS, and this division reflected the personalities of two particular fellows, Moran and Thomas Lord Horder. These two consulting physicians may have been the best-known doctors in Britain.[20] They were certainly the only two practising doctors then in the House of Lords, which gave each a distinguished official platform from which to speak. Both spoke freely, and to opposing purposes.

Horder was active in opposition to the NHS 'on behalf of the consultant side of the profession'.[21] He led, however, more than those consultants who were opposed. He was 'the leader of the doctors opposed to the Act'.[22] He led the medical charge against the NHS.[23] Most of the doctors who followed Horder were general practitioners, not consultants. For a few months in early 1948 he proclaimed: 'I am more and more a "BMA man".'[24] This was only a statement made in the heat of a passing passionate moment. He was not a trade unionist, but a member of the British medical establishment. If Horder loved any organization of doctors, it was the Royal College of Physicians, not the British Medical Association. Even that love, great as it was, was not absolute. Looking back on *Fifty Years of Medicine*, he saw: 'My own interests have been concerned with the individual rather than the group.'[25] Even while he was still at the heart of the British medical establishment, Horder was not apologetic for valuing individuals over institutions: 'It is the vision of the *individual*, not the adherence of the propagandized mass, that saves the public from perishing.'[26]

Speaking for, and supported by, no significant pressure group, from 1946 Horder nevertheless became the leader not only of doctors, but many other Britons as well, opposed to the NHS. He may well have been 'foremost among those who opposed the National Health Service'.[27] Without any significant institutional hat, he relied essentially on his own prestige. He had achieved deserved eminence in his profession. He had become not only Britain's leading consultant physician, but quite probably the most distinguished of all British physicians of his time. His was a household name in Britain. He was the medical personality best known to the general public.[28] He was known even outside Britain. Addressing an august medical assembly in 1936 in Edinburgh, he could not resist crowing: 'When I arrived in New York a few months ago, the pressmen crowded into my cabin, as they usually do.'[29]

The disagreement between Horder and Moran over the creation of the NHS was therefore a battle of medical giants. It was also only one battle in a war that lasted for at least the last 35 years of Horder's lifetime (1871–1955). If there had been no earlier battles in this war, their battle over the NHS might not have taken place. Because this battle did take place, and ending as it did, the remaining lives of both combatants were profoundly affected. One emerged triumphant, yet again, and the other totally defeated. After this battle, only one giant remained fit to do battle. Winners often loom larger, but Moran had the further advantage after 1948 of outliving Horder by 22 years. Earlier, long before 1945–48, the advantage had been Horder's. Moran was 11 years younger. More relevant, perhaps, for combatants in the same profession, Horder had been registered to practise medicine in 1896, and Moran in 1908.[30] Horder was therefore the senior combatant, deserving pride of place in what follows.

NOTES

1. A. Sked and C. Cook, *Post-war Britain: A Political History*, 2nd edn (Harmondsworth: Penguin, 1984), p. 41.
2. D. Owen, *In Sickness and In Health: The Politics of Medicine* (London: Quartet Books, 1976), p. 96.
3. P. Hatcher, 'The Health System of the United Kingdom', in M. Raffel (ed.), *Health Care and Reform in Industrialized Countries* (University Park, PA: Pennsylvania State University Press, 1997), p. 245.
4. P. Clarke, *Hope and Glory: Britain 1900–1990* (London: Penguin, 1997), p. 223; J. Fry, *General Practice and Primary Health Care 1940s–1980s* (London: Nuffield Provincial Hospitals Trust, 1988), p. 10; P. Hennessy, *Never Again: Britain 1945–1951* (London: Vintage, 1993), p. 140; R. Klein, *The Politics of the National Health Service* (London: Longman, 1983), p. 20; R. Lowe, *The Welfare State in Britain since 1945*, 2nd edn (London: Macmillan, 1999), p. 168; W. Mackenzie, *Power and Responsibility in Health Care: The National Health Service as a Political Institution* (Oxford: Oxford University Press, 1979), pp. 62–3; R. Stevens, *Medical Practice in Modern England: The Impact of Specialization and State Medicine* (New Haven, CT: Yale University Press, 1966), p. 77; R. Stevenson, *Morell Mackenzie: The Story of a Victorian Tragedy* (London: William Heinemann Medical Books, 1946), p. 47; D. Widgery, *Health in Danger: The Crisis in the National Health Service* (Hamden, CT: Archon, 1979), p. 29; A. Willcocks, *The Creation of the National Health Service: A Study of Pressure Groups and a Major Social Policy Decision* (London: Routledge & Kegan Paul, 1967), p. 30.
5. D. Fox, *Health Policies, Health Politics: The British and American Experience 1911–1965* (Princeton, NJ: Princeton University Press, 1986), p. 133.
6. P. Hollis, *Jennie Lee: A Life* (Oxford: Oxford University Press, 1997), p. 129.
7. Lowe, *Welfare State*, p. 168.
8. G. Forsyth, *Doctors and State Medicine: A Study of the British Health Service* (London: Pitman Medical Publishing, 1966), p. 2.
9. C. Ham, *Health Policy in Britain: The Politics and Organisation of the National Health Service*, 2nd edn (London: Macmillan, 1985), p. 16.
10. H. Eckstein, *Pressure Group Politics: The Case of the British Medical Association* (Stanford, CA: Stanford University Press, 1960).
11. A. Bevan, *In Place of Fear* (New York: Simon & Schuster, 1953), p. 91.
12. Fellowship for Freedom in Medicine, *The Medical Surrender (July, 1948): An Account of the Events Leading up to the Acceptance by the Medical Profession in Great Britain of the National Health Service Act* (London: FFM, 1951), p. 5; M. Foot, *Aneurin Bevan*, vol 2 (New York: Atheneum, 1974), p. 169; G. Goodman (ed.), *The State of the Nation: The Political Legacy of Aneurin Bevan* (London: Victor Gollancz, 1997), p. 55; C. Ham, *Health Policy in Britain*, p. 16; Mackenzie, *Power and Responsibility*, p. 77; Willcocks, *Creation of National Health Service*, p. 106.
13. M. Foot, *Aneurin Bevan*, vol. 1 (London: Granada, 1982), p. 166.
14. Lowe, *Welfare State*, p. 183.
15. Klein, *Politics of National Health Service*, p. 24.
16. R. Maxwell in J. Pater, *The Making of the National Health Service* (London: King Edward's Hospital Fund for London, 1981), p. v.
17. D. Fox in *Social History of Medicine*, 3, 1 (1990), p. 104.
18. Foot, *Aneurin Bevan*, vol. 2, p. 160.
19. Lowe, *Welfare State*, p. 170.
20. Foot, *Aneurin Bevan*, vol. 2, p. 159; R. Lovell, *Churchill's Doctor: A Biography of Lord Moran* (London: Royal Society of Medicine Services, 1992), p. 154.
21. A. Cooke, *A History of the Royal College of Physicians of London* (Oxford: Clarendon, 1972), vol. 3, p. 1, 115.
22. F. Honigsbaum, *The Division in British Medicine: A History of the Separation of General Practice from Hospital Care 1911–1968* (London: Kogan Page, 1979), p. 296.
23. Foot, *Aneurin Bevan*, vol. 2, pp. 159, 173, 196, 204, 207, 211.
24. Supplement to *British Medical Journal*, 27 March 1948, p. 50.
25. Lord Horder, *Fifty Years of Medicine* (London: Gerald Duckworth, 1953), p. 22.

26. Lord Horder, *Obscurantism* (London: Watts, 1938), p. 5.
27. B. Watkin, *The National Health Service: The First Phase 1948–1974 and After* (London: George Allen & Unwin, 1978), p. 3.
28. *British Medical Journal*, 20 August 1955, p. 493; 27 August 1955, p. 566; W. Cruden, 'Lord Horder – The Clinician', *St Bartholomew's Hospital Journal*, 61, 8 (1957), p. 247; D. Gullick, 'Forty Years of the NHS: The Act, the Minister, and the Editors', *British Medical Journal*, 297 (1988), p. 56; Lord Hill, *Both Sides of the Hill* (London: Heinemann, 1964), p. 92; R. Lamont-Brown, *Royal Poxes and Potions: The Lives of Court Physicians, Surgeons and Apothecaries* (Stroud: Sutton, 2001), p. 235; Lovell, *Churchill's Doctor*, p. 154; V. Medvei and J. Thornton (eds), *The Royal Hospital of Saint Bartholomew 1123–1973* (London: Royal Hospital of Saint Bartholomew, 1974), p. 195; H. Oxbury, *Great Britons: Twentieth-century Lives* (Oxford: Oxford University Press, 1985), p. 171; L. Witts, 'Thomas Jeeves Horder', in E. Williams and H. Palmer (eds), *The Dictionary of National Biography 1951–1960* (London: Oxford University Press, 1971), p. 502; Earl of Woolton, *The Memoirs of the Rt Hon. The Earl of Woolton* (London: Cassell, 1959), p. 279.
29. Lord Horder, *Health and a Day: Addresses* (London: J. M. Dent, 1937), p. 51.
30. *Medical Register, 1897* (London: General Medical Council, 1897), p. 710; *Medical Register, 1909* (London: General Medical Council, 1909), p. 1, 805.

7

A Royal Physician

In the winter of 1936 the medical community at St Bartholomew's Hospital, London, gathered for a farewell lecture by its retiring senior physician. 'Bart's' had seen many such ceremonies. Founded in the twelfth century as part of the Priory of St Bartholomew, the hospital survived appropriation of monasteries during the Protestant Reformation by using its new connection with the City of London to become one of the most important of London's many charitable institutions. By the eighteenth century Bart's prestige was so great that one of its governors, William Hogarth, bred in its shadow, was willing without payment to adorn its walls with his murals to advertise his work. Bart's medical research and the superior quality of its medical care eventually gave it far more than local fame. So did its medical teaching. Rising above their location next to Butchers Hall, Bart's doctors proudly relished their status as guardians of Britain's oldest hospital. Their individual incomes were impressive, and their students were the first British medical students to be housed in hospital-owned residences.[1]

Even in such a setting, the retirement of Thomas Lord Horder as physician to St Bartholomew's Hospital was a special occasion. Horder was genuinely a 'Bart's man', whose entire adult life had been centred on one institution. He had studied medicine there, finding a mentor, Samuel Gee, whom Horder would hardly have described as 'the eccentric clinician'.[2] Gee was fully worthy of his student's respect. Horder was to articulate that respect in his own professional publications. Those publications, relatively numerous, demonstrated a capacity for, as well as a serious interest in, medical research. Horder's research, however, was almost always directed at using the laboratory for improving clinical diagnosis and treatment of patients. His science was applied, not pure.[3] Horder's teaching, like Gee's, was also patient-centred, without losing respect for his students. He became a teacher of distinction, intellectually incisive and personally kind.[4]

As a junior physician Horder had served in several staff roles at Bart's including casualty physician, medical registrar, and demonstrator of morbid anatomy, before becoming assistant physician and, in 1921, full physician. Early in, and then again near the end of, his Bart's career, Horder had also served on the staff of the Royal (earlier Great) Northern Hospital. His heart was always at Bart's, nevertheless. Even throughout the First World War he met his obligations there while he also served, assigned to London, in the Royal Army Military Corps.[5]

At the emotional end of his farewell lecture Horder sounded an appropriate note of institutional continuity by dramatically addressing his successor, Geoffrey Evans, a former student: 'So now I doff my ward coat and hand it to you, Evans, my friend.' That Horder was not merely a company man had been suggested a few moments earlier, when he addressed all those in his audience who had been his students: 'I trust my methods and my teaching have conformed in some measure to the great traditions of this place. But they have been largely, and of necessity, myself.'[6]

Fidelity to Bart's was not only a sentimental matter to Horder. While serving his hospital in an unpaid position Horder, like British consulting hospital physicians generally, hoped to attract substantial numbers of paying patients to his separate private office. The institutional prestige provided by a hospital appointment, especially at a teaching hospital, was expected to produce personal wealth. In Horder's case it did. Not for nothing was his surname derived from the Old English word for 'keeper of the hoard'.[7] Horder's private practice was large even by Bart's standards. One of his eulogists was eventually to argue that Horder 'could never have had an enemy'.[8] That was far from true among his professional rivals, beginning with those at Bart's, where the size of Horder's private practice did not escape envious notice. Attention, not always favourable, was also attracted by many examples of Horder's conspicuous consumption. Not many young British doctors can have started married life with four (later at least six) household servants. Those servants had plenty to do, not only in Horder's London home but also in a succession of comfortable country houses.[9] Of the typical successful London doctor, Bernard Shaw had written in 1911: 'His house, his servants, and his equipage (or autopage) must be on the scale to which his patients are accustomed.'[10] His private patients were often accustomed to the best, but Horder did not need Shaw's tart advice. He had already furnished his private office, in his London home, with no fewer than six paintings by J. M. W. Turner. Horder's preferences in wines were equally fastidious. Even conspicuous consumption can be tasteful. The most visible and audible, and perhaps most widely envied, sign of Horder's affluence was his fleet of fashionable automobiles. Not all London physicians were as willing to make house calls on their patients as was Horder, but few of them could so conveniently drive up, as he regularly did, in a chauffeured Rolls-Royce, or, equally conveniently, blame their late arrival on their driver's having become lost. Since, as Horder's mordant sense of humour grasped, he was often consulted as a diagnostic last resort about a dying patient, his Rolls-Royce may have appeared to some knowledgeable members of the British establishment as a hearse.[11]

Horder's private patients were not only numerous, but notable. In 1910, first called, probably at the suggestion of his mentor Gee, to see a royal patient, he unhesitatingly corrected a diagnostic error by Edward VII's more senior physicians. Court doctors were not necessarily the best doctors. The best doctors might neverthe- less, become court doctors. That is what happened to Horder, whose later royal patients included George V, Edward VIII, George VI and Elizabeth II. Horder cornered a large part of the British market for royal patients, even visiting royalty. In the 1930s he presided over a distinguished team of surgeons at a London clinic who were removing a tooth from the king of Siam.[12] As Bernard Shaw also saw, the career of a British doctor called in to treat a royal patient 'is made'.[13] After he visited Edward VII, Horder had all the private patients he could handle. Indeed, there may have been more than that number. Horder seldom drew a line against a new patient. As he put it: 'I should be ready to treat Beelzebub himself if he came to my consulting room.'[14] More than one Lord of the Flies entered there, for their great consult, without finding a new recruit. Horder had few illusions about his powerful, wealthy and prestigious patients. He saw them as 'but poor navigators of their own ship'.[15]

Some of Horder's many private patients were non-royal nobles, one of whom, David Thomas, Viscount Rhondda left Horder £10,000 in his will, which bequest Inland Revenue judged to be payment for medical services rendered.[16] The most demand- ing of this group of patients was doubtless Alfred Harmsworth, Viscount Northcliffe, a dubious lord but a genuine press baron. Visiting his new patient, Horder was greeted by a reluctant and recumbent viscount shouting 'One of Lloyd George's bloody

Knights',[17] while reaching under his pillow for a pistol. A male nurse deflected the latter, but the verbal hostility was at least based on fact. Sir Thomas Horder (not yet ennobled) had indeed been knighted by Prime Minister David Lloyd George, who had also, however, elevated Northcliffe to his viscountcy. Even after this unpromising beginning, Horder faithfully made 54 professional visits to Northcliffe in the last two months of the latter's life. During those visits, Horder twice refused to witness his patient's new will, presumably because of his doubts as to the would-be testator's sanity. Eventually, however, Horder signed a statement, sought by Northcliffe's relatives, that no certificate of insanity had been issued.[18]

Only slightly less trouble was another substantial group of Horder's private patients: past, present or future British prime ministers. The first such patient, in 1908, was a dying Henry Campbell-Bannerman.[19] Although responsible for Horder's knight-hood, David Lloyd George was the patient of Bertrand Lord Dawson of Penn, Horder's illustrious immediate predecessor among British court physicians. In 1918, Dawson was among those meeting privately with Prime Minister Lloyd George to advise him on postwar health policy.[20] In 1920, with his ennoble-ment by Lloyd George, Dawson began speaking for the medical profession in the House of Lords. In the same year his advisory role became both more official and more public with an *Interim Report of the Consultative Council on Medical and Allied Services*, sub-mitted to the Ministry of Health. This document became known as the Dawson Report, after the council's chairman. This identifi-cation was apt, for it was essentially Dawson's report,[21] just as the Beveridge Report would be Beveridge's report. Dawson's report urged regionalizing health care, which was seen as involving both curative medicine and preventive medicine (the latter producing physical fitness).[22] This report was widely discussed, even though it recommended no detailed regional administrative mechanism. Dawson's council was only advisory,[23] and the Ministry of Health did not much care for his advice. No final version of the report was issued, and the council withered away.[24] The Cabinet was by then busy avoiding new health care expenditures.[25] Dawson's report remained on the shelf until at least the Second World War.[26] Lloyd George remained personally faithful to Dawson if not his public policy advice, even though Horder was intellectually superior and Dawson had been memorably satirized by Bernard Shaw.[27] Lloyd George's continued personal reliance on Dawson was encouraged by Frances Stevenson, Lloyd George's mistress, who liked Dawson's 'easy manner and understanding of human nature' as 'as a man of the world'.[28] Only in late 1940, when he wanted a doctor at short notice to support medically his disinclination to accept Prime Minister Winston Churchill's nomination to be ambassador to the United States, did Lloyd George consult Horder professionally. Lloyd George got what he wanted from Horder, but it was Dawson who would eventually confirm the diagnosis of Lloyd George's cancer, which in early 1945 proved fatal 19 days after Dawson himself died.[29]

Lloyd George's successor as prime minister, Andrew Bonar Law, was Horder's patient while still Lloyd George's loyal Coalition Cabinet lieutenant.[30] Pressured in October 1922 by many of his fellow Conservatives to abandon his support for Lloyd George to become prime minister himself, Bonar Law consulted Horder in the hope of getting a medical excuse for not so becoming. Horder, then at the height of his career, declined to provide such an excuse,[31] and Bonar Law became prime minister. A few months later, Horder travelled to Paris to examine an ailing Bonar Law. Now Horder diagnosed throat cancer, which was soon fatal.[32] Sir George Newman, chief medical officer at the Ministry of Health, later severely criticized Horder's advice to Bonar Law of October 1922,[33] but there seems to be no evidence that Horder had then missed a diagnosis. Such a failure would certainly have been atypical. Diagnostic skill was Horder's greatest strength as a physician, and the basis for his professional reputation. Confident in his diagnostic skills, he stood out as a hospital physician even at Bart's in personally entering his own diagnoses, in ink, on ward sheets. Whatever the circumstances of Bonar Law's death, his Rolls-Royce was soon Horder's property.[34]

Other prime ministers did not hesitate to follow Bonar Law into Horder's care. Ramsay MacDonald was among them. The claim that Horder and Prime Minister MacDonald breakfasted weekly throughout 1929–35 may be exaggerated, but they were frequent social companions, and it was MacDonald who ennobled Horder as a baron.[35] MacDonald was nevertheless not Horder's favourite prime minister. That honour fell to Neville Chamberlain,[36] who might not have appreciated Horder's rationale: 'I was very fond of him. I like all unlovable men.'[37] Chamberlain was Horder's patient for the dramatic last 12 months (November 1939–November 1940) of Chamberlain's life,[38] even though Horder's appointment books did not so reveal.[39] That silence is no surprise, for Horder kept no records of his more eminent private patients, and regularly shredded other, less notable, private patients' record cards and correspondence.[40] This shredding, too, is unsurprising, as failure to keep proper medical case notes was the norm among British physicians in private practice at least as late as 1940.[41]

Horder's relationship with Chamberlain's prime ministerial successor was both much longer and much more opaque than with Chamberlain. Horder's patients included some of Winston Churchill's extended family, including his politically active cousin Frederick Guest.[42] The claim by her grandson that it was Horder who in 1921 amputated the leg of Churchill's mother[43] was, however, at least imprecise. That amputation was followed by septicaemia and death, so this claim might suggest that Horder was at least indirectly responsible for the death of Lady Randolph Churchill. That both of her sons would later choose a doctor whom they suspected of responsibility for their mother's death is highly unlikely. At least in 1922, shortly after his mother's death, Winston Churchill was Horder's patient.[44] For many years after Lady Randolph Churchill's death her younger son, John Strange Churchill, was Horder's patient.[45] John Strange Churchill's son, who identified Horder as the surgeon involved in his grandmother's fatal illness, played an organ prelude at the memorial service for Horder. That prelude was written by Ralph Vaughan Williams, who also, with many other member of Britain's cultural establishment, perhaps inevitably, had been Horder's private patient.[46] Horder was certainly not qualified as a surgeon. While in training at Bart's he had avoided all the expected surgical portions of his curriculum, probably because of a deep fear of performing surgery.[47] He was entirely a physician, and never a surgeon. This was a professional line he would not cross, let alone in the case of the widow of one major politician and the mother of another.

When Winston Churchill became prime minister in May 1940 it was widely assumed that his doctor was still Horder, or if not, would now be Horder.[48] Churchill had certainly thought of Horder in the years since 1922. In 1936, for instance, hoping to delay Prime Minister Stanley Baldwin's removal of Edward VIII, Churchill tried unsuccessfully to get Dawson and Horder, as the king's physicians, to attest to his medical incapacity to make any hasty decision about marrying Wallis Simpson.[49] That Churchill was out of touch with Horder at the time was indicated, however, by his reference to 'Sir Thomas Horder',[50] although Horder had been ennobled three years earlier. After Churchill became prime minister, he did not entirely ignore Horder. During the Battle of

Britain Horder served as chairman of the Committee on Health in Air Raid Shelters. Horder's major recommendations were quickly implemented, at least in London.[51] The next year he was appointed expert adviser on medical aspects of food problems to the minister of food. This appointment was entirely fitting for one of Britain's leading medical experts on nutrition.[52] In 1943, having been persuaded by Horder that Sir Ronald Adam allowed too much power to psychiatrists on military personnel matters, Churchill attempted, without success, to remove Adam as adjutant-general of the British Army.[53]

NOTES

1. P. Addison, *Now the War is Over: A Social History of Britain 1945–51* (London: British Broadcasting Corporation, 1985), p. 93; T. Bonner, *Becoming a Physician: Medical Education in Britain, France, Germany, and the United States 1750–1945* (New York: Oxford University Press, 1995), pp. 77, 90, 170, 201, 227, 273–4; R. Boxill, *Shaw and the Doctors* (New York: Basic Books, 1969), p. 89; E. Frazer, *A History of English Public Health 1834–1939* (London: Baillière, Tindall & Cox, 1950), p. 29; M. Horder, *The Little Genius: A Memoir of the First Lord Horder* (London: Gerald Duckworth, 1966), p. 15; S. Inwood, *A History of London* (New York: Carroll & Graf, 1998), p. 83; W. Jordan, *The Charities of London, 1480–1660: The Aspirations and the Achievements of the Urban Society* (London: George Allen & Unwin, 1960), pp. 187–8; R. Porter, *Bodies Politic: Disease, Death and Doctors in Britain, 1650–1900* (Ithaca, NY: Cornell University Press, 2001), pp. 92, 292, n10; R. Porter, *The Greatest Benefit to Mankind: A Medical History of Humanity* (New York: W. W. Norton, 1998), pp. 198, 298, 317; J. Uglow, *Hogarth: A Life and a World* (New York: Farrar, Straus & Giroux, 1997), pp. 5, 30, 268, 278, 282–6.
2. Bonner, *Becoming a Physician*, p. 275.
3. *British Medical Journal*, 20 August 1955, p. 495; L. Garrod, 'Mervyn Henry Gordon', in Williams and Palmer, *Dictionary of National Biography 1951–1960*, p. 422; S. Gee, *Medical Lectures and Aphorisms*, 2nd edn (London: Henry Frowde and Hodder & Stoughton, 1907), pp. 243–304; T. Horder, *Clinical Pathology in Practice* (London: Henry Frowde and Hodder & Stoughton, 1910), p. vi; T. Horder, 'On Vaccine Therapy', *Practitioner*, 85 (1910), p. 292; T. Horder, *Medical Notes* (London: Henry Frowde and Hodder & Stoughton, 1921), p. vii; E. Jewesbury, *The Royal Northern Hospital 1856–1956* (London: H. K. Lewis, 1956), pp. 60–1; *Lancet*, 5 May 1906, p. 1, 245; 6 November 1920, pp. 948–9; 19 February 1921, p. 388; Medvei and Thornton, *Royal Hospital*, pp. 178, 188–9, 191; N. Moore, 'Samuel Jones Gee', in S. Lee (ed.), *The Dictionary of National Biography: Supplement January 1901–December 1911*, vol. 2 (London: Oxford University Press, 1939), p. 92; Porter, *Greatest Benefit*, p. 532; Witts, 'Thomas Jeeves Horder', p. 502. An early example of Horder's practical clinical emphasis is T. Horder, 'Observations upon the Importance of Blood-cultures, with an Account of the Technique Recommended', *Practitioner* (1905), pp. 611–22. Some later important examples are T. Horder, 'Rat-bite Fever', *Quarterly Journal of Medicine*, 3 (1910), pp. 121–5; T. Horder, 'Diagnostic Significance of Nerve Symptoms in Acute Infections', *Lancet*, 200 (1920), pp. 174–8; T. Horder and A. Gow, *The Essentials of Medical Diagnosis* (London: Cassell, 1928); T. Horder and others, *Rose Research on Lymphadenoma* (Bristol: John Wright & Sons, 1932).
4. G. Bourne, *We Met at Bart's: The Autobiography of a Physician* (London: Frederick Muller, 1963), pp. 75, 141, 167–8, 213; Lovell, *Churchill's Doctor*, p. 154; Medvei and Thornton, *Royal Hospital*, pp. 189, 195.
5. M. Horder, *Little Genius*, p. 18; Jewesbury, *Royal Northern Hospital*, pp. 74, 138; Medvei

and Thornton, *Royal Hospital*, p. 387; N. Moore, *The History of St Bartholomew's Hospital*, vol. 2 (London: C. Arthur Pearson, 1918), pp. 399, 819.

6. Lord Horder, 'Clinical Medicine: A Farewell Lecture at St Bartholomew's Hospital', *British Medical Journal*, 25 January 1936, p. 165.

7. P. Reaney, *A Dictionary of British Surnames* (London: Routledge & Kegan Paul, 1958), p. 169.

8. *British Medical Journal*, 27 August 1955, p. 566.

9. Bourne, *We Met at Bart's*, pp. 139–40, 213; M. Horder, *Little Genius*, pp. 36, 44, 50, 112, 128; C. Newman, 'The History of Postgraduate Medical Education at the West London Hospital', *Medical History*, 10 (1966), p. 344; K. Young (ed.), *The Diaries of Sir Robert Bruce Lockhart* (London: Macmillan, 1974), vol. 1, p. 250.

10. G. B. Shaw, *The Doctor's Dilemma: A Tragedy* (London: Penguin, 1987), p. 73.

11. Bourne, *We Met at Bart's*, p. 43; A. Cox, *Among the Doctors* (London: Christopher Johnson, 1950), p. 195; M. Horder, *Little Genius*, pp. 25, 47, 66–7, 87, 128.

12. A. Barrow, *Gossip: A History of High Society from 1920 to 1970* (New York: Coward, McCann & Geoghegan, 1979), p. 145; D. Bennett, *Margot: A Life of the Countess of Oxford and Asquith* (New York: Franklin Watts, 1985), p. 193; *British Medical Journal*, 26 January 1901, p. 233; M. Gilbert, *Winston S. Churchill*, vol. 5 (Boston, MA: Houghton Mifflin, 1977), p. 816; M. Horder, *Little Genius*, pp. 14, 25–7, 75–6; T. Horder, 'Favourite Prescriptions', *Practitioner*, 165 (1950), p. 5; Lamont-Brown, *Royal Poxes*, pp. 235, 238; Medvei and Thornton, *Royal Hospital*, p. 189; Oxbury, *Great Britons*, p. 171; R. Pound, *Gillies: Surgeon Extraordinary* (London: Michael Joseph, 1964), p. 115; F. Watson, *Dawson of Penn* (London: Chatto & Windus, 1950), p. 285; J. Wheeler-Bennett, *King George VI: His Life and Reign* (London: Macmillan, 1958), p. 654n.

13. Shaw, *Doctor's Dilemma*, p. 11.

14. M. Horder, *Little Genius*, p. 125.

15. T. Horder, 'Individuality in Medicine', *St Bartholomew's Hospital Journal*, 34, 1 (1926), p. 7.

16. Barrow, *Gossip*, pp. 17, 80; M. Horder, *Little Genius*, p. 77.

17. P. Ferris, *The House of Northcliffe: A Biography of an Empire* (New York: World, 1972), p. 270.

18. Ibid., pp. 267, 271–2; Lord Beaverbrook, *Men and Power 1917–1918* (London: Hutchinson, 1956), pp. 90, 357–8; M. Horder, *Little Genius*, p. 79; R. Pound and G. Harmsworth, *Northcliffe* (New York: Frederick A. Praeger, 1960), pp. 872, 881.

19. H. L'Etang, *The Pathology of Leadership* (London: William Heinemann Medical Books, 1969), p. 69.

20. T. Jones, *Lloyd George* (London: Oxford University Press, 1951), p. 156; Lamont-Brown, *Royal Poxes*, pp. xi, 220, 232; K. Morgan, *Consensus and Disunity: The Lloyd George Coalition Government 1918–1922* (Oxford: Clarendon, 1986), p. 25.

21. Lamont-Brown, *Royal Poxes*, pp. 221, 224; C. Webster, 'Conflict and Consensus: Explaining the British Health Service', *Twentieth Century British History*, 1, 2 (1990), pp. 121–2.

22. Ibid., pp. 122–3.

23. Lowe, *Welfare State*, p. 171.

24. Webster, 'Conflict and Consensus', p. 126.

25. Morgan, *Consensus and Disunity*, p. 20.

26. Webster, 'Conflict and Consensus', p. 126.

27. Jones, *Lloyd George*, pp. 244, 247, 276; D. Judd, *King George VI, 1895–1952* (New York: Franklin Watts, 1983), pp. 109, 123, 152; Robert Lord Platt, *Private and Controversial* (London: Cassell, 1972), p. 104; M. Reid, *Ask Sir James: Sir James Reid, Personal Physician to Queen Victoria and Physician-in-Ordinary to Three Monarchs* (New York: Viking, 1989), pp. 241, 249; K. Rose, *King George V* (New York: Alfred A. Knopf, 1984), p. 361; B. Shaw, *Doctors' Delusions, Crude Criminology, and Sham Education* (London: Constable, 1950), p. 159; F. Stevenson, *Lloyd George: A Diary*, A. Taylor, ed. (London: Hutchinson, 1971), pp. 276–7; Watson, *Dawson of Penn*, p. 287.

28. F. Stevenson, *Lloyd George*, pp. 276–7.

29. A. Eden, *The Reckoning* (Boston, MA: Houghton Mifflin, 1965), p. 210; M. Gilbert, *Winston S. Churchill*, vol 6 (Boston, MA: Houghton Mifflin, 1983), p. 952; Lamont-Brown, *Royal Poxes*, p. 248; F. Owen, *Tempestuous Journey: Lloyd George, His Life and Times* (London: Hutchinson, 1954), p. 754.

30. Lord Beaverbrook, *The Decline and Fall of Lloyd George: And Great was the Fall Thereof* (London: Collins, 1966), pp. 116, 225; L. Iremonger, *The Fiery Chariot: A Study of British Prime Ministers and the Search for Love* (London: Secker & Warburg, 1970), pp. 252, 297; L'Etang, *Pathology of Leadership*, p. 68; F. Stevenson, *Lloyd George*, p. 236; N. Waterhouse, *Private and Official* (London: Jonathan Cape, 1942), p. 214.

31. Beaverbrook, *Decline and Fall*, pp. 191–2; A. Chisholm and M. Davie, *Lord Beaverbrook: A Life* (New York: Alfred A. Knopf, 1993), pp. 190, 196; D. Dilks, *Neville Chamberlain*, vol. 1 (Cambridge: Cambridge University Press, 1984), p. 296; R. James, *Memoirs of a Conservative: J. C. C. Davidson's Memoirs and Papers, 1910–37* (New York: Macmillan, 1970), p. 123; M. Pugh, *State and Society: British Political and Social History 1870–1992* (London: Edward Arnold, 1994), p. 179.

32. Chisholm and Davie, *Lord Beaverbrook*, pp. 198–9; M. Horder, *Little Genius*, p. 909; James, *Memoirs of a Conservative*, pp. 149–50; T. Jones, *Whitehall Diary*, K. Middemas, ed. (London: Oxford University Press, 1969), p. 242; P. Rowland, *Lloyd George* (London: Barrie & Jenkins, 1975), p. 597; A. Taylor, *Beaverbrook* (New York: Simon & Schuster, 1972), p. 208; Waterhouse, *Private and Official*, p. 258.

33. T. Jones, *Whitehall Diary*, p. 279; H. L'Etang, *Ailing Leaders in Power 1914–1994* (London: Royal Society of Medicine, 1995), p. 9.

34. M. Horder, *Little Genius*, pp. 64, 67, 103; Witts, 'Thomas Jeeves Horder', p. 501.

35. M. Horder, *Little Genius*, p. 79; Iremonger, *Fiery Chariot*, p. 297; T. Jones, *A Diary with Letters 1931–1950* (London: Oxford University Press, 1954), p. 122; D. Marquand, *Ramsay MacDonald* (London: Jonathan Cape, 1977), pp. 694–5, 699, 760, 762, 768, 775; B. Park, *The Impact of Illness on World Leaders* (Philadelphia, PA: University of Pennsylvania Press, 1986), pp. 100, 111; F. Stevenson, *Lloyd George*, pp. 263, 265.

36. M. Horder, *Little Genius*, p. 79.

37. Iremonger, *Fiery Chariot*, p. 297; I. Macleod, *Neville Chamberlain* (London: Federick Muller, 1962), p. 23.

38. K. Feiling, *The Life of Neville Chamberlain* (Hamden, CT: Archon, 1970), p. 456; Gilbert, *Winston S. Churchill*, vol. 6, p. 817; M. Horder, *Little Genius*, p. 79; Iremonger, *Fiery Chariot*, p. 297; Macleod, *Neville Chamberlain*, p. 293.

39. L'Etang, *Ailing Leaders*, p. 21.

40. M. Horder, *Little Genius*, pp. x, 27–8, 64.

41. R. Lewis and A. Maude, *Professional People in England* (Cambridge, MA: Harvard University Press, 1953), p. 180.

42. C. Coote, *Editorial: The Memoirs of Colin R. Coote* (London: Eyre & Spottiswoode, 1965), p. 91.

43. J. Churchill, *A Churchill Canvas* (Boston, MA: Little, Brown, 1961), p. 245.

44. Chisholm and Davie, *Lord Beaverbrook*, p. 190.

45. J. Churchill, *A Churchill Canvas*, pp. 245–6.

46. M. Horder, *Little Genius*, pp. 30, 78, 120.

47. Ibid., pp. x, 10.

48. J. Colville, *Winston Churchill and His Inner Circle* (New York: Wyndham, 1981), p. 240; Lovell, *Churchill's Doctor*, p. 155; J. Wheeler-Bennett (ed.), *Action This Day: Working with Churchill* (London: Macmillan, 1968), p. 109.

49. J. Colville, *Footprints in Time* (London: Collins, 1976), p. 202; Gilbert, *Winston S. Churchill*, vol. 5, p. 816.

50. M. Gilbert, *Winston S. Churchill* (London: Heinemann, 1982), vol. 5 companion part 3 Documents, p. 454.

51. Inwood, *History of London*, p. 800.

52. Lord Horder, C. Dodds and T. Moran, *Bread: The Chemistry and Nutrition of Flour and Bread, with an Introduction to their History and Technology* (London: Constable, 1954), especially p. 180.

53. P. Addison, *Churchill on the Home Front 1900–1955* (London: Pimlico, 1993), pp. 353–4; *British Medical Journal*, 26 July 1941, p. 148; N. Goodman, *Wilson Jameson: Architect of National Health* (London: George Allen & Unwin, 1970), p. 84; Horder, Dodds and Moran, *Bread*, p. vi; Woolton, *Memoirs*, pp. 224–7.

8

A Royal College

Horder's contacts with Churchill in and after 1940 were nevertheless infrequent and relatively tangential to both. When Churchill became prime minister, Horder was supplanted as his physician, if he was still such, by another of London's leading consultant physicians, known since 1938 as Sir Charles Wilson, who would be ennobled in 1943 by his most famous patient as Baron Moran of Manton. Moran would remain Churchill's doctor for the last quarter-century of the patient's life. The new doctor's candidacy had been initially pushed, probably *via* Clementine Churchill, by Max Aitken, Lord Beaverbrook,[1] another of Britain's press lords, who had in the 1920s begun to see Moran professionally after the latter correctly made an emergency diagnosis of appendicitis in Beaverbrook's son. As a hypochondriac Beaverbrook's choice of doctor mattered intensely to him. In this case, he chose a doctor who was also a hypochondriac.[2] During the Second World War, Moran would not give Beaverbrook a medical excuse for not becoming, or resigning as, minister of aircraft production.[3]

Much earlier Beaverbrook had chosen another doctor, who showed no sign of hypochondria. That earlier doctor was Horder. In 1910, the year Horder had first been consulted in a royal illness, Beaverbrook became, and remained for many years, Horder's patient.[4] Beaverbrook then saw Horder as 'the great doctor'.[5] Patient and doctor even shared long foreign holidays. Relations cooled, however, after Gladys Lady Beaverbrook died of a brain tumour while also Horder's patient, although Horder continued as a dinner guest in Beaverbrook's home.[6] Horder was presumably not present when an embittered Beaverbrook proclaimed: 'All doctors are frauds anyway.'[7] Neither, presumably, was Moran, who also dined at Beaverbrook's home.[8] Long before his death, Beaverbrook hoped his obituaries would not 'say anything about doctor's orders to me. Doctors may advise me. They cannot order me.'[9]

Even more than he feared illness Beaverbrook loved power, which he achieved in overfull measure. The twin bases of his power were his vast press holdings and his personal relationships with members of a variety of British elites. Often those two bases intersected, as they did in Moran's case. Beaverbrook saw Moran as he had once seen Horder, as a gifted rising star whom it would be worthwhile to assist on his way up. If used properly, Moran should prove useful. Beaverbrook often used his money to buy personal influence. He was generous to Moran personally, sometimes by cheque, sometimes with hundreds of one-pound notes.[10] Since Moran's highest value was not his own wealth, Beaverbrook used more substantial sums of money to solve the financial problems of the institution with which Moran was most closely connected. Beaverbrook became the most generous donor to St Mary's Hospital Medical School, London, of which Moran was dean during 1920–45.[11]

Moran was also tempted with wider prestige and power. Beaverbrook, not known for flowery compliments, gushed, in a letter to Moran's wife:

> I think your husband is a great figure – the greatest in London among professional men. I have been most anxious, again and again, to tell the public about him. But he always makes such a big objection that I cannot be bothered to fight for publication.[12]

Coming from Britain's most powerful press lord, this offer of wider favourable publicity to a doctor not yet widely known outside his own hospital, which as the newest of London's large voluntary hospitals was still among the less prestigious,[13] might have tempted even a more ascetic doctor than Moran. When the latter tergiversated, he was directly addressed: 'Now the good doctors in the world are few, and you are the best of all of them. The most honest, the most simple, the most clever and the most upright.'[14] The best doctor in the world was surely even more worthy of favourable publicity and consequent power than someone who was merely the best doctor in London, although even Beaverbrook could not guarantee global recognition, let alone global power. When Moran was ennobled, Beaverbrook advised him to speak early and often in House of Lords debates.[15]

Moran learned Beaverbrook's lesson so well that he became known in the medical profession as 'Corkscrew Charlie'. Although its origin is unknown, by this term Moran's enemies signified an unscrupulous deviousness, and his friends a sensitive problem-solving creativity.[16] By the Second World War the tempted may have outdistanced his tempter. Moran wrote to Beaverbrook in 1943, urging him to become minister of health with Moran as 'your Chief of Staff', to reform 'radically' the medical profession so that every Briton would be able to consult appropriate medical specialists when needed.[17] Beaverbrook, who had no desire to create a new world, only to dominate the existing world, responded enigmatically. That Moran sought substantial wider power had already become apparent the previous year, when he unsuccessfully urged appointment of an expert co-ordinator of all medical decisions by the British government, who would obviously be Moran himself.[18] He had long desired 'the control of men', but had assumed that becoming a doctor precluded such control.[19] Beaverbrook's prodding not only awakened that sleeping desire, but sharpened his understanding of how that desire could be fulfilled by a doctor.

Moran came to recognize that the power of institutions can be based on the prestige of those institutions.[20] Personal prestige, he also saw, could lead to personal power. Most distinctively, he came to understand that the prestige of institutions could be used to advance the personal power of an individual human being. For him prestige was useful rather than ornamental, having instrumental, if not inherent, value.[21] In early 1938 he wrote to Beaverbrook: 'I have slowly become persuaded – you told me this years ago – that to get things done in medicine one must be known as Dawson and Horder are known.'[22] Dawson and Horder were both known as members of the House of Lords. One of the other ways that Dawson was known was as president, since 1931, of the Royal College of Physicians (London). That institution would become Moran's power base for the next decade.[23]

Moran chose his institutional power base well. In British medicine one institution stood out as the most prestigious: the Royal College of Physicians (London), founded in 1518 by Henry VIII.[24] The college was soon one of the buttresses of a hierarchical society, surviving even the English Civil War.[25] It was to Winston Churchill 'a veritable pillar of the State'.[26] To Moran the college was the link between the government and the medical profession.[27] Of this august body Moran had long been a fellow, without playing any conspicuous part in college affairs. Now, in mid-1938, campaigning, at 55, as the candidate of younger fellows, he was elected college treasurer, succeeding one of his own teachers, who was 87.[28] In 1941, having campaigned vigorously, Moran was elected president of the Royal College of Physicians (RCP). As the youngest president in many years, his chief internal support came from the Younger Fellows Club and his chief external support came from biased coverage of the two leading candidates in newspapers owned by Beaverbrook.[29] Moran saw this election as the most significant event of his career,[30] because his presidency made him 'head of the medical profession for the time being'[31] and 'leader of the profession for the moment'.[32] His election certainly made him a powerful figure in the medical world. He was now at the top of his profession,[33] although he was not alone there. Dawson and Horder were both still alive, and still his seniors.

Moran wanted his moment to last, and it did. On each Palm Sunday until 1949, he was re-elected RCP president. This may have been an unprecedented succession of college presidential victories.[34] Of the nine elections, that in 1948, at the height of the public campaign by the British Medical Association against scheduled implementation later that year of the National Health Service Act, was the occasion of the largest turnout of college fellows, as well as the narrowest margin of victory after the most intensive campaigning by both Moran and his chief defeated rival. Dorothy Lady Moran was forced to provide overnight London lodging for provincial voters.[35] Even though that in 1948 was the most dramatic, Moran's re-election campaigns were always energetic.[36]

In all these nine elections Moran's chief defeated rival was Thomas Lord Horder.[37] By 1941, Horder was a veteran within the college, having become a fellow in 1906 and having served as an examiner, a council member, and censor.[38] His influence within the college had been substantial enough to win election to an honorary fellowship for Havelock Ellis, who did not have a proper medical degree, but who was, along with his mistress, Horder's patient.[39] Moran considered his election to the RCP presidency the most significant event of his career; Horder's greatest ambition had long been to be elected to that office.[40] As the latter told the opening assembly of the Westminster Hospital Medical School in 1936: 'I want what all honest men want, to be judged by my peers.'[41] His real peers were, of course, the other fellows of the Royal College of Physicians, not the other members of the House of Lords. Of the judgement of his real peers Horder had never before feared.

Horder's greatest dream was nevertheless to remain unrealized.[42] For this denial he blamed Moran as the willing instrument of Beaverbrook. Horder could keep his patients' secrets, but not his own. He shared, sometimes unexpectedly, his personal frustrations with others. In late 1944, Hugh Dalton, who became chancellor of the exchequer in the new Labour Cabinet a few months later, visited Horder professionally for the first time.[43] That evening Dalton described this visit:

> He tells me how Beaverbrook pushed him aside both from being the present PM's Medical Adviser – which he had been before the latter became PM – and also stopped him from becoming President of the Royal College of Physicians, which he would normally have been in succession to Dawson of Penn. The Beaver successfully ran Charlie Wilson, now Lord Moran, for both these honours.[44]

Even after this unusual initiation, Dalton did not hesitate to become Horder's patient.[45] Dalton soon persuaded his junior party colleague, Hugh Gaitskell, who would eventually become leader of the Labour Party, to consult Horder about his continuing medical problems. After being elected to the House of Commons in 1945, Gaitskell decided not to seek junior ministerial office after again seeing, at short notice, Horder, sharing an appointment time previously made by Dalton. Horder had needed no introduction to his newer patient, since Gaitskell had as a young man visited Horder's office in 1930.[46]

These were not the only members of the Labour Party elite of 1945–48 known professionally by Horder. He was also consulted[47] in the serious illnesses of Herbert Morrison: in 1940, when leader of the London County Council, and in 1947 when lord president of the Council and leader of the House of Commons. While Morrison was the Labour Party boss in London, Horder had praised London's local government as compelling 'the admiration of the world'.[48] Soon after offering this public praise, Horder was named medical adviser to London Transport.[49]

At least one other member of the Labour Party front bench in the new 1945 House of Commons had been Horder's patient. That was the minister of health, Aneurin Bevan. Many years before, probably when he was a student at the Central Labour College in London, Bevan had visited Horder on an urgent medical matter.[50] Some years after that visit, in 1932, Bevan, now a Labour Member of Parliament, had been ill while spending a weekend at Beaverbrook's home. His alert host later sympathetically suggested: 'If you have not yet thrown off your trouble, will you let me arrange for the St Mary's Hospital staff to look into it? I have a long connection with that hospital.' That connection, of course, was with Moran, whose recruiting agent Beaverbrook had now become. Bevan, at least equally alert, did not care to fall quite so fully into Beaverbrook's web, so he waited two weeks to report that he had 'recovered' and thus had 'no need to avail myself of your kind offer to consult your medical advisers'.[51] When Bevan finally did again consult Moran, the patient was all of Britain, not Aneurin Bevan. The latter continued, however, to visit Beaverbrook's table until press reports revealed his presence during a fire at Beaverbrook's home. After 1943, they seem not to have met, to at least Beaverbrook's regret.[52]

NOTES

1. Chisholm and Davie, *Lord Beaverbrook*, p. 378; Colville, *Winston Churchill*, p. 241; Gilbert, *Winston S. Churchill*, vol. 6, p. 390; Lovell, *Churchill's Doctor*, p. 155.
2. Chisholm and Davie, *Lord Beaverbrook*, 376; Z. Cope, *The History of St Mary's Hospital Medical School, or a Century of Medical Education* (London: William Heinemann, 1954), p. 66; Lovell, *Churchill's Doctor*, pp. 97–9, 109; Lord Moran, *Churchill: Taken from the Diaries of Lord Moran: The Struggle for Survival 1940–1965* (Boston, MA: Houghton Mifflin, 1966), p. 10; 'Lord Moran in conversation with Dr C. E. Newman, 26 July 1980', Royal College of Physicians archives.
3. Chisholm and Davie, *Lord Beaverbrook*, p. 397; Moran, *Churchill*, pp. 31–2.
4. Chisholm and Davie, *Lord Beaverbrook*, p. 116; M. Horder, *Little Genius*, p. 77; Taylor, *Beaverbrook*, p. 52.
5. Chisholm and Davie, *Lord Beaverbrook*, p. 199.
6. Ibid., pp. 241, 257–9, 312; Young, *Diaries of Robert Bruce Lockhart*, vol. 1, p. 115.
7. Young, *Diaries of Robert Bruce Lockhart*, vol. 1, p. 193.
8. Lovell, *Churchill's Doctor*, p. 99.
9. Young, *Diaries of Robert Bruce Lockhart*, vol. 1, p. 154.
10. Lovell, *Churchill's Doctor*, pp. 107, 243.
11. Ibid., pp. 100–1; G. Macfarlane, *Alexander Fleming: The Man and the Myth* (Cambridge, MA: Harvard University Press, 1984), pp. 112, 144–5; A. Maurois, *The Life of Sir Alexander Fleming, Discoverer of Penicillin*, G. Hopkins, trans. (New York: E. P. Dutton), p. 106; 'Lord Moran in conversation'; R. Pollitt and H. Curry, *Portraits in British History* (Homewood, IL: Dorsey, 1975), p. 315; Taylor, *Beaverbrook*, pp. 258–9, 331.
12. Lovell, *Churchill's Doctor*, p. 105.
13. Ibid., p. 8; R. Hare, *The Birth of Penicillin and the Disarming of Microbes* (London: George Allen & Unwin, 1970), p. 22; L'Etang, *Ailing Leaders*, p. 24; D. Wilson, *Penicillin in Perspective* (London: Faber & Faber, 1976), p. 39.
14. Lovell, *Churchill's Doctor*, p. 155.
15. Ibid., p. 190.
16. Ibid., pp. xi, 308; Addison, *Now the War is Over*, p. 100; Foot, *Aneurin Bevan*, vol. 2, p. 124; S. Grimes, *The British National Health Service: State Intervention in the Medical Marketplace, 1911–1948* (New York: Garland, 1991), p. 136; Gullick, 'Forty Years of the NHS', pp. 55–6; Hennessy, *Never Again*, p. 142; K. Morgan, *Labour in Power 1945–1951* (Oxford: Oxford University Press, 1985), p. 153.
17. Lovell, *Churchill's Doctor*, p. 212.
18. Ibid., p. 172.
19. Ibid., p. 68.
20. A. Cooke, *History of Royal College of Physicians*, vol. 3, p. 1, 207; Stevens, *Medical Practice*, p. 109.
21. *Lancet*, 15 April 1950, p. 722.
22. Lovell, *Churchill's Doctor*, p. 140.
23. Ibid., p. 143.

24. Bonner, *Becoming a Physician*, p. 183; Eckstein, *Pressure Group Politics*, p. 50n; Foot, *Aneurin Bevan*, vol. 2, p. 124; Forsyth, *Doctors and State Medicine*, pp. 3–4; D. Gill, *The British National Health Service: A Sociologist's Perspective* (Bethesda, MD: National Institutes of Health, 1980), p. 11; F. Honingsbaum, *Health, Happiness, and Security: The Creation of the National Health Service* (London: Routledge, 1989), p. 115; R. Porter, *London: A Social History* (Cambridge, MA: Harvard University Press, 1995), p. 60; Mackenzie, *Power and Responsibility*, pp. 61, 73.
25. H. Cook, 'Policing the Health of London: The College of Physicians and the Early Stuart Monarchy', *Social History of Medicine*, 2, 1 (1989), pp. 1–33; Porter, *London*, p. 79.
26. R. James (ed.), *Winston S. Churchill: His Complete Speeches* (New York: Chelsea House, 1974), vol. 7, p. 6, 896.
27. 'Lord Moran in conversation'.
28. Lovell, *Churchill's Doctor*, pp. 143–4.
29. *British Medical Journal*, 23 April 1977, p. 1, 088; D. Hubble, 'Lord Moran and James Boswell: The Two Diarists Compared and Contrasted', *Medical History*, 13 (1969), p. 8; T. Hunt, 'Moran', in G. Wolstenholme (ed.), *Lives of the Fellows of the Royal College of Physicians of London continued to 1983* (Oxford: IRL Press, 1984), p. 409; B. Pimlott (ed.), *The Second World War Diary of Hugh Dalton, 1940–45* (London: Jonathan Cape, 1986), p. 806; Taylor, *Beaverbrook*, p. 259.
30. Lovell, *Churchill's Doctor*, p. 153.
31. Ibid., p. 225.
32. Ibid., p. 41.
33. Hubble, 'Moran and Boswell', p. 5; Porter, *Greatest Benefit*, p. 350; T. Williams, *Howard Florey: Penicillin and After* (Oxford: Oxford University Press, 1984), p. 206.
34. Foot, *Aneurin Bevan*, vol. 2, p. 124.
35. Lovell, *Churchill's Doctor*, pp. 302, 305–6; Pater, *Making of National Health Service*, p. 158.
36. *British Medical Journal*, 23 April 1977, p. 1,088; Honigsbaum, *Health*, p. 137.
37. Grimes, *British National Health Service*, p. 109; Lovell, *Churchill's Doctor*, p. 153; Moran, *Churchill*, p. 691.
38. *British Medical Journal*, 20 August 1955, pp. 493–4; M. Horder, *Little Genius*, p. 17.
39. P. Grosskurth, *Havelock Ellis: A Biography* (New York: Alfred A. Knopf, 1980), pp. 427–9, 438.
40. M. Horder, *Little Genius*, pp. 95, 106.
41. T. Horder, *Health and a Day*, p. 27.
42. L'Etang, *Pathology of Leadership*, p. 69.
43. B. Pimlott, *Hugh Dalton* (London: Jonathan Cape, 1985), p. 384; Pimlott, *Second World War Diary of Hugh Dalton*, pp. 805–6.
44. Pimlott, *Second World War Diary of Hugh Dalton*, p. 806.
45. Ibid., pp. 828–9; B. Pimlott (ed.), *The Political Diary of Hugh Dalton: 1918–40, 1945–60* (London: Jonathan Cape, 1986).
46. Pimlott, *Second World War Diary of Hugh Dalton*, pp. 853, 863; P. Williams, *Hugh Gaitskell: A Political Biography* (London: Jonathan Cape, 1979), pp. 35, 37, 125–6, 130; P. Williams (ed.), *The Diary of Hugh Gaitskell 1945–1956* (London: Jonathan Cape, 1983), pp. 8–9.
47. B. Donoughue and G. Jones, *Herbert Morrison: Portrait of a Politician* (London: Weidenfeld & Nicolson, 1973), p. 393; Lord Morrison, *Herbert Morrison: An Autobiography* (London: Odhams, 1960), p. 257.
48. Lord Horder, 'Foreword', in *Britain's Health: Prepared by S. Mervyn Herbert on the Basis of the Report on the British Health Services by PEP (Political and Economic Planning)* (Harmondsworth: Penguin, 1939); Supplement to *Medical World*, 21 July 1939, p. 2.
49. Oxbury, *Great Britons*, p. 171.
50. Foot, *Aneurin Bevan*, vol. 1, pp. 38–45; M. Horder, *Little Genius*, p. 98; K. Morgan, *Rebirth of a Nation: Wales 1880–1980* (Oxford: Oxford University Press, 1987), pp. 195–7.
51. Chisholm and Davie, *Lord Beaverbrook*, p. 360.
52. Ibid., p. 361; Taylor, *Beaverbrook*, pp. 164, 304, 334, 531–2, 574, 640.

9

A Royal Speech

When the new Labour Cabinet began in the summer of 1945 to reconstruct British society, Horder had a wide acquaintanceship with Britain's new leaders, deepened in several cases by the special bond formed between a patient and his or her physician. Most members of the British establishment knew that Horder had been ennobled by a Labour prime minister, but not all of them knew the extent of Horder's personal and professional relationships with senior Labourites after the era of Ramsay MacDonald, who had died in 1937. Among those who had not so realized was Moran. After the opening of the new Parliament in August 1945, a surprised Moran recorded his impressions of the king's speech in the House of Lords:

> Just before the arrival of the King and Queen, Horder entered. If I'd been in his place I'd have crept to a seat – if there was one – in the back row. But my Lord Horder is made of sterner stuff. Slowly he passed along the government bench, stopping to talk to Addison, Nathan and someone to whom I could put no name. For five years he has had no say in things. Now he will have another fling …[1]

That Horder greeted fellow lords whom he knew well should have been no surprise. Christopher Lord Addison, Prime Minister Lloyd George's choice as Britain's first minister of health, now Labour leader of the House of Lords, was a 'Bart's man' of Horder's generation,[2] so he and Horder had studied and first practised medicine together. Horder and Harry Lord Nathan, a prominent London solicitor, moved in the same social circles.

Horder would probably have been pleased that his grand entrance was not only noticed but gave Moran a rude shock, and even more pleased that Moran feared for his own future influence. Worried Moran certainly was. That there was a lord on the government front bench known to and by Horder but not himself was by itself worrisome. The politically active lords were relatively few, and frontbench Labour lords even fewer. The politics of personal influence could hardly be practised without matching the names and faces of the players. Throughout the Second World War, Moran had been flying high, including literally as Churchill's doctor to major international conferences. Sometimes his medical reasoning affected the arrival route chosen.[3] These travels did occasion, as he understood, criticism that he was deserting his post as president of the Royal College of Physicians,[4] but such criticism may have been compensated for by the 'Medical News' column of the *British Medical Journal*, which reported that Moran 'is a member of the British delegation to Washington'.[5] Sometimes he travelled without his prime ministerial patient, but with Beaverbrook, to be a British signatory to important international agreements.[6] Now, however, Moran's descent seemed possible, even probable. His Beaverbrook connection was hardly likely to be helpful in the immediate future. Indeed, that connection could now do great harm to his own influence. Beaverbrook was widely, if probably unfairly, blamed for Churchill's disastrous campaign claim that a Labour Party victory would result in the creation of 'a political police', in 'some form of *Gestapo*'.[7]

Being physician to the leader of His Majesty's Loyal Opposition would not be quite the same as being physician to the prime minister. In the latter role Moran had been inattentive not only to the RCP but to his private practice, which had essentially disappeared,[8] and also to his duties as dean of St Mary's Hospital Medical School. Never enthusiastic about administrative details,[9] his wartime visits to St Mary's had been brief and infrequent, although to characterize him already in 1942 as a former dean[10] is exaggerated. Virtually the only wartime service Moran had performed for St Mary's was to mobilize, in 1942, an enormously successful propaganda campaign to give Alexander Fleming the lion's share of public recognition for the development of penicillin. Fleming had been appointed professor of bacteriology, and given free research rein, at St Mary's by Dean Moran. They had been professional colleagues since their medical student years together at St Mary's.[11] Fleming had certainly discovered, in 1928, penicillin there.[12] The clinical development of penicillin, however, was only later made possible by an Oxford University research team including Howard Florey.[13] Moran was blamed by Florey for slighting the work of the Oxford team, and this suspicion was justified.[14] A few months earlier, Moran had been an unsuccessful candidate for appointment as regius professor of medicine at Oxford University.[15] In 1942 St Mary's suddenly became one of the world's most famous hospitals.[16] When in April 1951 the terminal disintegration of his Cabinet finally began, Prime Minister Clement Attlee, seriously ill with a peptic ulcer,[17] was, appropriately, a patient in St Mary's Hospital. It was Moran who had made St Mary's fashionable. He had learned well Beaverbrook's lesson in public relations. In a radio broadcast on 1 July 1945, on the centenary of St Mary's Hospital, Moran asserted that two doctors, Sir (as he was now) Alexander Fleming and Sir Almoth Wright, working in the same laboratory at St Mary's, had saved more soldiers' lives than anyone else in the world. Crediting Wright, whom he detested and who had obstructed his deanly policies,[18] could not have been easy for Moran. Wright had had an earlier brush with fame when he was caricatured as the leading character in Bernard Shaw's *The Doctor's Dilemma*.[19] Wright's strident antifeminism was also widely known.[20] Wright's research had been on a typhoid vaccine, but he got extra credit from reports that 'Penicillin was introduced in 1943 by a student of Wright's, Alexander Fleming.'[21] Moran's public relations efforts were so successful that Prime Minister Churchill publicly congratulated St Mary's Hospital on its association with penicillin without mentioning Oxford University.[22] Patients whose lives were saved by penicillin were grateful to 'Sir Alexander Fleming, the man who discovered penicillin'.[23] Fleming's role was magnified even in medical circles. Horder came to believe that the Oxford researchers were 'immediate colleagues' of 'Fleming himself'.[24] Wright and Fleming (in that order), working 'in association with'[25] Florey, were given credit for penicillin, although Wright was sometimes misnamed.[26] Even Moran appeared to share in the credit.[27] His public relations successes for St Mary's did not save Moran from being sacked, by letter, as dean in September 1945, although he remained on the hospital staff for two more years.[28] By war's end, Moran's influence therefore appeared to be essentially past. His private practice and his deanship were gone. He had already been RCP president for four years, and each year his re-election was bitterly contested by Horder, who was hardly likely to abandon his own hopes so long as Moran continued in the office Horder saw as rightfully his. Moran's moment seemed at the very least to be passing.

Moran's assumption in August 1945 that Horder would now 'have another fling' was also sensible. Horder was not only well connected to the Labour Party elite, but he would have been a most appropriate medical godfather to the creation of a national health service. He had never been a prisoner of the past. His openness to medical innovation was, especially for an established and establishment physician, impressive. He may well have been the most important British pioneer in clinical pathology.[29] His medical hero, the Prussian Rudolf Virchow, was far from conservative. Virchow was not only one of the founders of the Progressive Party but its leader, serving in the Prussian House of Representatives. Virchow sought to democratize German medicine because he saw medicine as a social science. By this, Virchow meant not only that promoting conventional public health measures was part of a doctor's task, but also that social medicine should fight those health problems, such as poor nutrition and poor housing, created by poverty. For him it was a physician's responsibility to serve as an 'attorney for the poor'.[30] Having been trained in a military hospital, Virchow did not fear state medicine. Even Virchow's natural science was riddled with, and perhaps weakened by, his democratic ideology. It was no accident that he would eventually be viewed as a hero in the German Democratic Republic.[31]

Horder too saw medicine as a social science.[32] In this respect his views resembled those of the Victorian RCP in pressing Prime Minister Benjamin Disraeli to the Cross Act of 1875, requiring replacement of slum housing on public health grounds. That college had already helped introduce Victorian Britons to the idea of state intervention in health matters by administering smallpox vaccinations for the government, which eventually assigned that task to the Local Government Board.[33] To Horder the ideal doctor would be 'a public servant' whose expertise should be 'available for the guidance of those who administer the State'.[34] Medicine 'should infiltrate Politics, but it is disastrous for Politics to attempt to infiltrate medicine'.[35] Because part of being a doctor was being both a social reformer and a legislator, medical schools should teach matters of social significance as part of their curricula. Medical schools and students should further be substantially subsidized by government.[36]

If prescribing political remedies was part of being a doctor, Horder had long made clear what his prescription would include. That prescription was developed with particular clarity in speeches and writings during the latter half of the 1930s, after his retirement from an official position at St Bartholomew's Hospital. Horder used his long-delayed maiden speech in the House of Lords, in late 1936, to summarize his prescription: '... my own lead, if I may put it that way, would be that the government should speed up all those social services upon the results of which depend the health and happiness of the people.'[37] Later, looking back on his long career, he praised advances in rehabilitative medicine, drawing the conclusion: 'Government action has aided all this in powerful fashion.'[38] Speaking of British health services to the Medical Practitioners' Union, of which he had been an early member before it became affiliated with the Trades Union Congress, Horder referred to 'the anomaly introduced by the economic factor'.[39] Elsewhere, but in a similar vein, he argued that the health of workers could not 'be divorced from economic considerations'.[40] It was urbanization and industrialization 'that have lowered the general hygiene, rather than any change in the capacity of the human body to be fit'.[41] These considerations overlapped with health. Millions of Britons still lacked proper food, shelter and work. Repairing these social deficiencies in the national health was the responsibility of government.[42] This responsibility, Horder was convinced, could be met, because it was not outside 'the statesman's control'. The means of health 'should be open to every citizen, independent of his income'.[43] Access to both preventive and curative services 'to every member of the community is paramount'.[44] To encourage such access, regional co-ordination of hospital facilities and staff, for instance, was both desirable and practicable.[45] Not only did St Bartholomew's Hospital not stand alone, for Horder preventive medicine foreshadowed environmental medicine. He was president of the Smoke Abatement Society and chairman of the Noise Abatement League. Pleading for that latter cause, he described noise as 'the result of an unplanning community in respect of its physical requirements'.[46] For Horder, educating the public on health matters was as important as training doctors.

NOTES

1. Lovell, *Churchill's Doctor*, p. 272.
2. Oxbury, *Great Britons*, p. 2.
3. G. Pawle, *The War and Colonel Warden* (New York: Alfred A. Knopf, 1963), p. 183.
4. Barron, *Gossip*, p. 114; Lovell, *Churchill's Doctor*, p. 230.
5. 3 January 1942, p. 29.
6. H. Balfour, *Wings Over Westminster* (London: Hutchinson, 1973), p. 166; Gilbert, *Winston S. Churchill*, vol. 6, p. 1, 211.
7. Chisholm and Davie, *Lord Beaverbrook*, pp. 453–4; James, *Winston S. Churchill*, vol. 7, p. 7, 172.
8. Lovell, *Churchill's Doctor*, pp. 256, 274.
9. Ibid., p. 277.

10. Fox, *Health Policies*, p. 101.
11. L. Ludovici, *Fleming: Discoverer of Penicillin* (London: Andrew Dakers, 1952), pp. 32, 110; R. Hare, 'The Scientific Activities of Alexander Fleming, other than the Discovery of Penicillin', *Medical History*, 27 (1983), p. 356; Macfarlane, *Alexander Fleming*, p. 36; Maurois, *Life of Alexander Fleming*, p. 32.
12. G. Macfarlane, *Howard Florey: The Making of a Great Scientist* (Oxford: Oxford University Press, 1979), p. 349; J. Simmons, *Doctors and Discoveries: Lives that Created Today's Medicine* (Boston, MA: Houghton Mifflin, 2002), p. 170n; M. Wainwright, 'The History of the Therapeutic Use of Crude Penicillin', *Medical History*, 31 (1987), p. 42; H. Wyatt, 'Robert Pulvertaft's Use of Crude Penicillin in Cairo', *Medical History*, 34 (1990), p. 320.
13. Simmons, *Doctors and Discoveries*, pp. 246, 249; Wainwright, 'History of Therapeutic Use', p. 41.
14. Hare, 'Scientific Activities of Alexander Fleming', pp. 366–7; Macfarlane, *Alexander Fleming*, pp. 207, 255; A. Weisse, *Medical Odysseys: The Different and Sometimes Unexpected Pathways to Twentieth-century Medical Discoveries* (Brunswick, NJ: Rutgers University Press, 1991), p. 83; T. Williams, *Howard Florey*, pp. 204–6, 208.
15. Lovell, *Churchill's Doctor*, pp. 173–4.
16. Macfarlane, *Alexander Fleming*, p. 26.
17. L'Etang, *Ailing Leaders*, p. 9.
18. Macfarlane, *Alexander Fleming*, pp. 113–14; Moran to M. Greenwood, 30 March 1948, RCP archives.
19. Boxill, *Shaw and the Doctors*, pp. 24, 107, 134; Macfarlane, *Alexander Fleming*, p. 218.
20. V. Brittain, *Envoy Extraordinary: A Study of Vijaya Lakshini Pandit and Her Contribution to Modern India* (London: George Allen & Unwin, 1965), p. 16.
21. Boxill, *Shaw and the Doctors*, p. 170.
22. James, *Winston S. Churchill*, vol. 7, p. 6, 895.
23. K. Norris, *The Cloister Walk* (New York: Riverhead Books, 1996), p. 87.
24. T. Horder, *Fifty Years of Medicine*, p. 11.
25. A. Ives, *British Hospitals* (London: Collins, 1948), pp. 49–50.
26. Wainwright, 'History of Therapeutic Use', p. 43.
27. Hare, 'Scientific Activities of Alexander Fleming', p. 351.
28. Lovell, *Churchill's Doctor*, pp. 277–8, 291.
29. Bourne, *We Met at Bart's*, pp. 111, 142–3, 183; *British Medical Journal*, 20 August 1955, pp. 479, 493–4; M. Horder, *Little Genius*, pp. 13, 17; Medvei and Thornton, *Royal Hospital*, p. 189.
30. Porter, *Greatest Benefit*, p. 415.
31. E. Ackerknecht, *Rudolf Virchow: Doctor, Statesman, Anthropologist* (Madison, WI: University of Wisconsin Press, 1953), pp. 46, 247; Bonner, *Becoming a Physician*, p. 55; J. Hollingsworth, *A Political Economy of Medicine: Great Britain and the United States* (Baltimore, MD: Johns Hopkins University Press, 1986), p. 96; L. Payer, *Medicine and Culture: Notions of Health and Sickness in Britain, the US, France, and West Germany* (London: Victor Gollancz, 1990), pp. 89, 92, 94; Porter, *Greatest Benefit*, pp. 332, 643; M. Ramsey, 'The Politics of Professional Monopoly in Nineteenth-century Medicine: The French Model and Its Rivals', in G. Geison (ed.), *Professions and the French State, 1700–1900* (Philadelphia, PA: University of Pennsylvania Press, 1984), pp. 256, 258, 295; G. Silver, 'Virchow, The Heroic Model in Medicine: Health Policy by Accolade', *American Journal of Public Health*, 77, 1 (1987), pp. 84, 86; R. Whalen, *Bitter Wounds: German Victims of the Great War, 1914–1939* (Ithaca, NY: Cornell University Press, 1984), pp. 6, 65.
32. *British Medical Journal*, 20 August 1955, pp. 479, 494.
33. Frazer, *History of English Public Health*, p. 172; A. Wohl, *Endangered Lives: Public Health in Victorian Britain* (Cambridge, MA: Harvard University Press, 1983), pp. 132, 314.
34. Lord Horder, *Health and a Day*, p. 61; T. Horder, 'Foreword', in *Britain's Health*, p. xii.
35. Lord Horder, 'Medicine and the State', *Lancet*, 248, 1 (1945), p. 296.
36. Lord Horder, *Obscurantism*, p. 29; Supplement to *Medical World*, 21 July 1939, p. 3.
37. Lord Horder, *Obscurantism*, p. 149.
38. Lord Horder, *Fifty Years of Medicine*, p. 32.
39. Supplement to *Medical World*, 21 July 1939, p. 2.
40. Lord Horder, *Obscurantism*, p. 25.

41. Ibid.
42. Ibid.; Lord Horder, *Health and a Day*, pp. 54, 111; Lord Horder, 'Foreword', in *Britain's Health*, pp. viii–x, xiii–xiv.
43. Supplement to *Medical World*, 21 July 1939, p. 21.
44. Lord Horder, 'Foreword', in *Britain's Health*, p. xi.
45. Ibid., p. xvi.
46. Lord Horder, *Fifty Years of Medicine*, p. 55.

10

At the Café Royal

If Moran was initially stunned in August 1945 by the prospect that Horder, not he, would now be Britain's most influential doctor, he soon recovered. If he was insufficiently known to the new rulers of Britain he would make himself known, especially to the new minister of health, whom he invited to his home for an amiable dinner for two.[1] Moran also carefully supervised preparations for the October 1945 version of an annual RCP dinner in memory of William Harvey, patron saint of British medicine, at which post-war austerity would be challenged. Prime Minister Clement Attlee, minister of health Aneurin Bevan and other Cabinet members were invited. At this convivial occasion the prime minister toasted the college, and the president of the college toasted the prime minister. Wisely the president did not here articulate his conviction that he was personally descended from William Harvey. The president did speak at length, and impressively, on the similarity of personal qualities needed for success in medicine and politics.[2] Since few of the politicians present hoped to become doctors, it is not surprising if some of them were privately to contemplate the possibility of a doctor becoming involved in politics. None of the politicians present could have known, however, that the president had recently written: 'The truth is I have always hoped Winston would give me some job which would take me out of medicine.' Even when that did not happen 'I went on hoping'.[3] That hope lasted until at least 1951. Churchill returned to the prime ministership, but did not name his doctor to be the new minister of health. Moran angrily complained to his patient.[4]

Moran did not permit the change in government in 1945, at least, to render him hopeless. He also made sure to attend the first meeting of the new minister of health with doctors to discuss informally the creation of a national health service.[5] This seminal gathering took place at the Café Royal in London in late October 1945. It had been arranged by Charles (later Lord) Hill, secretary of the British Medical Association, most of whose members were general practitioners without hospital appointments. Though he had not practised medicine for over a decade, Hill had used his fame as the wartime British Broadcasting Corporation 'Radio Doctor' to gain his full-time BMA position in 1944. Before Bevan became minister of health, he had not met Hill.[6] This is not surprising. Not only had Hill been working outside London, as deputy medical officer in Oxford, but he was an enthusiastic Conservative.[7] While BMA secretary he sought nomination as a Conservative candidate for the 1945 general election, but was rejected by both the constituency parties which interviewed him.[8] In 1947, Hill was finally accepted as its candidate by a constituency party, but did not resign from his BMA position until elected to the House of Commons in the 1950 general election, after giving one of the Conservative Party's national campaign radio speeches.[9]

The choice of restaurant for this gathering reflected Bevan's preference. He had long frequented the Café Royal, where in 1934 Jennie Lee had accepted his proposal of marriage.[10] The choice of medical guests in 1945 was, however, Hill's.[11] All those doctors invited by Hill were members of a standing Negotiating Committee intended to speak for the medical profession in all dealings with the Ministry of Health. This Negotiating Committee included representatives of eight different organizations of doctors, with a majority of members representing the BMA,[12] but the doctors chosen by Hill to dine at the Café Royal were only one-sixth of the total membership of the Negotiating Committee. Among the diners, Guy Dain, chairman of the BMA Council, was a general practitioner from Birmingham. J. B. Miller was a physician from Bishopbriggs. Sir Henry Souttar, president of the BMA, was surgeon to the London Hospital. Sir Alfred (later Lord) Webb-Johnson was president of the Royal College of Surgeons.[13] The final medical guest was Moran.[14]

The absence of some possible guests at the Café Royal, if perhaps predictable, was nevertheless revealing. All those present were male. Mary Esslemont, who represented the Medical Women's Federation on the Negotiating Committee, had not been invited by Hill. That failure would not have bothered Moran, who in 1924 as dean of St Mary's Hospital Medical School had, like other medical school administrators in London, ended admission, permitted during the First World War, of female students.[15] Horder, who approved of women both as doctors and as members of the House of Lords,[16] might have been bothered by the almost complete absence of female doctors from the corridors of power during the creation of the National Health Service. He might even have prodded the minister of health, who seems not to have noticed that absence.

Bevan's failure so to notice was not accidental. He shared Moran's bias against equality for women. Although he bitterly criticized H. H. Asquith's Liberal Cabinet for having opposed women's suffrage, Bevan treated female Members of Parliament of his own party with open contempt.[17] When one of them, Jean Mann, criticized him at a party meeting he told her to 'Contain your bile, woman'.[18] In the presence of another, Bessie Braddock, certainly the most formidable and perhaps the most worthy female Labour Member of Parliament, Bevan snarled to a delegation of working-class women: 'I'm not going to be dictated to by a lot of frustrated females.'[19] For Bevan equality meant an end to class, not gender, distinctions. Herbert Morrison, Bevan's most determined enemy within the Labour Party leadership, was more supportive of equality for women than was Bevan, whose priorities were fully shared by his wife, Jennie Lee, first elected to the House of Commons before she was old enough to vote, who died a member of the House of Lords.[20]

The corridors of British governmental power were profoundly different from the corridors of British hospitals, dominated by nurses. Florence Nightingale's successors, mostly female, were, like female doctors, mostly absent from the creation of the NHS. In almost all the debates, discussions and negotiations/consultations about the emerging NHS, the Royal College of Nursing, the Royal British Nurses' Association and the College of Midwives were unrepresented. It is therefore not surprising that in the NHS structure nurses had a subordinate position. The Negotiating Committee claimed to speak for the entire medical profession, but all its members were doctors. Many consultants certainly resented nurses' independence.[21] Geraldine Duggett, who had reluctantly given up her nursing career when she married a young Thomas Horder, might have prodded her husband to include nurses on this matter.[22] Bevan, who as minister of health substantially improved working conditions for nurses,[23] does not seem to have been offended by exclusion of nurses from the Negotiating Committee. For a brief time in 1946 the BMA , most of whose members did not work in hospitals, tried to enlist the political support of the Royal College of Nursing, but soon lost interest when nurses appeared to have a mind of their own.[24] This independence of nurses may not have been expected by the doctors' Negotiating Committee, whose official records refer to · 'nursing, secretarial and other ancillary staff'.[25] Nurses were at least 'staff'. The Patients Association and the College of Health not yet having been created, there was no organized voice for patients. Claims that patients were in fact represented by Parliament and government or by the doctors or the medical profession or by Moran individually[26] need much more evidence to be persuasive.

Not even all those dining at the Café Royal were to matter, let alone equally, in the creation of the NHS. Miller proved insignificant, and Souttar almost so. The latter, suspected of sympathy with Bevan's intentions, soon lost his BMA presidency. Hill, who became the leader of the BMA's campaign against the NHS, found Dain to be his most important ally within the BMA establishment. Hill would dedicate his 1949 doctors' guidebook to NHS structure and procedures to Dain 'with warmest admiration'.[27] Hill nevertheless later disparaged Dain's leadership gifts. Here Moran would have agreed.[28] There would, however, have been sharp disagreement between Hill and Moran about Webb-Johnson, whom the former saw as 'a born negotiator'.[29] Moran considered Webb-Johnson 'an oaf' and 'mulish' and was to warn Bevan privately that anything said confidentially in his presence would be leaked to the BMA.[30] Webb-Johnson nevertheless proved mostly pliant to Moran's desire to cloak his own actions in creating the NHS with a deceptive public cover of concerted action by all three royal colleges of doctors: Physicians, Surgeons and Obstetricians/Gynaecologists. Webb-Johnson perhaps was made more respectful of Moran by his own experiences as dean of the Middlesex Hospital Medical School.[31]

Moran's primacy within these three royal colleges was helped even more by the fact that in Britain physicians had long had greater prestige than surgeons. Physicians were seen as scholarly intellectuals, while surgeons were seen as manual workers.[32] Such a prestige system might have appealed even to Hippocrates, who, after all, had seen Apollo as a physician, not a surgeon. Moran's primacy was further helped by the RCP's greater wealth, which allowed him to pay the expenses of all three colleges' representatives in their dealings with the minister and Ministry of Health.[33] The Obstetricians/Gynaecologists' presidents, first Eardley Holland and then Sir William Gilliatt, as heads of the most junior, and most often ignored,[34] of these three colleges, may have appreciated Moran's public trinitarian stance. Uninvited to the Café Royal by Hill, Britain's chief obstetricians may have been grateful to be invited to be present at the birth, if not the conception, of the NHS. Moran's influence with Holland may have been especially unexpected in view of Holland's enthusiastic participation, like Horder's, in the Eugenics Society.[35] Horder not only served as president of the Eugenics Society, but also as chairman of the Joint Committee on Voluntary Sterilization, which in the 1930s urged eugenic policies on the Ministry of Health. In 1940, of all years, he argued that 'if a certain class, *qua* class, produces through heredity, as distinct from environment, a better race, then we have got to accept that, be it the poor, the middle or the upper class'. Not surprisingly, the Labour movement was the most determined opponent of eugenic policies in Britain.[36]

Of the doctors present at the Café Royal two would be, by far, the most influential: Hill and Moran. Between them there was an unbridgeable gulf.[37] Part of the distance between them was based on mutual personal antipathy. Neither respected the other. A year before the Café Royal dinner, Moran had written privately to the editor of *The Times*, describing Hill as 'a demagogue' whose 'mind is without depth or balance – not a wise man'.[38] Moran had also already complained to a senior official at the Ministry of Health of the BMA's 'arbitrary and provocative' behaviour under Hill's guidance.[39] Nothing that happened later changed Moran's judgement of Hill. When Beaverbrook told Moran in 1948 that if he were now to choose between Hill and Horder as his doctor, he would choose Hill, Moran responded that Beaverbrook must have developed suicidal tendencies.[40]

After Moran was dead, Hill chose to recall that before 1945 Moran 'had no experience' as a negotiator, and during the negotiations leading to the creation of the NHS 'did not really comprehend the procedures'.[41] The 'Radio Doctor' presumably had not listened to the BBC's wartime 'Brains Trust' programme, on which Moran appeared anonymously. Perhaps, Hill would not then have recognized the distinctive voice of the president of the Royal College of Physicians. In any event, Hill's argument that Moran was not intelligent enough to understand Hill's preferred procedures in 1945–8 was risible. If Hill's argument was intended seriously, the shoe was on the other foot. Moran's *modus operandi* was to bypass unhelpful procedures whenever necessary to achieve his desired result. His goal was success, not procedural propriety.[42] Group decisions were of little interest to him, which offended the organization man in Hill. As one of his eulogists was to put it, Moran found private discussion with trusted friends more valuable than a committee of senior statesmen. He paid as little attention to the seniority as to the committee aspect.[43]

Even though personal initiatives, not bureaucratic procedures, were his preferred way, Moran was fortunate in his institutional power base. His presidency of the RCP assured him a seat at the decision-making tables. Hill could not afford to exclude him. Within the college a closed circle of fellows led the non-voting members, and the president led the fellows. The weakness of representative structures within the college permitted him wide leeway of action without immediately endangering his institutional primacy.[44] He was, after all, a president, not a prime minister. Once elected president, he was essentially free to act until the next presidential election. That is why the college's presidential elections were so important to him – and to Horder. Previous RCP presidents, notably Sir William Jenner, had also dominated the college. Moran, however, carried college presidential leadership to new heights or depths.[45] He was later to concede that if a poll had been taken within the college most fellows would have been against the creation of the NHS.[46] This did not bother him. Decades earlier, he had confessed: 'I dislike my fellow consultant more and more as a class.'[47]

Almost the only thing Hill and Moran had in common in October 1945 was a lack of desire to involve Horder in the NHS negotiations. The absence of the latter from the Café Royal was, and is, striking. Horder was not a member of the Negotiating Committee, but Hill could easily have arranged such membership for Horder as a BMA representative if Hill had so wanted. All Moran would have had to do to make Horder a RCP representative was to remove from the Negotiating Committee his institutional *locum tenens*, Harold Boldero, whom he had made RCP registrar.[48] Hill's and Moran's motivations for passing over Horder were very different. Hill's reasons were entirely situational. As far as Hill could have known in October 1945, Horder would be likely to support the emerging NHS. Furthermore, as Britain's most successful consulting physician Horder had little in common with the general practitioners who were the essential BMA clientele. He had paid relatively little attention to the BMA over his long career. Mostly his connection was intermittently with its leading publication, the *British Medical Journal*. He would contribute one of his brief, less-significant articles,[49] or correct the *Journal*'s reporting of House of Lords matters.[50] Some of Horder's experiences with the *Journal* had been more significant and most unpleasant. The *Journal* never embraced eugenics, which cause

Horder advocated so enthusiastically.[51] A *Journal* editorial had bitterly criticized Horder's 1941 'scheme' for a specialized clinical medical attack on rheumatism for making 'still another inroad' into the incomes of general practitioners, already threatened by too many 'child welfare and ante-natal clinics'.[52] This unimpressive attack had enraged Horder, who was not only chairman of the Empire Rheumatism Council, but also proud author of an oft-revised medical text, *Rheumatism*. In 1947, while battling against the NHS, Horder returned to wage 'war on rheumatism', with his *Plan for National Action* against rheumatism diseases, to be funded by, among others, the national exchequer and local governments, 'subject to the strictest control' by these governmental levels.[53]

Unlike Hill, Moran's reasons for excluding Horder from NHS negotiations were personal, not situational. As far as Moran knew in October 1945, Horder would support the NHS. Horder and Moran, further, had much in common situationally. Both were eminent consulting physicians, closely identified with a particular teaching hospital. They lived in impressive homes, containing their private practice offices, a few doors away from each other on Harley Street, the preferred address of London's consulting physicians: Moran at 129, Horder at 141. If Horder's household had long been well-staffed with servants, so eventually was Moran's, with four servants. If Horder's chauffeur could have been seen from 129 waiting in the Rolls-Royce, so Moran's chauffeur could be seen from 141 waiting in Moran's Rolls-Royce.[54] If on Harley Street keeping up with the neighbours was mostly keeping up with the Horders, the Morans had met the challenge.

For at least two decades before 1945, nevertheless, relations between Moran and Horder had been strained. Long before Horder became Moran's chief rival for the RCP presidency, Horder was viewed unfavourably in the Moran household.[55] Frequently hypercritical of his fellow human beings,[56] Moran's special contempt for Horder was based on the success of the latter's private practice. Horder was already at the top of their common profession while the younger Moran was still struggling financially. When Moran spoke with disdain of doctors with high incomes, calling them medical grocers,[57] his most immediate target was obvious: Britain's most successful consulting physician. After Horder was long dead, even Moran conceded that he had been 'the consultant', with a 'wonderful practice'.[58] In 1924, Moran became much more explicit in identifying his target. When

Horder enthusiastically endorsed a new therapeutic device imported from the United States, Moran suggested that Horder had been paid by a newspaper for a related story, later failing to apologize to Horder.[59] Almost a half-century later, long after Horder's death, Moran was to display the beginning, but only that, of remorse: 'Horder was not a bad character, really. The idea grew up in medicine that he was a pure mercenary ... I don't think that was true.'[60] It was not true, but prominent among those who had fostered the 'idea' that 'grew up in medicine' was Moran. Reading, in 1966, a new biography of Horder by the latter's son, Moran confessed: 'I hadn't divined ... Horder's multiplicity of interests.'[61] Horder was no more a grocer than was Moran, although the servants from both households doubtless visited gourmet grocers. Sour grapes may have been on the Morans' list of purchases. A larger portion of Horder's total professional income came from private practice and a larger portion of Moran's total professional income came from administrative salaries, but both lived off, and necessarily so, their professional income. Moran's professional income was handsome. In 1940, the year he became Churchill's doctor, he was earning £5,000 annually from his private practice, £500 as dean of St Mary's Hospital Medical School, and £1,300 (plus allowances) as a wartime sector group officer of London-area hospitals. The latter salary was replaced in 1941 by £1,400 (later £1,200) as consultant adviser to the Ministry of Health, which title he held throughout the Second World War. In 1944 he accepted, briefly, editorship, then chairmanship, of the *Practitioner*, a monthly medical journal owned by Brendan Bracken, Winston Churchill's most loyal lieutenant, which carried an annual salary of £1,000. The next year he earned £500 from *The Sunday Times* for publication of excerpts from his *The Anatomy of Courage*, as well as 250 guineas for examining Rudolf Hess at Nuremberg.[62] In early 1945 he nevertheless lamented that because of his frequent attendance upon Prime Minister Churchill his annual income from private practice had dwindled to £70.[63] That was, of course, the material price he had willingly paid in exchange for further professional prestige and the possibility of power.

While Horder was busy at Bart's and Moran at St Mary's, their professional paths had seldom crossed. Before Moran became active in the Royal College of Physicians, their institutional encounters were therefore few. As soon as Moran became treasurer of the RCP, he and Horder, then not long retired from Bart's, crossed swords on college matters. By 1943, Moran was trying to hide some of his medical policy activities from Horder.[64] In that year, in what may have been the only olive branch offered by one combatant to the other, Horder wrote to Moran, congratulating the latter on Churchill's recent recovery from pneumonia. Moran apparently did not respond.[65] In January 1945 their mutual antagonism became even more visible and audible. They argued in the daily press over whether the RCP should move to a new building, and almost simultaneously at a college meeting Horder attacked no fewer than six times a council report written by Moran.[66]

The vigour of Moran's desire to influence Bevan in the latter's creation of a national health service was surely encouraged by a desire to defeat Horder yet again. Moran's belief in the desirability of a national health service was, nevertheless, sincere and entirely predictable. That belief was consistent with a lifetime of expressed opinions. A 1910 editorial, 'Hospitals and Democracy' in the *St Mary's Hospital Gazette*, referred to Bernard Shaw's argument, in his introduction to *The Doctor's Dilemma*, for a state medical service. The editor, challenging his charitable private-hospital readership, continued: 'It is not our intention to enter into the right or wrong of this control by the State. That this control is coming there can be no manner of doubt.'[67] The editor of the *Gazette* was a rising young doctor, Charles Wilson, who was soon to undergo, in France in 1914–18, the most important educational experience of his long life, in a state medical service, the Royal Army Medical Corps. Dealing for four years with endless fragile British casualties left Moran with much besides a Military Cross 'for conspicuous gallantry' at the Somme.[68] He learned there much about the human condition. Some of that learning could be, and was, expressed in clinical terms. Much of what he learned was psychological insight into stress, especially about fear and its overcoming, eventually summarized in his memorable *The Anatomy of Courage*, first published in 1945, and later supplemented by an address to the American College of Physicians.[69] Not all of Moran's judgements of military medicine were favourable, but long after 1918 he continued to take seriously the role of military medicine, and frequently lectured at British military colleges. In 1957 he was appointed chairman of the Army Medical Advisory Board, although his deep conviction that fear was the natural reaction of soldiers in battle could hardly have pleased the military establishment, any more than did his opposition to continuation of conscription after 1945.[70] Moran had been, of course, for an important part of his life, a doctor practising medicine in an army, not a combatant. The soldiers he had come to know the most intimately were his patients. Their fear of battle had been justified.

Upon returning to civilian life after his own war, Moran participated in several public debates about the future of medical care. In language strikingly similar to that used consistently by Horder before 1945, Moran told his fellow doctors in 1920 that they must in the future act as advisers to the British nation. One area needing such advice was the question of voluntary versus governmental hospitals. Moran declined to answer this question explicitly, but observed:

> ... the State hospital is the settled policy of a great party of the State – a party, incidentally, that has taken more interest in medical matters than their older rivals in politics. Moreover, it is a logical policy. It is in keeping with the very faith and creed of that party, it is certainly not a sudden move dictated by opportunism.[71]

Moran was here giving the Labour Party's frequent support for municipal hospitals much broader policy significance than was then justified, but this statement was, after all, an expression of Moran's, not the Labour Party's, expectation of the future. He was clearly not frightened by government hospitals. Indeed, in some parts of Britain, in his view, large municipal hospitals were already more important medically than smaller, more modest voluntary hospitals. Here Moran's view was prescient. After the Local Government Act of 1929, the initial relative inferiority of municipal to voluntary private hospitals began to disappear nationally.[72]

Shortly after speaking kindly of the Labour Party to doctors, Moran spoke kindly of its chief constituency, the working classes, to a wider audience. He saw British workers as then engaging in strikes because of 'lack of security' which would only 'be removed by the erection of machinery for settling trade disputes in which labour really believes'. He saw 'the mass of people' in Britain as simply wanting 'to better their conditions. It is important to meet this wish up to the very limit compatible with the industrial state.'[73] To Moran the 'industrial state' was an essentially capitalist state. This suggests that for Moran capitalism should remain but the British welfare state should be expanded as much as possible. Not many RCP fellows would then have so preached. Among those few others was Horder.

Moran's personal involvement in governmental medical planning took a large leap forward in the late 1930s, with the emerging possibility of another great European war, in which British cities, especially London, would be far more vulnerable to aerial bombing attacks than in 1914–18. A governmental committee, chaired by Moran, was named by the Home Office to develop a contingency plan for air-raid casualties needing hospitalization. This plan, implemented in 1939 as the Emergency Medical Service, divided London area hospitals into several sectors, each dominated by a teaching hospital. St Mary's Hospital, with its Medical School dean, was given authority over a generous sector. In 1941, Moran gave up his duties as sector officer and joined another government committee, to advise on allocation of doctors between military and civilian needs.[74] The consequence of these wartime emergency measures was that the administration of British medicine was centralized as never before. Emergency planning had been so effective that there were more hospital beds and staff available than were needed by civilian bombing casualties, so these extra beds and staff, already paid for by government funds, were allocated for ordinary civilian use, creating something like a national hospital service well before most Britons realized it.[75] Moran, primarily responsible for this achievement, fully so realized. The lessons he drew from the Emergency Medical Service were similar to those drawn in the Labour Party's 1943 *National Service for Health*.[76] Already in 1942, in a BBC broadcast to Sweden, Moran described a future British national health service which was remarkably similar to that outlined in the National Health Service bill introduced into the House of Commons in March 1946 by Aneurin Bevan.[77] Moran's maiden speech in the House of Lords in 1943 repeated most of the prescription he had earlier given his Swedish radio audience.[78] The main emphasis of this speech was not much different from Horder's maiden speech in the House of Lords.

NOTES

1. Foot, *Aneurin Bevan*, vol. 2, pp. 124–5; Lovell, *Churchill's Doctor*, p. 293.
2. A. Cooke, *History of the Royal College of Physicians*, vol. 3, p. 1, 102; Lovell, *Churchill's Doctor*, pp. 279–80, 316.
3. Lovell, *Churchill's Doctor*, p. 273.
4. Ibid., p. 334.
5. Ibid., p. 281; J. Campbell, *Aneurin Bevan and the Mirage of British Socialism* (New York: W. W. Norton, 1987), p. 171.
6. Lord Hill, *Behind the Screen: The Broadcasting Memoirs* (London: Sidgwick & Jackson, 1974).

7. C. King, *With Malice toward None: A War Diary* (London: Sidgwick & Jackson, 1970), p. 247; Morgan, *Labour in Power*, p. 159.
8. These rejections were apparently unknown to a successful Labour nominee, Barbara Castle, even long after the 1945 general election. G. Goodman, *State of the Nation*, pp. 56–7.
9. Hill, *Both Sides*, pp. 4–15; H. Nicholas, *The British General Election of 1950* (London: Macmillan, 1951), pp. 107–8, 137.
10. Hollis, *Jennie Lee*, pp. 82, 152; Morgan, *Labour in Power*, p. 153.
11. Honigsbaum, *Health*, p. 119; Pater, *Making of National Health Service*, p. 107.
12. C. Webster, *The Health Services and the War*, vol. 1 (London: Her Majesty's Stationery Office, 1988), p. 67.
13. Not the Royal College of Obstetricians, as reported by K. Morgan, *The People's Peace: British History 1945–1950* (Oxford: Oxford University Press, 1992), p. 38.
14. Lovell, *Churchill's Doctor*, p. 293.
15. Ibid., p. 96; Bonner, *Becoming a Physician*, pp. 314, 338; Cope, *History of St Mary's Hospital Medical School*, p. 69; Hare, 'Scientific Activities of Alexander Fleming', p. 352; Porter, *Greatest Benefit*, p. 358.
16. P. Brookes, *Women at Westminster: An Account of Women in the British Parliament 1918–1966* (London: Peter Davies, 1967), pp. 208–9; *The Medical World*, 21 July 1939, p. 3.
17. A. Bevan, *In Place of Fear*, pp. 8–9; Hollis, *Jennie Lee*, pp. 152–3, 191.
18. Hollis, *Jennie Lee*, p. 152.
19. Ibid., pp. 152–3; I. Bulmer-Thomas, *The Growth of the British Party System* (London: John Baker, 1965), vol. 2, p. 175.
20. Brookes, *Women at Westminster*, pp. 66, 237; Hollis, *Jennie Lee*, pp. viii, 140, 149–50, 158; Inwood, *History of London*, p. 758.
21. Lowe, *Welfare State*, pp. 36, 192.
22. M. Horder, *Little Genius*, pp. 34–5.
23. Foot, *Aneurin Bevan*, vol. 2, pp. 128n, 129.
24. E. Grey-Turner and F. Sutherland, *History of the British Medical Association*, vol. 2 (London: British Medical Association, 1982), p. 54.
25. Negotiating Committee, *Minutes*, 17 January 1946, p. 3, RCP archives.
26. For Parliament and government, see Willcocks, *Creation of National Health Service*, p. 33; for 'the doctors' see F. Honigsbaum, 'The Evolution of the NHS', *British Medical Journal*, 301, 6, 754 (1990), p. 698; for 'the profession' see RCP Comitia, *Minutes*, 16 May 1946, p. 65; for Moran, see D. Black, 'Foreword', in Lovell, *Churchill's Doctor*, p. vii.
27. C. Hill and J. Woodcock, *The National Health Service* (London: Christopher Johnson, 1949).
28. Hill, *Both Sides*, p. 90; Lovell, *Churchill's Doctor*, p. 238.
29. *British Medical Journal*, 1 July 1978, p. 31.
30. Lovell, *Churchill's Doctor*, pp. 255, 299, 301.
31. Z. Cope, *The Royal College of Surgeons of England: A History* (London: Anthony Blond, 1959), p. 207.
32. Bonner, *Becoming a Physician*, p. 63; Frazer, *History of English Public Health*, p. 158; Honigsbaum, *Health*, p. 113; C. Lawrence and S. Shapin (eds), *Science Incarnate: Historical Embodiments of Natural Knowledge* (Chicago, IL: University of Chicago Press, 1998), pp. 11–12, 156–61, 165, 171, 173, 177, 183–7; Payer, *Medicine and Culture*, p. 36; W. Reader, *Professional Men: The Rise of the Professional Classes in Nineteenth-century England* (New York: Basic Books, 1966), p. 16; Reid, *Ask Sir James*, p. 171; Shaw, *Doctor's Dilemma*, p. 113; R. Stevenson, *Morell Mackenzie*, p. 54.
33. Honigsbaum, *Health*, p. 119.
34. Even by careful scholars, as in K. Morgan, *Labour People: Leaders and Lieutenants, Hardie to Kinnock* (Oxford: Oxford University Press, 1987), p. 209.
35. R. Soloway, *Demography and Degeneration: Eugenics and the Declining Birthrate in Twentieth-century Britain* (Chapel Hill, NC: University of North Carolina Press, 1995), pp. 206, 342.
36. Ibid., pp. 158, 189, 194, 201, 206–7, 267, 272–3, 342; J. Macnicol, 'Eugenics and the Campaign for Voluntary Sterilization in Britain between the Wars', *Social History of Medicine*, 2, 2 (1989), p. 162.

37. Lovell, *Churchill's Doctor*, p. 291.
38. Ibid., p. 239.
39. Webster, *Health Services and War*, vol. 1, p. 412.
40. Lovell, *Churchill's Doctor*, pp. 289, 291.
41. *British Medical Journal*, 1 July 1978, p. 31.
42. Hill, *Both Sides*, p. 91; Honigsbaum, *Health*, p. 116.
43. Robert, Lord Platt in *British Medical Journal*, 23 April 1977, p. 1,088; Platt, *Private and Controversial*, p. 105.
44. Gullick, 'Forty Years of NHS', p. 56; Honigsbaum, *Health*, p. 118; Mackenzie, *Power and Responsibility*, p. 74.
45. Honigsbaum, *Health*, p. 216; R. Stevenson, *Morell Mackenzie*, p. 40.
46. 'Lord Moran in conversation'.
47. Lovell, *Churchill's Doctor*, p. 92.
48. Ibid., p. 180.
49. T. Horder and N. Ferry, 'A Search for an Ideal Antigen for Therapeutic Immunization', *British Medical Journal*, 31 July 1926, pp. 177–80; T. Horder, 'New Treatments for Old', *British Medical Journal*, 20 May 1933, pp. 859–863.
50. *British Medical Journal*, 11 June 1938, p. 1,287; 18 June 1938, p. 1, 341.
51. Soloway, *Demography and Degeneration*, pp. 206–7.
52. *British Medical Journal*, 3 May 1941, p. 674.
53. Lord Horder, *Rheumatism: A Plan for National Action*, 5th edn (London: H. K. Lewis, 1947), pp. 5, 50, 53, 61.
54. Lovell, *Churchill's Doctor*, pp. 107–8.
55. Ibid., p. 117.
56. Colville, *Winston Churchill*, p. 243; J. Colville, *The Fringes of Power: 10 Downing Street Diaries 1939–1955* (New York: W. W. Norton, 1986), pp. 518, 758; M. Gilbert, *Winston S. Churchill*, vol. 7 (Boston, MA: Houghton Mifflin, 1986), p. 967; Hubble, 'Moran and Boswell', p. 4.
57. Lovell, *Churchill's Doctor*, p. 117.
58. 'Lord Moran in Conversation'.
59. Lovell, *Churchill's Doctor*, p. 117.
60. 'Lord Moran in Conversation'.
61. Ibid.; Lovell, *Churchill's Doctor*, p. 384.
62. Lovell, *Churchill's Doctor*, pp. 92–3, 147–8, 243, 256, 263–4, 281, 289.
63. Ibid., p. 256.
64. Ibid., pp. 145, 151, 234.
65. Ibid., p. 199.
66. Ibid., pp. 257–8.
67. Ibid., p. 20.
68. Ibid., p. 49; Oxbury, *Great Britons*, p. 353.
69. Lord Moran, 'Wear and Tear', *Lancet*, 258 (1950), pp. 1,099–101.
70. Hunt, 'Moran', pp. 408, 410; Lovell, *Churchill's Doctor*, pp. 137–8, 285–6.
71. *Lancet*, 25 December 1920, p. 1,288.
72. Ibid., pp. 1,287–8; Hollingsworth, *Political Economy of Medicine*, p. 28.
73. *Lancet*, 4 June 1921, pp. 1,195–6.
74. Cope, *History of S. Mary's Hospital Medical School*, p. 71; Hare, 'Scientific Activities of Alexander Fleming', p. 363; Lovell, *Churchill's Doctor*, pp. 140–1, 146, 148; G. Shakespeare, *Let Candles Be Brought In* (London: Macdonald, 1949), p. 279.
75. N. Goodman, *Wilson Jameson: Architect of National Health* (London: George Allen & Unwin, 1970), p. 95; O. Keidan, 'The Health Services', in A. Forder (ed.), *Penelope Hall's Social Services of England and Wales* (New York: Routledge & Kegan Paul, 1969), p. 153; Widgery, *Health in Danger*, p. 26.
76. Labour Party, *National Service for Health* (London: Labour Party, 1943), p. 10.
77. Lovell, *Churchill's Doctor*, p. 190.
78. Ibid., pp. 204–5.

11

Away from the Café Royal

In autumn 1945, the president of the Royal College of Physicians had no hesitancy in becoming the ally[1] of the minister of health, who was to describe himself as the 'tribune of the people'.[2] Not only did Moran and Bevan become allies, Moran became Bevan's closest as well as most important ally in creating the NHS. Other than with Moran, Bevan largely kept his own counsel while drafting the NHS bill. The minister of health told the full membership of the doctors' Negotiating Committee he would not 'negotiate' within them, but he would 'consult' them in composing his bill. His responsibility, as he saw it, after all, was not to doctors but to Parliament.[3] When Charles Hill urged particular language for a statement by Bevan to the House of Commons, the minister retorted that he did not wish to be told what words he would use in announcing government policy to Parliament.[4] This was more ministerial than parliamentary, or even collective Cabinet, sovereignty, however. Bevan wrote that 'the authority of Parliament is part of the social and political climate of Britain',[5] but as minister he engaged in climate control. To backbench, including Labour, Members of Parliament, Bevan was no more forthcoming than to the Negotiating Committee. The health policy group of Labour Members of Parliament formally complained to the Liaison Committee of the Parliamentary Labour Party that the minister of health refused to discuss with them possible details of his forthcoming bill.[6]

With Moran, outside the office, it was another matter. The two allies would meet privately in the evenings at Pruniers, another fashionable London restaurant.[7] It was no accident that Bevan was widely known as 'the Bollinger Bolshevik'. He liked expensive wines and food,[8] perhaps even more than did his great enemy Herbert Morrison.[9] Bevan went to the best restaurants whenever he could.[10] Now he could. Occasional reports of Bevan and Moran dining together were misinterpreted in hostile medical circles as late-night carousals.[11] Even such misleading reports cannot have been many, for much later, after reading a biography of Bevan, Charles Hill acknowledged that such private meetings had been 'quite unknown' to him at the time.[12]

Although private meetings between Bevan and Moran were not primarily social occasions, they were probably enjoyable occasions to both allies. Bevan, Moran soon realized, got his information by talking to people rather than by reading documents.[13] There were many things the new minister of health wanted and needed to learn about medical matters. He had a long-standing genuine commitment to equalized access for all Britons to high-quality medical care, but he did not yet fully see how that goal could best be reached. Moran could be an extremely effective teacher when he so chose. Now he certainly so chose. Rather than lecturing his students, he drew them out conversationally.[14] That teaching style matched Bevan's learning style. Moran appreciated a bright student, and he gave Bevan's intellect high marks: 'He would come to the heart of my case almost before I had put it to him.'[15] Ernest Bevin was correct: Bevan was, as he himself understood, an intellectual.[16] Even in such pleasant circumstances, however, Moran never forgot 'my case'. Teachership can easily slip into leadership, and Moran's way of influencing, not merely, teaching, people was to talk to them.[17] His path to influencing Bevan was clear, and he made the most of his opportunity. Corkscrew Charlie was now teaching the Bollinger Bolshevik.

The first major topic discussed by Moran and Bevan was hospitals. That all British hospitals, voluntary private as well as municipal, should be nationalized had never before been seriously considered.[18] The intellectual origins of the idea of hospital nationalization are far from certain.[19] The implementation of that idea was the most innovative aspect of the creation of the NHS.[20] Nationalization of all hospitals was not only part of Bevan's eventual bill, but also his broadest legislative priority during 1945–48.[21] Already early on, he was at least considering it.[22] The claim that Bevan 'consulted various sections' of the medical profession before deciding to nationalize hospitals[23] is off the mark. Only one doctor was privy to the possible decision, and that doctor may have also been a party to that decision. Bevan may in fact have 'negotiated' with Moran. The major impetus for hospital nationalization may have come from Moran.[24] More precisely, perhaps, Bevan arrived at this decision with Moran's assistance.[25] For Moran, hospital nationalization was an apt solution to the serious problem of regional differences in quality among British hospitals.[26] Substantial regional differences there certainly were.[27] Because eliminating such regional differences was for Moran the key to a truly national health service, he saw Bevan's eventual bill, which shared that priority,[28] as the most appropriate possibility.[29]

Hospital buildings would not be much use without hospital doctors. Under Bevan's eventual NHS bill the latter would no longer need to play Robin Hood, overcharging a few rich patients in an impossible attempt fully to subsidize treatment of many poor patients. Hospital doctors would now receive substantial salaries, which would surely attract at least some consulting physicians and surgeons to nationalized hospitals. Those salaries, however, might not be attractive enough by themselves to attract the most ambitious consultants. Forgetting his antipathy to medical grocers, Moran therefore urged, and Bevan consented to, consultants in nationalized hospitals being permitted to accept payment for treating further, private patients.[30] Bevan was later to claim that this permission was a 'defect' which he had 'seen from the beginning'.[31] Perhaps he later thought he had been seduced by Moran. Perhaps he had.[32]

Even the most ambitious hospital consultants might not be the most gifted. Bevan and Moran therefore agreed on supplementing with continuing distinction awards the salaries of the most meritorious consultants. This supplement was suggested by Moran.[33] Distinction awards would be available only for hospital consultants, not to general practitioners.[34] This policy bias reflected Moran's personal bias. To him general practitioners were not capable of distinction. They were inferior to, indeed were often failed aspirant, hospital consultants.[35] Lacking proper training and experience (which Moran had no desire to have provided), general practitioners should in his view be totally excluded from pay wards in hospitals.[36]

Moran's proposal of distinction awards was acceptable to Bevan because such awards would gratify those whom he too saw as the leaders of the medical profession, the consultants.[37] That Bevan gratified 'the elite within the profession whom the Labour Party might have been expected to favour least' later raised scholarly eyebrows.[38] If he wanted British workers to have access to the best medical care, Bevan may have had no other option. Consultants were the key to the highest-quality medical care becoming possible for NHS patients.[39] As Bevan conceded, and perhaps boasted, to get consultants to participate in the NHS 'I stuffed their mouths with gold'.[40] In his agreement with Moran, however, Bevan ensured to hospital consultants not only future wealth, but also future prestige and future power.[41] Consultants would be free of the disciplinary system to be created to regulate the professional behaviour of general practitioners.[42] The NHS Bevan established was hospital-dominated, but its rulers can be more precisely identified. Those rulers were consultants.[43] The NHS did not create, but it did at least preserve and perhaps further widen, the gap between consultants and general practitioners.[44] Group practices of general practitioners, officially encouraged by the NHS Act, never blossomed, partly at least because Bevan did not want such group practices to compete for patients with outpatient departments of hospitals.[45]

Even among consultants some would be more equal than others. In addition to the inner circle of consultants who would receive distinction awards, there would be an even smaller inmost circle which would include only those consultants at British teaching hospitals, then 30 in number. This was only 1 per cent of the number of British hospitals nationalized in 1948.[46] Most teaching hospitals had accumulated substantial endowments, often used to finance medical research. These endowments would not be touched.[47] Except for the nine teaching hospitals in Scotland, the boards of governors of teaching hospitals would be nominated in a distinctively autonomous manner, and function independently of regional hospital boards.[48] A tripartite division of doctors, with general practitioners on the bottom, most hospital consultants in the middle, and a few full-time professors at medical schools on the top, had been Moran's vision of the future of British medicine, articulated a decade earlier.[49] The primacy of academic medicine was also evident in a draft of the 1945 Conservative Party election manifesto, Moranesque in language.[50] That elitist dream was now implemented in the NHS, with the addition of a further barrier, devised in 1946 by Moran himself, between those consultants who would, and those who would not, receive distinction awards.

Such awards in effect doubled the salaries of consultants receiving them. The salary range of consultants deemed the most meritorious eventually rose above the salary range of the most senior British civil servants, even permanent secretaries, into the range of Cabinet-level ministers and judges.[51] This was no surprise to Moran, who in 1947–8 was the chief architect of the structure and process for implementing his idea of distinction awards.[52] The system Moran then constructed may well be the most formalized of any national method used to reward doctors financially for their ability.[53] As soon as this machinery had been created Moran successfully further suggested himself to Bevan as the first, salaried, chairman of the Standing Awards Committee on Distinction Awards.[54] In this capacity he dominated until 1962 the awards selection process, frequently monopolizing both information and decision-making.[55] While so acting he was the most powerful doctor in Britain. Few doctors in any nation can have exercised so much administrative power for so long.

NOTES

1. K. Morgan, *The Red Dragon and the Red Flag: The Cases of James Griffiths and Aneurin Bevan* (Aberystwyth: National Library of Wales, 1989), p. 9.
2. Bevan, *In Place of Fear*, p. 6.
3. Negotiating Committee, *Minutes*, meeting with Minister 6 February 1946, p. 1, RCP archives.
4. Ibid., 4 December 1945, p. 3.
5. G. Goodman, *State of the Nation*, p. 43.
6. Donoughue and Jones, *Herbert Morrison*, p. 369.
7. B. Abel-Smith, *The Hospitals 1800–1948: A Study in Social Administration in England and Wales* (Cambridge, MA, Harvard University Press, 1964), pp. 486–7; Fox, *Health Policies*, p. 134; Honigsbaum, *Health*, pp. 174, 216.
8. A. Boyle, *Poor, Dear Brendan: The Quest for Brendan Bracken* (London: Hutchinson, 1974), p. 221; M. Foot, *Debts of Honour* (New York: Harper & Row, 1981), pp. 76–7; G. Goodman, *State of the Nation*, p. 37; Lovell, *Churchill's Doctor*, p. 293; P. Mair, *Shared Enthusiasm: The Story of Lord and Lady Beveridge* (Windlesham: Ascent, 1982), p. 105; Morgan, *Red Dragon and Red Flag*, p. 13.
9. H. Nicolson, *Diaries and Letters 1945–1962* (New York: Atheneum, 1968), p. 165.
10. Chisholm and Davie, *Lord Beaverbrook*, p. 362.
11. Widgery, *Health in Danger*, p. 30.
12. Lord Hill, 'Aneurin Bevan among the Doctors', *British Medical Journal*, 24 November 1973, p. 469.
13. *British Medical Journal*, 16 July 1960, p. 236.
14. Lovell, *Churchill's Doctor*, pp. xi, 92, 137.
15. *British Medical Journal*, 16 July 1960, p. 236.
16. H. Nicolson, *Diaries and Letters 1939–1945* (New York: Atheneum, 1967), p. 192; Nicolson, *Diaries and Letters 1945–1962*, p. 368; W. Rodgers and B. Donoughue, *The People into Parliament: A Concise History of the Labour Movement in Britain* (New York: Viking, 1966), p. 163.
17. Lovell, *Churchill's Doctor*, p. 116.
18. Foot, *Aneurin Bevan*, vol. 2, p. 133; Grimes, *British National Health Service*, p. 136; Honigsbaum, *Health*, p. 217; K. Laybourn, *The Rise of Labour: The British Labour Party 1890–1979* (London: Edward Arnold, 1988), pp. 115–16; Sked and Cook, *Post-war Britain*, p. 43.
19. G. Goodman, *State of the Nation*, p. 108.
20. Ibid., p. 107.
21. Clarke, *Hope and Glory*, p. 223.
22. Addison, *Now the War is Over*, p. 99; Campbell, *Aneurin Bevan*, p. 167; Fox, *Health Policies*, p. 135; G. Goodman, *State of the Nation*, p. 108.
23. G. Goodman, *State of the Nation*, p. 90.

24. Foot, *Aneurin Bevan*, vol. 2, p. 132; Hennessy, *Never Again*, p. 137; Honigsbaum, *Health*, p. 174.
25. Grimes, *British National Health Service*, p. 136.
26. Pater, *Making of National Health Service*, p. 175.
27. G. Godber, 'Forty Years of the NHS: Origins and Early Development', *British Medical Journal*, 297 (1988), p. 37; Ham, *Health Policy*, p. 20; A. Heidenheimer, H. Heclo and C. Adams, *Comparative Public Policy: The Politics of Social Choice in America, Europe, and Japan* (New York: St Martin's, 1990), p. 77; Keidan, 'Health Services', pp. 141, 161; M. Powell, 'Hospital Provision before the National Health Service: A Geographical Study of the 1945 Hospital Surveys', *Social History of Medicine*, 5, 3 (1992), pp. 483–504; Widgery, *Health in Danger*, p. 26.
28. Addison, *Now the War is Over*, p. 101; Fox, *Health Policies*, p. 134; G. Goodman, *State of the Nation*, p. 127.
29. Addison, *Now the War is Over*, p. 101; Webster, *Health Services and War*, vol. 1, p. 99.
30. Addison, *Now the War is Over*, p. 100; Campbell, *Aneurin Bevan*, p. 169; Foot, *Aneurin Bevan*, vol. 2, p. 137.
31. A. Bevan, *In Place of Fear*, p. 96.
32. Campbell, *Aneurin Bevan*, p. 168; Forsyth, *Doctors and State Medicine*, p. 2; H. Glennester, *British Social Policy since 1945* (Oxford: Blackwell, 1995), p. 50.
33. *Lancet*, 15 April 1950, p. 722; Klein, *Politics of National Health Service*, pp. 161, 175.
34. J. Hogarth, *The Payment of the Physician: Some European Comparisons* (New York: Macmillan, 1963), pp. 44, 47, 49.
35. Supplement to *British Medical Journal*, 25 January 1958, p. 29; Lovell, *Churchill's Doctor*, p. 364; Stevens, *Medical Practice*, p. 101.
36. Honigsbaum, *Division in British Medicine*, p. 142.
37. *British Medical Journal*, 2 July 1988, p. 14; B. Griffith, S. Iliffe and G. Rayner, *Banking on Sickness: Commercial Medicine in Britain and the USA* (London: Lawrence & Wishart, 1987), p. 27; Grimes, *British National Health Service*, p. 137; Webster, *Health Services and War*, vol. 1, p. 313.
38. Lowe, *Welfare State*, p. 177.
39. Grimes, *British National Health Service*, p. 6.
40. Campbell, *Aneurin Bevan*, p. 168.
41. Ibid.
42. Willcocks, *Creation of National Health Service*, p. 70.
43. Hollis, *Jennie Lee*, p. 130; Widgery, *Health in Danger*, p. 31.
44. Russell Lord Brain, *Medicine and Government* (London: Tavistock Publications, 1967), p. 5; Campbell, *Aneurin Bevan*, p. 177; A. J. Cronin, *The Citadel* (New York: Bantam Books, 1962), pp. 101, 192; Forsyth, *Doctors and State Medicine*, pp. 76, 97; Ham, *Health Policy*, p. 21; Lewis and Maude, *Professional People*, pp. 40, 181; Morgan, *Labour in Power*, p. 156; Porter, *Greatest Benefit*, p. 654; Widgery, *Health in Danger*, p. 31.
45. Bevan, *In Place of Fear*, p. 196; Ham, *Health Policy*, pp. 23–4.
46. T. Chester, *Organisation for Change: The British National Health Service* (Paris: Organisation for Economic Co-operation and Development, 1975), p. 8; Foot, *Aneurin Bevan*, vol. 2, p. 108.
47. A. Bevan, *In Place of Fear*, p. 198.
48. Ibid., p. 120; Foot, *Aneurin Bevan*, vol. 2, pp. 131–2; Glennester, *British Social Policy*, p. 50; N. Goodman, *Wilson Jameson*, p. 122n; Keidan, 'Health Services', p. 157; Porter, *Greatest Benefit*, p. 653; Widgery, *Health in Danger*, p. 31; Willcocks, *Creation of National Health Service*, p. 69. The 1946 National Health Service Act excluded Scotland, whose counterpart Act followed a year later. Willcocks, *Creation of National Health Service*, p. 12.
49. Lovell, *Churchill's Doctor*, p. 140.
50. Fox, *Health Policies*, p. 109n.
51. H. Clegg and T. Chester, *Wage Policy and the Health Service* (Oxford: Basil Blackwell, 1957), pp. 60–1; Lowe, *Welfare State*, p. 176.
52. Hunt, 'Moran', pp. 409–10; Stevens, *Medical Practice*, p. 214.
53. W. Glaser, *Paying the Doctor: Systems of Remuneration and their Effects* (Baltimore, MD: Johns Hopkins University Press, 1970), p. 216.
54. Lovell, *Churchill's Doctor*, pp. 290, 321–2.

55. Forsyth, *Doctors and State Medicine*, p. 30; A. Lindsey, *Socialized Medicine in England and Wales: The National Health Service 1948–1961* (Chapel Hill, NC: University of North Carolina Press, 1962), pp. 344–6; Lovell, *Churchill's Doctor*, pp. 370–1; Webster, *Health Services and War*, vol. 1, pp. 252, 314; Widgery, *Health in Danger*, p. 31.

12

A Battle Royal

It may well be that after Bevan and Moran had reached agreement on consultant staffing of nationalized hospitals, Bevan's ensuing 'long drawn-out tussle' with the British Medical Association over the status of general practitioners was 'an unseemly irrelevance'.[1] At the time, however, this hardly seemed to be the case. For two years many medical critics, particularly general practitioners in the BMA, campaigned vigorously against scheduled implementation in mid-1948 of the NHS. The tone of this public campaign was far from restrained, even in its beginnings. When the minister of health announced, in March 1946, his decision to nationalize all, including voluntary private, hospitals, Sir Bernard Docker, president of the British Hospital Association (BHA), charged him with mass murder.[2] Whether Docker was charging Bevan with causing the deaths of medical institutions or of their patients remained unclear, as may have been intended. Shortly thereafter a BHA resolution attacking Bevan's decision to 'extinguish the voluntary hospitals' was read verbatim in a House of Lords debate.[3] This resolution was probably no surprise to anyone in either medicine or politics. The identity of its reader may have been a surprise to many. Denied membership by Moran in the doctors' Negotiating Committee as a representative of his own Royal College of Physicians, Thomas Lord Horder had finally joined the public debate on Bevan's decisions, as a representative of the British Hospital Association. This was an unexpected institutional affiliation. Horder had never been known as an enthusiast for hospital administrators. As Moran acidly noted at a meeting of RCP fellows, with Horder present, the BHA was largely composed, not of doctors, but of hospital administrators who viewed unpaid consulting physicians as hospital employees. Later Moran used the same setting to point out that the treasurer of Horder's own St Bartholomew's Hospital was supporting

Bevan.[4] Such needling was intended to, and did, draw Horder's blood.

In the House of Lords, Horder had already attacked the emerging NHS. He only did so, however, after Moran, months before Bevan's NHS bill would reach the House of Lords, introduced there a resolution supporting Bevan's decisions about hospitals. In procedural terms this resolution was premature at best and meaningless at worst, and Moran withdrew it at the end of this Lords debate.[5] The resolution had already served its purpose. Having introduced it, Moran spoke first in the ensuing debate, giving what may have been the speech of his life, and thereby giving Bevan's bill an early as well as most valuable medical imprimatur.[6] Only late in this Lords debate did Horder rise to speak. He had not previously been eager to debate with another doctor in a political forum. In 1934, although president of the National Birth Control Association, he had remained silent in the Lords when Bertrand Lord Dawson introduced a bill to restrict sale, display and advertisement of contraceptives, because he wanted to avoid a public squabble between two medical peers.[7] Perhaps he should have followed his own precedent this time as well. He did not, in responding to Moran, give the speech of his life, perhaps because at such short notice he was not fully prepared for the occasion. He was certainly not fully prepared for the warmth of Moran's public embrace of Bevan's bill. He had, after all, been kept in the dark. Even if there had been hints in the press, Horder, who seldom bothered to read newspapers because 'if anything happens, people will always tell you'[8] would not have picked up on them.

In his Lords response to Moran, Horder attacked not only Bevan's bill, but Moran as well. The two attacks, political and personal, were, furthermore, so intertwined as to be inseparable. It was not immediately clear which, Bevan or Moran, was the greater sinner in Horder's eyes. Moran made effective use of this confusion when reporting, to the fellows of the Royal College of Physicians, Horder's accusation in the Lords debate that the college president did not represent his college. Moran added that such a statement would have come more appropriately from someone else. This editorial addition was a clear reference to Horder's (then) five consecutive defeats in college presidential elections, most recently by a more than three-to-one margin. Moran concluded his college report of Horder's Lords speech by claiming that after that speech an unnamed senior lord had privately regretted to Moran the 'venom' of Horder's attack, as 'alien to the spirit' of the House of Lords.[9]

Whether the suggestion that Horder was a snake was originally that of some still-anonymous third party, or Moran's own invention, the obsequious formal world of 'my noble Lord' had now been left far behind. This House of Lords debate was for both Moran and Horder one of what Carl Schmitt called those 'high points of politics' in which moment 'the enemy is, in concrete clarity, recognized as the enemy'.[10] This recognition, further, took place in full public view. Horder's hatred of Moran was displayed even more audibly in the House of Lords, and Moran's hatred of Horder was displayed even more audibly within the Royal College of Physicians. Attentive members of the British political and medical elites could now expect a battle royal. It was perhaps fortunate for both Horder and Moran that the other was a physician, not a surgeon. Whether they were trying to scratch each other's eyes out or engaging in an all-out wrestling match,[11] they were locked in mortal combat. Though it was in a political context, and had political significance, its causes were by conventional distinctions essentially personal not political.

This was not a party dispute. Neither Horder not Moran ever accepted a party whip in the House of Lords.[12] Discussing 'The Doctor and Public Happiness' in 1936, Horder had asserted: 'For the doctor there can be no left or right.'[13] The Earl of Woolton, the wartime Conservative minister of food whose expert adviser Horder had been, later testified to his 'complete freedom from a party bias'.[14] While privately allied during 1945–48 with a Labour minister of health, Moran remained physician to the leader of His Majesty's Loyal Opposition, whose party opposed, however ineffectively, the minister's NHS bill in Parliament. Neither Bevan nor Churchill seems to have raised a critical eyebrow to Moran about this fact.[15] Indeed, hosting Lord and Lady Moran on the day before the 1948 RCP presidential election, Churchill toasted the prospect of Horder's defeat yet again by Moran. The next evening both Clementine and Winston Churchill telephoned Moran to learn the RCP election results.[16] In 1951, Churchill told the RCP: 'Lord Moran in my view did his duty in recognizing that he should lead the college in a policy of co-operation with the government.'[17] Until shortly before Horder's death, Churchill continued to tease Moran about the long rivalry between the two medical lords.[18]

The personal warfare between Horder and Moran was waged on many fronts. Privately, Moran told RCP fellows of 'the unsuitability' of Horder for the college presidency.[19] Publicly, in the House of Lords, Moran argued that Bevan's position in his dispute with the British Medical Association should receive 'the loyal support of all reasonable members of the profession'.[20] The implications were clear: Horder, for one, was not 'reasonable', let alone 'loyal'. Loyal to Moran as RCP president Horder certainly was not, however much Moran thought Horder should be. Loyal to Bevan's decisions because those decisions were supported by the RCP president Horder could hardly be. On this particular occasion, Moran was supporting Bevan's decision on a particular matter which had been part of an earlier private agreement between Bevan and Moran.[21]

Such a sequence of events was representative. The Bevan–Moran alliance continued even after the essential hospital elements of the NHS bill had been forged. Moran's support fortified Bevan psychologically in the latter's struggle with the BMA.[22] Their relationship became more personal,[23] but the political aspect was undiminished. Moran was given advance copies of Bevan's Commons speeches, enabling him immediately to support Bevan's position in a Lords speech.[24] This meant that Moran often knew Bevan's position before the Commons, to whom the minister was politically responsible, knew. Not surprisingly, Bevan found one such speech 'the most helpful thing said by any doctor in the whole of this business'.[25] In a 'personal' message Moran warned Bevan against discussing any consultant matters with a BMA delegation including Horder, who had finally found, if only briefly, a seat on the BMA's side of the table.[26] This warning was hardly necessary. Bevan had earlier told Moran he could reveal ministerial intentions to some NHS opponents, but not to Horder. Bevan had given a similar instruction to the Labour leader of the House of Lords.[27] For Bevan, too, Horder had become not only an opponent but an enemy. In public Bevan described his *bête noire*: 'Horder has a heart of gold, but a mind of steel; and unfortunately it is the steel with which the government have to deal.'[28] In private Bevan was less flattering, at least in intent, characterizing Horder as 'an incontinent romantic'.[29] Horder's public response was at least as vigorous: Bevan was 'a clever and forceful party politician, actuated equally by fanatical faith in a political dogma and considerations of electoral expediency', whose 'very unfortunate intransigence' and 'unscrupulousness' had made him 'a subtle and powerful dictator' leading 'the mad march of totalitarianism'.[30]

Horder's greatest distress was not with Bevan himself, but the minister's close relationship with Moran, which closeness he only slowly came fully to perceive. The alliance between Beaverbrook and Moran had in his eyes deprived him not only of a choice prime ministerial patient, but the presidency of the Royal College of Physicians. Now the alliance between Bevan and Moran was depriving him of any influence over creation of the National Health Service. The only constant element in all these defeats was the presence of Moran. For his final, greatest, defeat Horder also blamed Moran. Horder's mind and life became filled with what amounted to a conspiracy theory. Bevan could have been defeated on the NHS, but 'the ball was passed to the other side, by whom I don't know'.[31] In his mind, of course, Horder knew the traitor's name. There had been 'machinations', 'meddlesome and mischievous', by 'men holding key positions' outside the BMA, which alone now to Horder spoke legitimately for doctors.[32] Since the most important 'key position', and its holder, were by now known to all, there was no need for Horder to speak the unmentionable name, any more than there would be for Winston Churchill to speak the name of Aneurin Bevan while campaigning in Wales in 1950.

When in mid-1948 the general practitioners in the BMA overwhelmingly accepted positions in the NHS, Horder continued his fight.[33] Now his attacks began to include those on the 'absolute leadership' of the BMA by 'Dr Guy Dain and Dr Charles Hill'.[34] Horder could speak those names in public because they were so tangential to his real life. Soon the rank-and-file BMA members were also accused of having 'surrendered' to Bevan 'like a rabble'.[35] Even Moran had never used such language about general practitioners. As the NHS was coming into administrative existence Horder urged all doctors who wished to join in his continuing struggle against the NHS to write to him.[36] To those respondents whom Horder judged sufficiently militant in tone he sent a printed invitation granting admission to a closed meeting in November 1948. Over 700 doctors attended, founding the Fellowship for Freedom in Medicine (FFM). Horder was unanimously elected the new fellowship's first chairman.[37] Horder clearly intended the fellowship to institutionalize his charisma. Dominate its meetings until his death in 1955 he certainly did. Whether the fellowship was actually a functioning institution is less certain. If his brief approach to the BMA leadership had involved a field marshal unable to fit into a non-commissioned officers' mess, his leadership of the FFM involved a field marshal with virtually no one between him and a substantial member of newly recruited privates. At its peak the fellowship claimed some 3,000 doctors as followers,[38] which concept was organizationally amorphous at best. There was little bureaucratic structure to the FFM. There appeared to be no functioning lieutenants. Only one other RCP fellow was visible in the new fellowship.[39] Whatever got done, Horder did. Perhaps he had no lieutenants because he needed to be not only omnipotent but omnipresent. Within the fellowship no one seems to have used the term 'absolute leadership', perhaps because Horder was always in attendance. His physical stamina was impressive. For the last eight years of his life he did not miss a meeting of a smaller discussion group of clinical physicians aptly named the Horder Society.[40]

The new fellowship played no significant role in British politics, although its chairman was widely and favourably noticed by American critics of national health insurance proposals. The fellowship, however, played a large role in Horder's last years, spent, as his son put it, fighting a rearguard action against the NHS.[41] After Geraldine Lady Horder's heart attack in 1950, the FFM became his real home. Obsessed with his political cause, he had no time to deal with patients or former professional colleagues. He had never frequented BMA House, and he had burned most of his personal bridges to the RCP. After losing that college's presidential election in 1948, he absented himself from the ensuing fellows' meeting, as well as that evening's traditional ceremonial dinner.[42] To Horder, Moran had now won everything, which meant he had been left with nothing. When, in 1950, for the first time since 1941, Moran did not seek re-election to the RCP presidency, Horder, also for the first time since 1941, was not the runner-up, coming third. In 1951 and 1953 he received one vote, and in 1952 two votes: in those last years Horder finally received more votes than Moran.[43]

The new fellows became his new family. His eightieth birthday was celebrated at a dinner attended by 'a representative gathering of FFM members',[44] many of whom he knew only slightly. He urged future biographers to focus on the pages of the FFM *Bulletin*, where they would find that his continued opposition to the NHS after 1948 'has not been free from some degree of heroism'.[45] The cult of personality was practised in FFM publications, which described Horder's speeches as 'powerful' and 'vigorously and ably presented'.[46] The speaker may well have been doubling as reporter here. For Horder heroes were certainly possible, as his belief in Samuel Gee and Rudolf Virchow demonstrated. If he was himself a hero, it was as an Aristotelian tragic hero, falling from grace because of a tragic flaw, causing pity and fear in the audience.

That Horder had a gift of grace would have been a tenable proposition before 1945. Few physicians, in Britain or elsewhere, were so deserving of respect and admiration. The Reverend H. R. L. Sheppard, Britain's most influential interwar pacifist, had considered Horder, whose patient he was, and who was short in physical stature, as one of the two biggest (the other was Richard Lord Haldane) human beings he had known.[47] After 1945 this kind of evaluation would have been much less likely, from even a sympathetic observer.

The key question about Horder's life was aptly asked, but not answered, by a careful scholar who observed that Horder's 'abrupt change of attitude toward state intervention in 1945 has never been explained'.[48] To envision, as Moran fearfully did in August 1945, Horder as the leading medical champion of the NHS is not difficult. That he became the great medical opponent of the NHS appears to have been the consequence of Moran's early embrace of the NHS. Horder's NHS would perhaps not have been much different from Moran's NHS, but the latter, in whatever form, was unacceptable to Horder. Contemplating the prospect of Moran's NHS, Horder was compelled to object. He came to oppose Bevan's NHS because it was also Moran's. Horder's life became dominated by his inner need finally to defeat Moran, who had so unfairly (in Horder's view) defeated him repeatedly.

It was no accident that the term *prima donna* was often used to describe both Horder and Moran. Operatic roles may be fictional, but the singers are real. Horder's perception of Moran as a dangerous enemy was no fantasy. Moran was seen as ruthless even by his chief lieutenant.[49] No one seems to have viewed Horder as ruthless. Lacking any religious faith, having abandoned his parents' Congregationalism, Horder's highest ethical value was 'being kind'.[50] That he had long been. Reckless he certainly became in 1945–55. In his eulogy of Moran, Robert Lord Platt could hardly avoid mentioning Horder, whom he described as 'of course the better clinician of the two', but nowhere near Moran 'as a medical politician'.[51] This was as astute a diagnosis as Platt ever made in his own distinguished medical career.

This truthful tribute would not have been enough for Horder. He could not accept Moran's triumph over the NHS as merely another defeat by a superior politician. It was a bitterly personal loss. He had never been merely a grocer. Wealth mattered to him, but no more than prestige and power. In losing them he lost part of himself. The loss of power after 1945 was hard enough. The loss of prestige was perhaps even more painful. As he had himself acknowledged, he needed to be respected. Already in 1947, while he and his wife were both patients in the London Clinic after an automobile accident, George VI asked after Lady, not but Lord, Horder.[52] An earlier royal patient, Edward VII, had given impetus to Horder's professional career. Now he was being snubbed by another royal patient. Courtiers, of course, easily fall from grace and favour. Horder had made himself unfashionable.

The most immediately visible aspect, however, of Horder's fall was financial. He had to sell his house on Harley Street and move his London office to a rented room. Soon even that room was too costly. Horder's last medical office was the borrowed boardroom, seldom used for its intended function, of one of the many organizations in which he had been active, and of which he was still president. This building also now served as the mailing address for the Fellowship for Freedom in Medicine.[53] His last London home was a room on the distant top floor of this building which now served as his bedroom. He was still living above the shop, but Harley Street this was not. 45 Nottingham Place was the headquarters of the Cremation Society, founded in 1874 by Sir Henry Thompson, a surgeon.[54] This setting killed, perhaps understandably, what little was still left of Horder's private practice. He had long been a supporter of cremation, and now he became its most enthusiastic British advocate.[55] He attended a meeting of the Royal College of Physicians in order to report having presided over a cremation conference in the beach resort of Blackpool, which had included a large cremation exhibition. Horder promised to report further on this subject at later RCP meetings.[56] He was not alone in this cause. Among the members of the Cremation Society was Winston Churchill. As minister of health Aneurin Bevan approved building more crematoria, and the Cabinet's interdepartmental Cremation Committee (1947–51) reported doubling of the cremation rate, to 9.1 per cent. In 1951, Aneurin Bevan attended the cremation of Ernest Bevin. A half-century later, most British funerals involved cremation.[57] Even in this winning battle, Horder's behaviour was distinctive. Privately, but still in his capacity as president of the Cremation Society, he picked up sackfuls of unclaimed ashes from crematoria to use as fertilizer for the mineral-deficient soil in the garden of his country home.[58]

NOTES

1. Campbell, *Aneurin Bevan*, p. 169.
2. Grimes, *British National Health Service*, p. 135.
3. *Parliamentary Debates*, House of Lords, 16 April 1946, p. 856.
4. RCP Comitia, *Minutes*, 15 April 1946, p. 27; 16 May 1946, p. 43, RCP archives.
5. *Parliamentary Debates*, House of Lords, 16 April 1946, p. 868.
6. N. Goodman, *Wilson Jameson*, p. 122; Grimes, *British National Health Service*, p. 136; Pater, *Making of National Health Service*, p. 124; Stevens, *Medical Practice*, pp. 78–9; Webster, *Health Services and War*, vol. 1, pp. 99–100.
7. Soloway, *Demography and Degeneration*, pp. 189, 207, 267.
8. M. Horder, *Little Genius*, p. 128.
9. RCP Comitia, *Minutes*, 16 May 1946, p. 49.
10. C. Schmitt, *The Concept of the Political*, G. Schwab, trans. (New Brunswick, NJ: Rutgers University Press, 1976), p. 67.
11. Foot, *Aneurin Bevan*, vol. 2, pp. 144, 158–9.
12. D. Johnson, Deputy Clerk of Records, House of Lords, writing to this author, November 1990; Lovell, *Churchill's Doctor*, p. 341.
13. Lord Horder, *Health and a Day*, p. 53.
14. Woolton, *Memoirs*, p. 279.
15. Lovell, *Churchill's Doctor*, pp. 301–2.
16. Ibid., pp. 285, 306.
17. R. James (ed.), *Winston S. Churchill: His Complete Speeches*, vol. 8 (New York: Chelsea House, 1974), p. 8, 225.
18. Moran, *Churchill*, p. 691.
19. Moran to W. H. Wynn, 4 March 1948, RCP archives.
20. Foot, *Aneurin Bevan*, vol. 2, p. 201.
21. Lovell, *Churchill's Doctor*, p. 304.
22. *British Medical Journal*, 2 July 1988, p. 14.
23. Lovell, *Churchill's Doctor*, p. 302.
24. Ibid., p. 307; Grimes, *British National Health Service*, p. 194.
25. Lovell, *Churchill's Doctor*, p. 307.
26. Moran to 'My dear Bevan', 6 May 1948, RCP archives; Webster, *Health Services and War*, vol. 1, p. 116.
27. Lovell, *Churchill's Doctor*, p. 304.
28. M. Horder, *Little Genius*, p. 98.
29. Ibid.
30. Supplement to *British Medical Journal*, 27 March 1948, p. 49; Fellowship for Freedom in Medicine, *Bulletin*, June 1949, p. 21; FFM, *Medical Surrender*, p. 40; Lord Horder, *Fifty Years of Medicine*, p. 43.
31. Foot, *Aneurin Bevan*, vol. 2, p. 207.
32. FFM, *Bulletin*, November 1948, p. 4.
33. Lindsey, *Socialized Medicine*, p. 63; Medvei and Thornton, *Royal Hospital*, p. 229; Pater, *Making of National Health Service*, p. 162.
34. FFM, *Medical Surrender*, p. 36.
35. FFM, *Bulletin*, November 1948, p. 4.
36. Foot, *Aneurin Bevan*, vol. 2, p. 207.
37. FFM, *Bulletin*, November 1948, pp. 1, 3–4; M. Horder, *Little Genius*, p. 100; Lovell, *Churchill's Doctor*, p. 308.
38. Webster, *Health Services and War*, vol. 1, p. 119.
39. FFM, *Memorandum of Evidence Submitted to the Committee of Inquiry into the Costs of the National Health Service* (London: Fellowship for Freedom in Medicine, 1954), p. 2.
40. *Minutes* of the Horder Society, pp. 1, 6–7, 34, RCP archives.
41. M. Horder, *Little Genius*, p. 97.
42. Lovell, *Churchill's Doctor*, p. 306.
43. Ibid., p. 311; M. Horder, *Little Genius*, p. 95; RCP, *Annals*, 63, p. 99; 64, p. 17; 64, p. 85, RCP archives.
44. FFM, *Bulletin*, April 1951, p. 8.

45. Lord Horder, *Fifty Years of Medicine*, p. 43.
46. FFM, *Medical Surrender*, pp. 17, 31–2.
47. R. Roberts, *H. R. L. Sheppard: Life and Letters* (London: John Murray, 1942), pp. 209, 211.
48. Honigsbaum, *Health*, p. 152.
49. Lovell, *Churchill's Doctor*, p. 174.
50. M. Horder, *Little Genius*, p. 5; Lord Horder, *Obscurantism*, p. 47.
51. *British Medical Journal*, 23 April 1977, p. 1,088.
52. M. Horder, *Little Genius*, p. 43n.
53. FFM, *Medical Surrender*; FFM, *Memorandum of Evidence*, p. 2; *Medical Directory, 1955* (London: J. & A. Churchill, 1955), p. 971.
54. M. Horder, *Little Genius*, pp. 29, 32, 121; P. Jalland, 'Victorian Death and its Decline: 1850–1918', in P. Jupp and C. Gittings (eds), *Death in England: An Illustrated History* (New Brunswick, NJ: Rutgers University Press, 2000), pp. 249–50.
55. *British Medical Journal*, 17 May 1941, p. 761; Lord Horder, *Health and a Day*, p. 55; Lord Horder, *Fifty Years of Medicine*, pp. 52–3.
56. RCP, *Annals*, 1950–1951, pp. 71, 72c.
57. P. Jupp and T. Walter, 'The Healthy Society: 1918–98', in Jupp and Gittings (eds), *Death in England*, pp. 260, 264–5.
58. J. Huxley, *Memories* (New York: Harper & Row, 1970), p. 226.
    Thomas Lord Horder closed his account of *Fifty Years in Medicine* 'on an auto-biographical note' with lines from Alfred Lord Tennyson's *Ulysses*:

How dull it is to pause, to make an end,
To rust unburnish'd, not to shine in use …

Part III:

Disciples Decide

'Who shall decide when doctors disagree?'
Alexander Pope, *Moral Essays*

13

Disciples Decide

Democratic politics can be, and often is, seen as mass politics. At least in stable democratic political systems the masses can be, and often are, seen as integrated into the formal decision-making process either directly by referenda or indirectly by representative institutions such as parties and pressure groups. Unlike in much of the rest of western Europe, referenda have never taken root in British soil. There has been only one system-wide referendum in the United Kingdom, that in 1975 asking voters whether they wished the United Kingdom to leave the European Economic Community which its government had already joined. This avoidance of referenda has been no accident. Professional politicians, determined to preserve their power, were, and are, firmly in control of the United Kingdom. Winston Churchill accurately articulated the dominant view of the British members of his profession when he argued in 1911 that referenda 'would lead to complete irresponsibility' among ministers as well as Members of Parliament.[1] According to Churchill, disaster would follow use of referenda: 'Parliamentary and representative institutions which have been the historic glory of these islands would be swept away, and in their places, we would have the worst forms of Jacobinism, Caesarism, and Anarchy'.[2] Churchill may here have confused different forms of dictatorship with each other and with the absence of government, but the main point of his argument was and is broadly accepted among British politicians. That main point was never distinctive to conservative British critics of democracy. In 1911, Churchill was the chief lieutenant of the leader of the Liberal left. Almost eight decades later, Leo Abse, one of the most deeply egalitarian Labour Members of Parliament, echoed Churchill's main point when he referred to his own 'distaste for referenda, which by their nature diminish the role of Parliament, making Members mere delegates not representatives'.[3] Since deference to professional politicians is so great in British political culture, Churchill's main point was and is probably at least acceptable to most Britons. Whatever else British politics may have been or be, populist it was or is not. Members of the political elite are expected to, and do, govern Britain. The anarchy feared by Churchill has not triumphed.

That British democracy is not direct does not mean it cannot be representative. The party that governs is, after all, empowered in a competitive free election. Whatever the possible distorting efforts of the British electoral system, the general election of 1945 certainly clearly articulated the preference of the British electorate. That representative democracy is less democratic than direct democracy is by no means clear. In the creation of the National Health Service, however, the masses of Britons were not even indirectly involved. There was no great public debate between or among parties and/or pressure groups. Only one long-standing major pressure group, the British Medical Association, was actively involved as an institution in making relevant public pronouncements, and those pronouncements were not couched in diction encouraging dialogue with possible supporters, or even other potential opponents, of the NHS. The BMA could not join forces with the Conservative Party because of Churchill's deep hostility to the BMA dating from 1911. Churchill made no move to create a new organization to propagandize against the NHS, nor does he appear to have wanted to abort the NHS. Bevan, in turn, made no significant effort to use any existing pressure group to mobilize popular support for his bill. Nor did he attempt to create an *ad hoc* organization to generate such support, as Chancellor David Lloyd George had done in 1911 by creating the Liberal Insurance Committee under Christopher Addison, and as G. D. H. Cole had done in 1942 by creating the Social Security League to agitate for the Beveridge Report. Quite likely, Bevan preferred to exercise a monopoly as the tribune of the people, as Churchill wished to avoid becoming prisoner of the doctors. The tribune, however, spoke surprisingly little in public, even after receiving Cabinet approval of his bill.

The major parties were not much more effective than were pressure groups in speaking to, or for, the masses of Britons on health policy during the creation of the NHS. Television was not yet useful as a medium of mass communication, and the state radio system essentially confined political debates to general election campaigns, not particular policy-making differences. Party organizations had, further, been substantially weakened during the Second World War. Real public debate opportunities were therefore confined essentially to Parliament. The NHS debates in the House of Commons were, especially in this context, disappointing. The public was not educated on medical policy by either the Government or the Opposition. The responsible minister revealed his legislative decisions with precision and clarity, but surprisingly little passion, while the leader of the Opposition remained silent and his subordinates were neither precise nor clear. The debates between Moran and Horder in the House of Lords were much livelier than those in the Commons. Neither Moran nor Horder spoke for a party, however, and the evident personal animosity of each for the other did not encourage many of their fellow lords to join in even the substantive aspects of the debate. This spectacle was hardly instructive. The conduct of the two distinguished medical lords in this debate did nothing to support the case for involving experts in legislative policy debates. One of the lords spiritual should perhaps have risen to interject the judgement reported by a third physician, in Luke 4:23.

The most intellectually interesting discussions about the emerging NHS were quite likely the extended conversations between Bevan and Moran. At the time, however, they were not only private but secret. There were probably no flies on the well-kept walls of Pruniers restaurant. In their discussions neither Bevan nor Moran drew on or appealed to public opinion, nor were they debating. It was, indeed, the easy private agreement of the two participants which made their discussions politically significant. The most important real debate occurred almost equally secretly as the discussions at Pruniers, in the Cabinet room. In that debate the losing side, led by Herbert Morrison, may well have represented at least opinion within the Labour Party more accurately than did the winning side, led by Bevan. Considering how little inherent value party loyalty had for Bevan, this possibility may not have bothered him any more than did his possible disconnection from British public opinion generally. The only parts of that public that mattered much to him were the working classes, which he clearly distinguished from their institutional expression in the Labour Party.

The views of the many did not much matter to Bevan situationally because he understood that the fate of his National Health Service bill would be determined by the views of a few, his Cabinet colleagues. That bill, he was confident, after and perhaps because of his discussions with Moran, was an effective instrument

for the achievement of his inherent values. An institutional structure that had the blessing of the hypercritical intelligence of
Charles Wilson, Lord Moran might well prove capable of
longevity. Moran may have instructed him on how to achieve his
inherent values, but Bevan no longer felt he needed other persons,
in whatever number, to instruct him on those inherent values. The
latter had been socialized into him long before, in Tredegar.

Bevan's self-knowledge was as substantial as his self-confidence.
When visited, while minister of health, by Geoffrey Fisher,
Archbishop of Canterbury, Bevan greeted his visitor: 'I'm a
Welsh Baptist myself.'[4] This statement was probably Bevan's most
accurate self-revelation, and it was appropriately made to a
member of the clergy, Church of England though Fisher was.
Bevan's parting shot in this conversation suggests that his con-
fession had been proud not penitent: 'You leave it to me, I'll look
after the Protestants.'[5] This barb conveyed, as it was meant to, that
Fisher was too high church to be listened to by Protestant
Christians. This corollary, surely unfair to Fisher's ecumenism,
followed from Bevan's major reminder to the archbishop, that
his own origins were Protestant nonconformist, not Church of
England. The argument that 'Aneurin was very Welsh'[6] is incom-
plete at best. Bevan could not speak Welsh,[7] and this lack seems
never to have bothered him. Wales was mentioned to Fisher by
Bevan only because Welsh nonconformists were so numerous
that the Church of England had three decades earlier been
disestablished (by David Lloyd George) in Wales.

Bevan had appropriately addressed the archbishop in the
present tense. That he had been nurtured in nonconformity had
not been forgotten by the minister. At the 1949 Labour Party
conference Bevan addressed complaints that Labour's outlook
was too materialistic, lacking in vision:

> I would point out that in some way or another the conception
> of religious dedication must find concrete expression, and I
> say that never in the history of mankind have the best ideas
> found more concrete expression than in the programme that
> we are carrying out. 'Suffer the little children to come unto
> me' is not now something which is said only from the pulpit.
> We have woven it into the warp and woof of our national life,
> and we have made the claims of the children come first. What
> is national planning but an insistence that human beings
> shall make ethical choices on a national scale? ... The
> language of priorities is the religion of Socialism.[8]

This speech aroused Archbishop Fisher to an angry public rebuke. Politicians, Fisher said, should not quote 'the words of the New Testament and especially the words of our Lord. Such quotations are out of place and cause discomfort and distress.'[9] Bevan was not put off by such unscriptural criticism, nor did he mind causing discomfort and distress within the established church. When told later that Archbishop Fisher wished to meet again with him, Bevan expressed pleasure at the prospect: 'There is no reason why I should not bring about conversions in the highest places.'[10]

Bevan was equally confident, with perhaps better reason, in entering the Cabinet room to argue his case for the NHS with the powerful few. He had no illusions about his uneasy, even hostile personal relationship with many of his Cabinet colleagues, but he knew there were people in the Cabinet room who shared his inherent values because they had been socialized, including politically, in an environment essentially similar to that in Tredegar. There would be other Protestant nonconformist disciples in his most important audience, enough to matter. They would join in the last great triumph of nonconformist values in British politics. With those listeners Bevan's task would be practical, not ideological, conversion. It was undeniably true that by 1945 Protestant nonconformity, including Baptists, Congregationalists and Methodists, had been greatly weakened by widespread secularization of British society, and had consequently lost its earlier dominant position within the British left, first attained within the Liberal Party and then also in the new Labour Party.[11] After the First World War, except in south Wales, Protestant nonconformity was not decisively Labour at the polls, but the chapels still produced Labour parliamentary candidates.[12] As late as the 1950 general election, of nonconformist parliamentary candidates, 61 were Labour, 59 were Liberal, and only six were Conservative.[13] During that campaign, even many of the Labour candidates claimed to be heirs of the 'great Liberal governments' of 1906 and 1910.[14] In policy terms, that claim was justified. Those were the governments which, dominated by Lloyd George and Churchill, had created the British welfare state, including old-age pensions in the 1909 Budget and unemployment as well as health insurance in the National Insurance Act of 1911.

If Bevan, youngest member of Attlee's Cabinet, was old enough to have been socialized politically in his formative years in a nonconformist chapel, he was far from alone in that Cabinet. James Griffiths, now minister of national insurance and prime mover behind the 1943 Labour Party report, *National Service for Health*, had personal roots similar to Bevan's. Griffiths was a coalminer's son from south Wales who had himself started working in a coalmine at age 13, with the hope of eventually training for the Congregational ministry. That hope remained unrealized, but he had become another kind of minister. The young Griffiths had moved directly and naturally from chapel activities to socialist activities, becoming a miner's agent who went, as Bevan did, to the Central Labour College in London to study socialism more intensively.[15]

Another nonconformist in Attlee's Cabinet was Ellen Wilkinson, minister of education and perhaps the most principled of Bevan's Cabinet colleagues in support of his NHS bill, in spite of her personal closeness to Herbert Morrison. Wilkinson remained a deeply convinced Methodist.[16] In 1939 she had perhaps startled the more secularized members of the Left Book Club when she told them: 'I am still a Methodist, you can never get its special glow out of your blood.'[17] Another nonconformist in Attlee's Cabinet mattered even more to the eventual Cabinet acceptance of Bevan's NHS bill. That was Ernest Bevin, who had attended a Methodist Sunday school as a child. After his early entrance into manual labour, Bevin joined a Baptist chapel, becoming a Sunday-school teacher himself. As a young adult he preached at open-air evangelical meetings and, like Griffiths, considered taking a theological course to become a minister. The British Socialist Society he joined in his political baptism flowed as naturally from his chapel life[18] as had similar progressions by his nonconformist Cabinet colleagues.

In the same Cabinet room in which in late 1945 Aneurin Bevan gained acceptance for his National Health Service bill, David Lloyd George had, in spring 1911, gained acceptance from his Cabinet colleagues for his National Insurance bill. Lloyd George's ambulance wagon, small and of limited itinerary as it was, had also emerged from a Welsh Baptist chapel. It was in the pulpit of the Disciples of Christ chapel in Criccieth that the adolescent Lloyd George had learned to speak in public. It was also there that he learned what to say. The most important of his political speeches were in fact sermons which freely used 'the words of the New Testament and especially the words of our Lord'. Among the achievements of the most powerful political voice of British nonconformity was, besides disestablishment · in Wales of the Church of England, implementation of a British welfare state which he so memorably depicted to Winston Churchill in Wales in the summer of 1908. That year the new chancellor of the exchequer was not too busy to accept election as president of the Welsh Baptist Union.[19] An alert 10-year-old boy at Sunday school in Tredegar now became part of the president's flock, and there he remained, in spirit if not always in body. He would give the main speech at the inaugural meeting of the Christian Socialist Movement in 1960.[20]

When his former president died, Aneurin Bevan, soon to become minister of health, rose to tell the House of Commons:

> We have lost our most distinguished member, and Wales her greatest son. He was, like the Prime Minister, a most formidable and even terrifying debater, but he also possessed what the Prime Minister possesses – the generosity of greatness. We have lost in his death the most irridescent [*sic*] figure that ever illuminated the British political scene.[21]

Bevan did more than eulogize the creators of the National Insurance Act of 1911. He fulfilled Lloyd George's hope that national health insurance for the employed would be replaced by national entitlement for all Britons to free medical care. With Bevan's act, Lloyd George's ambulance wagon should now be large enough to pick up all ill and injured would-be passengers, to take them, if medically appropriate, to Harley Street or, if medically necessary, to St Mary's Hospital or even to St Bartholomew's Hospital, where Harley Street would be waiting for them. They would no longer need to remain 'in the alleys, the homes where they lie stricken'.

Entitlements are not always enforced. Not all of the higher hopes raised by Bevan's larger ambulance wagon were fully realized. Ticket takers soon appeared, barring free entry to some parts of the vehicle. Fees were charged for such NHS services as prescriptions and spectacles. The first such fee, a one-penny container charge as a deposit on prescription medicine bottles, was conceded in principle (if not implemented) already in 1949 by minister of health Bevan himself. Bevan justified this violation of the principle of free access by his need to gain support for the housing construction goals for which he was also ministerially responsible, and to which he was now paying perhaps belated attention.[22] In 1951, shortly after being shifted to minister of labour, Bevan resigned, never to return to ministerial office, to protest at Cabinet acceptance of dental and ophthalmic charges by the NHS. Other fees have followed, but patient payments have always been a relatively small part of NHS income, never exceeding 4.8 per cent (in the early 1960s). In 1996, for instance, fees provided only 2.3 per cent of NHS income.[23]

A much more important impediment to full realization of Bevan's goals for the NHS may have been that his ambulance wagon did not reach all 'the alleys, the homes' which held ill and injured potential passengers. Spatial distribution of medical services throughout Britain had been seriously uneven long before the NHS was created. Such regional inequalities were perhaps Moran's most important reason for becoming Bevan's ally. As a former medical school teacher and dean, Moran was most concerned with improving the quality of doctors, especially hospital doctors, throughout Britain. He was still busy at this mission, dominating merit awards to doctors, when Bevan died in 1960. The NHS certainly substantially improved the distribution of both doctors and diagnostic equipment.[24] There was 'a considerable leveling-up of services'.[25] Many regional differences, in both health and access to health services, nevertheless continued to exist, documented especially in the 1980 report of the Working Group on Inequalities in Health, chaired by Sir Douglas Black, former president of the Royal College of Physicians.[26]

Since spatial and social class inequalities in health often overlap in Britain,[27] such regional inequalities raise the possibility of substantial social class inequalities in the effectiveness of the NHS. That possibility has been a noteworthy reality.[28] Social class differentials have been especially visible in preventive medicine.[29] The judgement that under the NHS the medical care received by working-class people 'is as good as that secured by the other social classes'[30] is considerably exaggerated. Especially striking was the increase, after the first few years of the NHS' existence, in the mortality rate of unskilled male workers.[31] Bevan had in 1945 rejected local government administration of the NHS precisely because there would tend to be 'a better service in the richer areas, a worse service in the poorer'.[32] Bevan's fear was realized even with the nationalization of hospitals. Underserved poorer areas did not get sufficient compensatory resources. The existing municipal and private voluntary hospitals were taken over in 1948, but no new hospitals were built under the NHS until the 1960s.[33] Late in that decade, Richard Crossman as secretary of state for social services responsible for the Ministry of Health, was told by his senior civil servants that almost all of the NHS hospital budget was committed to preserving the *status quo*: 'A terrific lot of money goes into the teaching hospitals, most of which are in the South, and this shifts the balance even more in favour of the

London hospitals, with great unfairness to Sheffield, Newcastle, and Birmingham, which are really greatly under-financed.'[34] Crossman was warned by his staff that he could not shift resources to 'sub-normal' hospitals 'without upsetting the consultants and having a blow-up in the medical service'.[35] The minister nevertheless made a modest attempt at such a spatial shift of resources, getting virtually nowhere with the regional hospital boards,[36] dominated by, as he discovered, 'self-perpetuating oligarchies'.[37] Oligarchs are generally satisfied with the *status quo*.

Teaching hospitals, especially those in London, were certainly favoured within the structure of the NHS. That would not have distressed Moran, who had worked hard during and after the creation of the NHS to achieve precisely that favoured position. Even within the teaching hospitals some medical needs were more favoured than others. These, too, reflected Moran's professional priorities, which often approached personal prejudices. In the 1970s a student at St Mary's Hospital Medical School, Moran's own former hospital, lamented that 'our department of obstetrics and gynaecology and the school of nursing are housed in converted stables that used to belong to Paddington station, and our department of general practice is located in a building on the premises of a second-hand car dealer'.[38] Moran had seen general practitioners as at the bottom of the medical profession, and (mostly female) nurses as outside that profession. The distinctive illnesses of women were of little more interest to him than were their possible professional contributions.

If the winter of 1945–6 was a time to heal Britain, it was apparently not yet the time to heal all of Britain. Perhaps it might have been if the minister of health had consulted a second 'swell doctor' from Harley Street. The young and powerless Aneurin Bevan had found his way to a helpful visit at Number 141. Perhaps privately calling on the consulting physician still at that address would have helped the newly powerful minister find a more direct path to his political goal. At least he might have avoided much ministerial grief from Number 141. Thomas Lord Horder deserved to be consulted, and he did not deserve the wound he received from Bevan as well as Moran. A distinguished medical historian would later judge Horder as a worthy successor to the tradition of Hippocrates and William Harvey,[39] patron saints of world and British medicine respectively. Unlike Moran, Horder was humble enough not to claim personal descent from Harvey. Horder's professional vision was, further, broad enough not to disdain general practitioners or nurses, or the particular medical needs of women. It might have been difficult, however, for Horder, as a life-long committed 'Bart's man' to disagree with Moran's focus on teaching hospitals centred in urban areas, especially London. St Bartholomew's Hospital had long served well the poor of its part of London, but Horder did not know well other impovished areas of Britain.

To be reminded of the pressing medical needs of Britons outside major urban centres, Bevan might well have also visited one of David Lloyd George's 'mist-laden valleys', the Ebbw Vale division of Monmouthshire. The Tredegar Working Men's Medical Aid Society might not be an apt national model, but the general practitioners, nurses and patients of Tredegar might well have been worth consulting for useful perspectives and suggestions, especially on the need for prevention of occupational illnesses. They may even have earned the right to be so consulted. They were, after all, not only the minister's own faithful parliamentary constituents, but Aneurin Bevan's own people. If they could advise better about ends than means, at least they might have strengthened his resolve to attain equality in all aspects of health care.

Best of all for Bevan might have been a visit to David Lloyd George himself. Wales' greatest son now rested, however, alone, under a great stone on the banks of the River Dwyfor. Lloyd George's greatest gift was probably his capacity and eagerness to ask questions of, and genuinely listen to, a wide variety of his fellow human beings. Aneurin Bevan, not often accused of listening too much to other people, might have benefited from such mentoring. Coming from Lloyd George, he might even have followed the advice. In creating the National Health Service, however, the minister of health prematurely closed his ears to all other voices except one.

NOTES

1. R. Churchill, *Winston S. Churchill*, vol. 2, companion part 2 (London: Heinemann, 1969), p. 1,071.
2. A. Johnson, *Viscount Halifax: A Biography* (London: Robert Hale, 1941), p. 78.
3. L. Abse, *Margaret, Daughter of Beatrice: A Politician's Psycho-biography of Margaret Thatcher* (London: Jonathan Cape, 1989), p. 178.
4. Michael Foot, *Aneurin Bevan*, vol. 2 (New York: Atheneum, 1974), p. 127.
5. Ibid.; S. Koss, *Nonconformity in Modern British Politics* (London: B. T. Batsford, 1975), p. 39.
6. A. Rowse, *Glimpses of the Great* (Lanham, MD: University Press of America, 1985), p. 67.

7. C. Cross (ed.), *Life with Lloyd George: The Diary of A. J. Sylvester 1931–45* (New York: Barnes & Noble, 1975), p. 78n.
8. Foot, *Aneurin Bevan*, vol. 2, p. 263.
9. Ibid., p. 264.
10. Ibid., p. 410.
11. Koss, *Nonconformity*.
12. P. Catterall, 'Morality and Politics: The Free Churches and the Labour Party between the Wars', *Historical Journal*, 3, 3 (1993), pp. 677–9.
13. H. Nicholas, *The British General Election of 1950* (London: Macmillan, 1951), p. 58.
14. Ibid., p. 222.
15. T. Jarman, *Socialism in Britain: From the Industrial Revolution to the Present Day* (New York: Taplinger, 1972), p. 113; K. Morgan, *Labour People: Leaders and Lieutenants, Hardie to Kinnock* (Oxford: Oxford University Press, 1987), p. 198.
16. D. Edwards, *Christian England: From the Eighteenth Century to the First World War* (Grand Rapids, MI: William B. Eerdmans, 1985), p. 238.
17. Morgan, *Labour People*, p. 103.
18. A. Bullock, *The Life and Times of Ernest Bevin*, vol. 1 (London: Heinemann, 1960), pp. 3–4, 8–10, 21; Jarman, *Socialism in Britain*, pp. 111–12; Rowse, *Glimpses*, pp. 35–6; F. Williams, *Ernest Bevin: Portrait of a Great Englishman* (London: Hutchinson, 1952), pp. 13–14, 21–5.
19. K. Morgan, *Wales in British Politics 1868–1922* (Cardiff: University of Wales Press, 1980), p. 238.
20. Catterall, 'Morality and Politics', pp. 679–80.
21. P. Rowland, *Lloyd George* (London: Barrie & Jenkins, 1975), p. 804.
22. J. Eversley, 'The History of NHS Charges', *Contemporary British History*, 15, 2 (2001), pp. 59, 61; Foot, *Aneurin Bevan*, vol. 2, p. 338.
23. Eversley, 'History of NHS Charges', p. 56.
24. Russell Lord Brain, *The Doctor's Place in Society* (London: London School of Economics and Political Science, 1963), pp. 5–6; A. Heidenheimer, H. Heclo and C. Adams, *Comparative Public Policy: The Politics of Social Choice in America, Europe, and Japan* (New York: St Martin's, 1990), p. 77; D. Widgery, *Health in Danger: The Crisis in the National Health Service* (Hamden, CT: Archon, 1979), pp. 34–5.
25. R. Porter, *The Greatest Benefit to Mankind: A Medical History of Humanity* (New York: W. W. Norton, 1998), p. 654.
26. C. Ham, *Health Policy in Britain: The Politics and Organisation of the National Health Service*, 2nd edn (London: Macmillan, 1985), pp. 166–73; P. Townsend and N. Davidson (eds), *Inequalities in Health: The Black Report* (London: Penguin, 1990), pp. 49–50; M. Whitehead, *Inequalities in Health: The Health Divide* (London: Penguin, 1990), pp. 245–8, 321.
27. Townsend and Davidson, *Inequalities in Health*, pp. 78–9; Whitehead, *Inequalities in Health*, pp. 246–7; Widgery, *Health in Danger*, p. 146.
28. Ham, *Health Policy*, pp. 173–80; Townsend and Davidson, *Inequalities in Health*, pp. 43–8, 52–6, 68, 80–1; Whitehead, *Inequalities in Health*, pp. 228–243, 254, 264–5; Widgery, *Health in Danger*, pp. 39–40.
29. Townsend and Davidson, *Inequalities in Health*, pp. 73–5, 80.
30. Heidenheimer, Heclo and Adams, *Comparative Public Policy*, p. 75.
31. Townsend and Davidson, *Inequalities in Health*, pp. 58–9, 66.
32. G. Bevan, H. Copeman, J. Perrin and R. Rosser, *Health Care Priorities and Management* (London: Croom Helm, 1980), p. 31.
33. M. Powell, 'An Expanding Service: Municipal Acute Medicine in the 1930s', *Twentieth Century British History*, 8, 3 (1997), p. 343.
34. R. Crossman, *The Diaries of a Cabinet Minister*, vol. 3 (London: Hamish Hamilton and Jonathan Cape, 1977), p. 466.
35. Ibid., p. 455.
36. Ibid., pp. 466, 571.
37. Ibid., p. 613.
38. Widgery, *Health in Danger*, p. 147.
39. Porter, *Greatest Benefit*, p. 717.

Bibliography

Abel-Smith, B., *The Hospitals 1800–1948: A Study in Social Administration in England and Wales* (Cambridge, MA: Harvard University Press, 1964).

Ackerknecht, E., *Rudolf Virchow: Doctor, Statesman, Anthropologist* (Madison, WI: University of Wisconsin Press, 1953).

Addison, P., *Now the War is Over: A Social History of Britain 1945–51* (London: British Broadcasting Corporation, 1985).

Addison, P., *Churchill on the Home Front 1900–1955* (London: Pimlico, 1993).

Attlee, C., *As It Happened* (New York: Viking, 1954).

Bevan, A., *In Place of Fear* (New York: Simon & Schuster, 1953).

Bevan, G., H. Copeman, J. Perrin and R. Rosser, *Health Care Priorities and Management* (London: Croom Helm, 1980).

Beveridge, W., *The Pillars of Security: And Other War-time Essays and Addresses* (New York: Macmillan, 1943).

Beveridge, W., *The Price of Peace* (New York: W. W. Norton, 1945).

Beveridge, W., *Power and Influence* (New York: Beechhurst, 1955).

Beveridge, W., *Social Insurance and Allied Services: Presented to Parliament by Command of His Majesty November 1942* (New York: Agathon, 1969).

Bonner, T., *Becoming a Physician: Medical Education in Britain, France, Germany, and the United States, 1750–1945* (New York: Oxford University Press, 1995).

Bourne, G., *We Met at Bart's: The Autobiography of a Physician* (London: Frederick Muller, 1963).

Boxill, R., *Shaw and the Doctors* (New York: Basic Books, 1969).

Brain, Lord, *The Doctor's Place in Society* (London: London School of Economics and Political Science, 1963).

Brain, Lord, *Medicine and Government* (London: Tavistock Publications, 1967).

Brand, J., *Doctors and the State: The British Medical Profession and*

Government Action in Public Health, 1879–1912 (Baltimore, MD: Johns Hopkins University Press, 1965).

Brookes, P., *Women at Westminster: An Account of Women in the British Parliament 1918–1966* (London: Peter Davies, 1967).

Bruce, M., *The Coming of the Welfare State* (London: B. T. Batsford, 1961).

Bullock, A., *The Life and Times of Ernest Bevin*, vol. 1 (London: Heinemann, 1960).

Bullock, A., *The Life and Times of Ernest Bevin*, vol. 2 (London: Heinemann, 1967).

Bullock, A., *Ernest Bevin: Foreign Secretary 1945–1951* (New York: W. W. Norton, 1983).

Bulmer-Thomas, I., *The Growth of the British Party System*, 2 vols (London: John Baker, 1965).

Burridge, T., *Clement Attlee: A Political Biography* (London: Jonathan Cape, 1985).

Butler, R., *The Art of the Possible: The Memoirs of Lord Butler* (Harmondsworth: Penguin, 1973).

Callaghan, J., *Time and Change* (London: Fontana, 1988).

Campbell, J., *Aneurin Bevan and the Mirage of British Socialism* (New York: W. W. Norton, 1987).

Carr-Saunders, A. and P. Wilson, *The Professions* (Oxford: Clarendon, 1933).

Catterall, P., 'Morality and Politics: The Free Churches and the Labour Party between the Wars', *Historical Journal*, 3, 3 (1993), pp. 667–85.

Chamberlain, A., *Politics from Inside: An Epistolary Chronicle 1906–1914* (New Haven, CT: Yale University Press, 1937).

Chester, T., *Organisation for Change: The British National Health Service* (Paris: Organisation for Economic Co-operation and Development, 1975).

Chisholm, A. and M. Davie, *Lord Beaverbrook: A Life* (New York: Alfred A. Knopf, 1993).

Churchill, R., *Winston S. Churchill*, vol. 2 (Boston, MA: Houghton Mifflin, 1967).

Churchill, R., *Winston S. Churchill*, vol. 2, companion part 2 (London: Heinemann, 1969).

Clarke, P., *Hope and Glory: Britain 1900–1990* (London: Penguin, 1997).

Clegg, H., *Medicine in Britain*, 4th edn (London: Longmans, Green, 1951).

Clegg, H. and T. Chester, *Wage Policy and the Health Service* (Oxford: Basil Blackwell, 1957).

Cole, G., *Great Britain in the Post-war World* (London: Victor Gollancz, 1942).

Cole, M., *The Life of G. D. H. Cole* (London: Macmillan, 1971).

Cooke, A., *A History of the Royal College of Physicians of London*, vol. 3 (Oxford: Clarendon, 1972).

Cooke, C., *The Life of Richard Stafford Cripps* (London: Hodder & Stoughton, 1957).

Cope, Z., *The History of St Mary's Hospital Medical School, or a Century of Medical Education* (London: William Heinemann, 1954).

Cope, Z., *The Royal College of Surgeons of England: A History* (London: Anthony Blond, 1959).

Cox, A., *Among the Doctors* (London: Christopher Johnson, 1950).

Craig, F. (ed.), *British General Election Manifestos 1900–1974* (London: Macmillan, 1975).

Cregier, D., *Bounder from Wales: Lloyd George's Career before the First World War* (Columbia, MO: University of Missouri Press, 1976).

Cronin, A. J., *The Citadel* (New York: Bantam Books, 1962).

Cronin, A. J., *Shannon's Way* (Boston, MA: Little, Brown, 1983).

Crossman, R., *The Diaries of a Cabinet Minister*, vol. 3 (London: Hamish Hamilton and Jonathan Cape, 1977).

Cruden, W., 'Lord Horder – The Clinician', *St Bartholomew's Hospital Journal*, 61, 8 (1957), pp. 247–50.

Dalton, H., *The Fateful Years: Memoirs 1931–1945* (London: Frederick Muller, 1957).

Dalton, H., *High Tide and After: Memoirs 1945–1960* (London: Frederick Muller, 1962).

DeGroot, G., *Liberal Crusader: The Age of Sir Archibald Sinclair* (London: Hurst, 1993).

Dilks, D., *Neville Chamberlain*, vol. 1 (Cambridge: Cambridge University Press, 1984).

Donoughue, B. and G. Jones, *Herbert Morrison: Portrait of a Politician* (London: Weidenfeld & Nicolson, 1973).

du Parcq, H., *Life of David Lloyd George*, vol. 1 (London: Caxton, 1912).

du Parcq, H., *Life of David Lloyd George*, vol. 2 (London: Caxton, 1912).

du Parcq, H., *Life of David Lloyd George*, vol. 3 (London: Caxton, 1913).

du Parcq, H., *Life of David Lloyd George*, vol. 4 (London: Caxton, 1913).

Eckstein, H., *Pressure Group Politics; The Case of the British Medical Association.* (Stanford, CA: Stanford University Press, 1960).

Estorick, E., *Stafford Cripps: Master Statesman* (New York: John Day, 1949).

Evans, T., *Bevin of Britain* (New York: W. W. Norton, 1946).

Eversley, J., 'The History of NHS Charges', *Contemporary British History*, 15, 2 (2001), pp. 53–75.

Fellowship for Freedom in Medicine (1948–71, irregularly), *Bulletin*, Nos 1–72.

Fellowship for Freedom in Medicine, *The Medical Surrender (July, 1948): An Account of the Events Leading up to the Acceptance by the Medical Profession in Great Britain of the National Health Service Act* (London: Fellowship for Freedom in Medicine, 1951).

Fellowship for Freedom in Medicine, *Memorandum of Evidence Submitted to the Committee of Inquiry into the Costs of the National Health Service* (London: Fellowship for Freedom in Medicine, 1954).

Ferris, P., *The House of Northcliffe: A Biography of an Empire* (New York: World, 1972).

Fielding, S., P. Thompson and N. Tiratsoo, *'England Arise!': The Labour Party and Popular Politics in 1940s Britain* (Manchester: Manchester University Press, 1995).

Foot, M., *Debts of Honour* (New York: Harper & Row, 1981).

Foot, M., *Aneurin Bevan*, vol. 1 (London: Granada, 1982).

Foote, G., *The Labour Party's Political Thought: A History*, 2nd edn (London: Croom Helm, 1986).

Forder, A. (ed.), *Penelope Hall's Social Services of England and Wales* (New York: Routledge & Kegan Paul, 1969).

Forsyth, G., *Doctors and State Medicine: A Study of the British Health Service* (London: Pitman Medical Publishing, 1966).

Fox, D., *Health Policies, Health Politics: The British and American Experience 1911–1965* (Princeton, NJ: Princeton University Press, 1986).

Fraser, D., *The Evolution of the British Welfare State: A History of Social Policy Since the Industrial Revolution* (London: Macmillan, 1973).

Frazer, E., *A History of English Public Health 1834–1939* (London: Baillière, Tindall & Cox, 1950).

Freedman, L., *Politics and Policy in Britain* (White Plains, NY: Longman, 1996).

Friedrich, C., *Man and His Government: An Empirical Theory of Politics* (New York: McGraw-Hill, 1963).

Fry, J., *General Practice and Primary Health Care 1940s–1980s* (London: Nuffield Provincial Hospitals Trust, 1988).

Gee, S., *Medical Lectures and Aphorisms*, 2nd edn (London: Henry Frowde and Hodder & Stoughton, 1907).

Gemmill, P., *Britain's Search for Health: The First Decade of the National Health Service* (Philadelphia, PA: University of Pennsylvania Press, 1960).

Gerth, H. and C. Mills (eds), *From Max Weber: Essays in Sociology* (New York: Oxford University Press, 1972).

Gilbert, M., *Winston S. Churchill*, vol. 7 (Boston, MA: Houghton Mifflin, 1986).

Gilbert, M., *Winston S. Churchill*, vol. 8 (London: Minerva, 1990).

Gill, D., *The British National Health Service: A Sociologist's Perspective* (Bethesda, MD: National Institutes of Health, 1980).

Glaser, W., *Paying the Doctor: Systems of Remuneration and Their Effects* (Baltimore, MD: Johns Hopkins University Press, 1970).

Glennester, H., *British Social Policy since 1945* (Oxford: Blackwell, 1995).

Godber, G., *The Health Service: Past, Present and Future* (London: Athlone, 1975).

Godber, G., 'Forty Years of the NHS: Origins and Early Development', *British Medical Journal*, 297 (1988), pp. 37–43.

Goodman, G. (ed.), *The State of the Nation: The Political Legacy of Aneurin Bevan* (London: Victor Gollancz, 1997).

Goodman, N., *Wilson Jameson: Architect of National Health* (London: George Allen & Unwin, 1970).

Gordon Walker, P., 'Attlee', in Lord Longford and J. Wheeler-Bennett (eds), *The History Makers* (New York: St Martin's, 1973), pp. 288–303.

Gray, F., 'How GPs Came to Heel in NHS', *Pulse*, 41, 48 (1981), p. 14.

Grey-Turner, E. and F. Sutherland, *History of the British Medical Association*, vol. 2 (London: British Medical Association, 1982).

Griffith, B., S. Iliffe and G. Rayner, *Banking on Sickness: Commercial Medicine in Britain and the USA* (London: Lawrence & Wishart, 1987).

Grigg, J., *The Young Lloyd George* (London: Eyre Methuen, 1973).

Grigg, J., *Lloyd George: The People's Champion 1902–1911* (Berkeley, CA: University of California Press, 1978).

Grigg, J., *Lloyd George: From Peace to War 1912–1916* (Berkeley, CA: University of California Press, 1985).

Grimes, S., *The British National Health Service: State Intervention in the Medical Marketplace, 1911–1948* (New York: Garland, 1991).

Grosskurth, P., *Havelock Ellis: A Biography* (New York: Alfred A. Knopf, 1980).

Gullick, D., 'Forty Years of the NHS: The Act, the Minister, and the Editors', *British Medical Journal*, 297 (1988), pp. 55–8.

Halévy, E., *The Rule of Democracy 1905–1914 (Book II)*, 2nd edn, trans. E. I. Watkins. (New York: Peter Smith, 1952).

Ham, C., *Health Policy in Britain: The Politics and Organisation of the National Health Service*, 2nd edn (London: Macmillan, 1985).

Hare, R., *The Birth of Penicillin and the Disarming of Microbes* (London: George Allen & Unwin, 1970).

Hare, R., 'The Scientific Activities of Alexander Fleming, other than the Discovery of Penicillin', *Medical History*, 27 (1983), pp. 347–72..

Harris, J., *William Beveridge: A Biography* (Oxford: Clarendon, 1977).

Harris, K., *Attlee* (London: Weidenfeld & Nicolson, 1984).

Harrop, M. (ed.), *Power and Policy in Liberal Democracies* (Cambridge: Cambridge University Press, 1992).

Hatcher, P., 'The Health System of the United Kingdom', in M. Raffel (ed.), *Health Care and Reform in Industrialized Countries* (University Park, PA: Pennsylvania State University Press, 1997), pp. 227–61.

Healey, D., *The Time of My Life* (New York: W. W. Norton, 1990).

Heidenheimer, A., H. Heclo and C. Adams, *Comparative Public Policy: The Politics of Social Choice in America, Europe, and Japan* (New York: St Martin's, 1990).

Hennessy, P., *Never Again: Britain 1945–1951* (London: Vintage, 1993).

Herman, V. and J. Alt (eds), *Cabinet Studies: A Reader* (New York: St Martin's, 1975).

Hill of Luton, Lord, *Both Sides of the Hill* (London: Heinemann, 1964).

Hill of Luton, Lord, 'Aneurin Bevan among the Doctors', *British Medical Journal*, November 24, 1973, pp. 468–9.

Hill of Luton, Lord, *Behind the Screen: The Broadcasting Memoirs* (London: Sidgwick & Jackson, 1974).

Hill, C. and J. Woodcock, *The National Health Service* (London: Christopher Johnson, 1949).

Hill, D. (ed.), *Tribune 40: The First Forty Years of a Socialist Newspaper* (London: Quartet Books, 1977).

Hoffman, J., *The Conservative Party in Opposition 1945–51* (London: Macgibbon & Kee, 1964).

Hogarth, J., *The Payment of the Physician: Some European Comparisons* (New York: Macmillan, 1963).

Hollingsworth, J., *A Political Economy of Medicine: Great Britain and the United States* (Baltimore, MD: Johns Hopkins University Press, 1986).

Hollingsworth, J., J. Hage and R. Hanneman, *State Intervention in Medical Care: Consequences for Britain, France, Sweden, and the United States, 1890–1970* (Ithaca, NY: Cornell University Press, 1990).

Hollis, P., *Jennie Lee: A Life* (Oxford: Oxford University Press, 1997).

Honigsbaum, F., *The Struggle for the Ministry of Health 1914–1919* (London: G. Bell, 1970).

Honigsbaum, F., *The Division in British Medicine: A History of the Separation of General Practice from Hospital Care 1911–1968* (London: Kogan Page, 1979).

Honigsbaum, F., *Health, Happiness, and Security: The Creation of the National Health Service* (London: Routledge, 1989).

Honigsbaum, F., 'The Evolution of the NHS', *British Medical Journal*, 301, 6, 754 (1990), pp. 694–99.

Hopkins, H., *The New Look: A Social History of the Forties and Fifties in Britain* (Boston, MA: Houghton Mifflin, 1964).

Horder, Lord, 'Clinical Medicine: A Farewell Lecture at St Bartholomew's Hospital', *British Medical Journal*, 25 January 1936, pp. 163–5.

Horder, Lord, *Health and a Day: Addresses* (London: J. M. Dent, 1937).

Horder, Lord, *Obscurantism* (London: Watts, 1938).

Horder, Lord, 'Foreword', in *Britain's Health: Prepared by S. Mervyn Herbert on the Basis of the Report on The British Health Services by PEP (Political and Economic Planning)* (Harmondsworth: Penguin, 1939).

Horder, Lord, 'Medicine and the State', *Lancet*, 248, 1 (1945), pp. 295–8.

Horder, Lord, *Rheumatism: A Plan for National Action*, 5th edn (London: H. K. Lewis, 1947).

Horder, Lord, *Fifty Years of Medicine* (London: Gerald Duckworth, 1953).

Horder, Lord, C. Dodds and T. Moran, *Bread: The Chemistry and Nutrition of Flour and Bread, with an Introduction to their History and Technology* (London: Constable, 1954).

Horder, M., *The Little Genius: A Memoir of the First Lord Horder* (London: Gerald Duckworth, 1966).

Horder, T., *Clinical Pathology in Practice* (London: Henry Frowde and Hodder & Stoughton, 1910).

Horder, T., 'On Vaccine Therapy', *Practitioner*, 85 (1910), pp. 291–6.

Horder, T., *Medical Notes* (London: Henry Frowde and Hodder & Stoughton, 1921).

Horder, T., 'Individuality in Medicine', *St Bartholomew's Hospital Journal*, 34, 1 (1926), pp. 3–7.

Horder, T., 'New Treatments for Old', *British Medical Journal*, 20 May 1933, pp. 859–63.

Horder, T. and N. Ferry, 'A Search for an Ideal Antigen for Therapeutic Immunization', *British Medical Journal*, 31 July 1926, pp. 177–80.

Horder Society, *Minutes*, 1947–55. Royal College of Physicians (London) archives.

Howard, C., '"After This, What?": To 1945 and Beyond', *Historical Journal*, 28, 3 (1985), pp. 763–70.

Howell, D., *British Social Democracy: A Study on Development and Decay* (London: Croom Helm, 1976).

Hubble, D., 'Lord Moran and James Boswell: The Two Diarists Compared and Contrasted', *Medical History*, 13 (1969), pp. 1–10.

Hunt, T., 'Moran', in Gordon Wolstenholme (ed.), *Lives of the Fellows of the Royal College of Physicians of London continued to 1983* (Oxford: IRL Press, 1984), pp. 407–12.

Inwood, S., *A History of London* (New York: Carroll & Graf, 1998).

Ives, A., *British Hospitals* (London: Collins, 1948).

Jackson, R., *Rebels and Whips: An Analysis of Dissension, Discipline and Cohesion in British Political Parties* (London: Macmillan, 1968).

James, R., *Memoirs of a Conservative: J. C. C. Davidson's Memoirs and Papers, 1910–37* (New York: Macmillan, 1970).

James, R. (ed.), *Winston S. Churchill: His Complete Speeches*, vols 2, 7, 8 (New York: Chelsea House, 1974).

Jarman, T., *Socialism in Britain: From the Industrial Revolution to the Present Day* (New York: Taplinger, 1972).

Jeffreys, K., *The Labour Party since 1945* (London: Macmillan, 1993).

Jeffreys, K., *The Churchill Coalition and Wartime Politics, 1940–1945* (Manchester: Manchester University Press, 1995).

Jenkins, R., *Nine Men of Power* (New York: British Book Centre, 1974).

Jennings, I., *Cabinet Government*, 3rd edn (Cambridge: Cambridge University Press, 1959).

Jewkes, J. and S. Jewkes, *The Genesis of the British National Health Service*, 2nd edn (Oxford: Basil Blackwell, 1962).

Jones, T., *Lloyd George* (London: Oxford University Press, 1951).

Jones, T., *A Diary with Letters 1931–1950* (London: Oxford University Press, 1954).

Jones, T., *Whitehall Diary*, ed. K. Middemas (London: Oxford University Press, 1969).

Kavanagh, D., 'The Postwar Consensus', *Twentieth Century British History*, 3, 2 (1992), pp. 175–90.

Keidan, O., 'The Health Services', in A. Forder (ed.), *Penelope Halls Social Services of England and Wales* (New York: Routledge & Kegan Paul, 1969), pp. 135–81.

Kent, J., *William Temple: Church, State and Society in Britain, 1880–1950* (Cambridge: Cambridge University Press, 1992).

Klein, R., *The Politics of the National Health Service* (London: Longman, 1983).

Koss, S., *Nonconformity in Modern British Politics* (London: B. T. Batsford, 1975).

Labour Party, *National Service for Health* (London: Labour Party, 1943).

Lamont-Brown, R., *Royal Poxes and Potions: The Lives of Court Physicians, Surgeons and Apothecaries* (Stroud: Sutton, 2001).

Lasswell, H., *Psychopathology and Politics* (New York: Viking, 1960).

Lasswell, H., *Power and Personality* (New York: Viking, 1969).

Laybourn, K., *The Rise of Labour: The British Labour Party 1890–1979* (London: Edward Arnold, 1988).

Lee, J., *My Life with Nye* (London: Jonathan Cape, 1980).

L'Etang, H., *The Pathology of Leadership* (London: William Heinemann Medical Books, 1969).

L'Etang, H., *Ailing Leaders in Power 1914–1994* (London: Royal Society of Medicine Press, 1995).

Lewis, R. and A. Maude, *Professional People in England* (Cambridge, MA: Harvard University Press, 1953).

Lindsay, T. and M. Harrington, *The Conservative Party 1918–1970* (New York: St Martin's, 1974).

Lindsey, A., *Socialized Medicine in England and Wales: The National Health Service, 1948–1961* (Chapel Hill, NC: University of North Carolina Press, 1962).

Lovell, R., *Churchill's Doctor: A Biography of Lord Moran* (London: Royal Society of Medicine Services, 1992).

Lowe, R., *The Welfare State in Britain since 1945*, 2nd edn (London: Macmillan, 1999).

Ludovici, L., *Fleming: Discoverer of Penicillin* (London: Andrew Dakers, 1952).

Macfarlane, G., *Howard Florey: The Making of a Great Scientist* (Oxford: Oxford University Press, 1979).

Macfarlane, G., *Alexander Fleming: The Man and the Myth* (Cambridge, MA: Harvard University Press, 1984).

Mackenzie, W., *Power and Responsibility in Health Care: The National*

Health Service as a Political Institution (Oxford: Oxford University Press, 1979).

Mackintosh, J., *The British Cabinet*, 3rd edn (London: Stevens, 1977).

Macmillan, H., *Tides of Fortune 1945–1955* (London: Macmillan, 1969).

MacNalty, A., *The History of State Medicine in England, being the Fitzpatrick Lectures of the Royal College of Physicians of London for the Years 1946 and 1947* (London: Royal Institute of Public Health and Hygiene, 1948).

Macnicol, J., 'Eugenics and the Campaign for Voluntary Sterilization in Britain between the Wars', *Social History of Medicine*, 2, 2 (1989), pp. 147–69.

Mair, P., *Shared Enthusiasm: The Story of Lord and Lady Beveridge* (Windlesham: Ascent, 1982).

Marquand, D., *Ramsay MacDonald* (London: Jonathan Cape, 1977).

McKenzie, R., *British Political Parties: The Distribution of Power within the Conservative and Labour Parties*, 2nd edn (New York: Frederick A. Praeger, 1963).

Medical Directory, 1955 (London: J. & A. Churchill, 1955).

Medical Register, 1897 (London: General Medical Council, 1987).

Medical Register, 1909 (London: General Medical Council, 1909).

Medvei, V. and J. Thornton (eds), *The Royal Hospital of Saint Bartholomew 1123–1973* (London: Royal Hospital of Saint Bartholomew, 1974).

Moore, N., *The History of St Bartholomew's Hospital*, vol. 2 (London: C. Arthur Pearson, 1918).

Moore, N., 'Samuel Jones Gee', in S. Lee, (ed.), *The Dictionary of National Biography: Supplement January 1901–December 1911*, vol. 2 (London: Oxford University Press, 1939), pp. 91–2.

Moran, Lord, 'Wear and Tear', *Lancet*, 258 (1950), pp. 1,099–1,101.

Moran, Lord, *Churchill: Taken from the Diaries of Lord Moran: The Struggle for Survival 1940–1965* (Boston, MA: Houghton Mifflin, 1966).

Moran, Lord, *The Anatomy of Courage* (Boston, MA: Houghton Mifflin, 1967).

Moran, Lord, 'Lord Moran in conversation with Dr C. E. Newman 26 July 1970', London: Royal College of Physicians (London) archives.

Morgan, K., *The Age of Lloyd George* (London: George Allen & Unwin, 1971).

Morgan, K. (ed.), *Lloyd George: Family Letters 1885–1936* (Cardiff: University of Wales Press and Oxford: Oxford University Press, 1973).

Morgan, K., *Labour in Power 1945–1951* (Oxford: Oxford University Press, 1985).

Morgan, K., *Consensus and Disunity: The Lloyd George Coalition Government 1918–1922* (Oxford: Clarendon, 1986).

Morgan, K., *Labour People: Leaders and Lieutenants, Hardie to Kinnock* (Oxford: Oxford University Press, 1987).

Morgan, K., *The Red Dragon and the Red Flag: The Cases of James Griffiths and Aneurin Bevan* (Aberystwyth: National Library of Wales, 1989).

Morgan, K., *The People's Peace: British History 1945–1950* (Oxford: Oxford University Press, 1992).

Morris-Jones, H., *Doctor in the Whips' Room* (London: Robert Hale, 1955).

Morrison of Lambeth, Lord, *Herbert Morrison: An Autobiography* (London: Odhams, 1960).

Morrison of Lambeth, Lord, *Government and Parliament: A Survey from the Inside*, 3rd edn (London: Oxford University Press, 1964).

National Health Service Act, 1946: 9 & 10 Geo. 6, Ch. 81 (London: Her Majesty's Stationery Office, no date).

Negotiating Committee, *Minutes*, 1945. Royal College of Physicians (London) archives.

Newman, C., 'The History of Postgraduate Medical Education at the West London Hospital', *Medical History*, 10 (1966), pp. 339–59.

Nicholas, H., *The British General Election of 1950* (London: Macmillan, 1951).

Owen, D., *In Sickness and In Health: The Politics of Medicine* (London: Quartet Books, 1976).

Owen, F., *Tempestuous Journey: Lloyd George, His Life and Times* (London: Hutchinson, 1954).

Oxbury, H., *Great Britons: Twentieth-century Lives* (Oxford: Oxford University Press, 1985).

Pater, J., *The Making of the National Health Service* (London: King Edward's Hospital Fund for London, 1981).

Payer, L., *Medicine & Culture: Notions of Health and Sickness in Britain, the US, France and West Germany* (London: Victor Gollancz, 1990).

Pearce, R., *Attlee* (London: Longman, 1997).

Pelling, H., *A Short History of the Labour Party*, 5th edn (New York: St Martin's, 1976).

Pelling, H., 'The 1945 General Election Reconsidered', *Historical Journal*, 23, 2 (1980), pp. 399–414.

Pimlott, B., *Hugh Dalton* (London: Jonathan Cape, 1985).

Pimlott, B. (ed.), *The Political Diary of Hugh Dalton: 1918–40, 1945–60* (London: Jonathan Cape, 1986).

Pimlott, B. (ed.), *The Second World War Diary of Hugh Dalton 1940–45* (London: Jonathan Cape, 1986).

Platt, Lord, *Private and Controversial* (London: Cassell, 1972).

Porter, R., *London: A Social History* (Cambridge, MA: Harvard University Press, 1995).

Porter, R., *The Greatest Benefit to Mankind: A Medical History of Humanity* (New York: W. W. Norton, 1998).

Porter, R., *Bodies Politic: Disease, Death and Doctors in Britain, 1650–1900* (Ithaca, NY: Cornell University Press, 2001).

Pound, R., *Gillies: Surgeon Extraordinary* (London: Michael Joseph, 1964).

Pound, R. and G. Harmsworth, *Northcliffe* (New York: Frederick A. Praeger, 1960).

Powell, M., 'Hospital Provision before the National Health Service: A Geographical Study of the 1945 Hospital Surveys', *Social History of Medicine*, 5, 3 (1992), pp. 483–504.

Powell, M., 'An Expanding Service: Municipal Acute Medicine in the 1930s', *Twentieth Century History*, 8, 3 (1997), pp. 334–57.

Pugh, M., *Lloyd George* (London: Longman, 1993).

Pugh, M., *State and Society: British Political and Social History 1870–1992* (London: Edward Arnold, 1994).

Reader, W., *Professional Men: The Rise of the Professional Classes in Nineteenth-Century England* (New York: Basic Books, 1966).

Reid, M., *Ask Sir James: Sir James Reid, Personal Physician to Queen Victoria and Physician-in-Ordinary to Three Monarchs* (New York: Viking, 1989).

Rintala, M., 'The Two Faces of Compromise', *Western Political Quarterly*, 22 (1969), pp. 326–32.

Rintala, M., 'Taking the Pledge: H. H. Asquith and Drink', *Biography*, 16 (1993), pp. 103–35.

Rintala, M., *Lloyd George and Churchill: How Friendship Changed Politics* (Lanham, MD: Madison Books, 1995).

Rivett, G., *The Development of the London Hospital System 1823–1982* (London: King Edward's Hospital Fund for London, 1986).

Rodgers, W. and B. Donoughue, *The People into Parliament: A Concise History of the Labour Movement in Britain* (New York: Viking, 1966).

Rowland, P., *Lloyd George* (London: Barrie & Jenkins, 1975).

Royal College of Physicians (London), *Annals*, 1940–51. RCP (L) archives.

Royal College of Physicians (London) Comitia, *Minutes*, 1945–8. RCP (L) archives.

Scally, R., *The Origins of the Lloyd George Coalition: The Politics of Social Imperialism, 1900–1918* (Princeton, NJ: Princeton University Press, 1975).

Schmitt, C., *The Concept of the Political*, trans. George Schwab, (New Brunswick, NJ: Rutgers University Press, 1976).

Searle, G., *The Quest for National Efficiency: A Study in British Politics and Political Thought, 1899–1914* (Berkeley, CA: University of California Press, 1971).

Self, R. (ed.), *The Neville Chamberlain Diary Letters*, vol. 1 (Aldershot: Ashgate, 2000).

Shaw, B., *Doctors' Delusions, Crude Criminology, and Sham Education* (London: Constable, 1950).

Shaw, B., *The Doctor's Dilemma: A Tragedy* (London: Penguin, 1987).

Shell, D. and R. Hodder-Williams (eds), *Churchill to Major: The British Prime Ministership since 1945* (Armonk, NY: M. E. Sharpe, 1995).

Silver, G., 'Virchow, the Heroic Model in Medicine: Health Policy by Accolade' *American Journal of Public Health*, 77, 1 (1987), pp. 82–8.

Sissons, M. and P. French (eds), *Age of Austerity 1945–51* (Harmondsworth: Penguin, 1964).

Sked, A. and C. Cook, *Post-war Britain: A Political History*, 2nd edn (Harmondsworth: Penguin, 1984).

Soloway, R., *Demography and Degeneration: Eugenics and the Declining Birthrate in Twentieth-century Britain* (Chapel Hill, NC: University of North Carolina Press, 1995).

Speller, S., *The National Health Service Act, 1946, Annotated, Together with Various Orders and Regulations Made Thereunder* (London: H. K. Lewis, 1948).

Speller, S., *The National Health Service Act, 1946, Annotated: Supplement to 1948 Edition, Including the 1949 Amending Act and Statutory Instrument* (London: H. K. Lewis, 1951).

Steinmo, S., K. Thelen and F. Longstreth (eds), *Structuring Politics: Historical Institutionalism in Comparative Analysis* (Cambridge: Cambridge University Press, 1997).

Stevens, R., *Medical Practice in Modern England: The Impact of Specialization and State Medicine* (New Haven, CT: Yale University Press, 1966).

Stevenson, F., *Lloyd George: A Diary*, ed. A. Taylor (London: Hutchinson, 1971).

Stevenson, J., *British Society 1914–45* (Harmondsworth: Penguin, 1984).

Stevenson, R., *Morell Mackenzie: The Story of a Victorian Tragedy* (London: William Heinemann Medical Books, 1946).

Strauss, P., *Cripps: Advocate Extraordinary* (New York: Duell, Sloan & Pearce, 1942).

Taylor, A., *Bismarck: The Man and the Statesman* (New York: Vintage, 1967).

Taylor, A. (ed.), *Lloyd George: Twelve Essays* (New York: Atheneum, 1971).

Taylor, A., *Beaverbrook* (New York: Simon & Schuster, 1972).

Taylor, A., *Politicians, Socialism and Historians* (New York: Stein & Day, 1982).

Thatcher, M., *The Downing Street Years* (New York: Harper Collins, 1993).

Thomson, M., *David Lloyd George: The Official Biography* (London: Hutchinson, 1948).

Townsend, P. and N. Davidson (eds), *Inequalities in Health: The Black Report* (London: Penguin, 1990).

Wainwright, M., 'The History of the Therapeutic Use of Crude Penicillin', *Medical History*, 31 (1987), pp. 41–50.

Watkin, B., *The National Health Service: The First Phase 1948–1974 and After* (London: George Allen & Unwin, 1978).

Watkins, S., *Medicine and Labour: The Politics of a Profession* (London: Lawrence & Wishart, 1987).

Watson, F., *Dawson of Penn* (London: Chatto & Windus, 1950).

Webb, S. and B., *The State and the Doctor* (London: Longmans, Green, 1910).

Webster, C., *The Health Services and the War*, vol. 1 (London: Her Majesty's Stationery Office, 1988).

Webster, C., 'Conflict and Consensus: Explaining the British Health Service', *Twentieth Century British History*, 1, 2 (1990), pp. 115–51.

Whitehead, M., *Inequalities in Health: The Health Divide* (London: Penguin, 1990), pp. 215–81.

Widgery, D., *Health in Danger: The Crisis in the National Health Service* (Hamden, CT: Archon, 1979).

Willcocks, A., *The Creation of the National Health Service: A Study of Pressure Groups and a Major Social Policy Decision* (London: Routledge & Kegan Paul, 1967).

Williams, F., *Press, Parliament and People* (London: William Heinemann, 1946).

Williams, F., *Ernest Bevin: Portrait of a Great Englishman* (London: Hutchinson, 1952).

Williams, F., *A Prime Minister Remembers: The War and Post-war Memoirs of the Rt Hon. Earl Attlee* (London: Heinemann, 1961).

Williams, P., *Hugh Gaitskell: A Political Biography* (London: Jonathan Cape, 1979).

Williams, P. (ed.), *The Diary of Hugh Gaitskell 1945–1956* (London: Jonathan Cape, 1983).

Williams, T., *Howard Florey: Penicillin and After* (Oxford: Oxford University Press, 1984).

Wilson, D., *Penicillin in Perspective* (London: Faber & Faber, 1976).

Wilson, H., *A Personal Record: The Labour Government 1964–1970* (Boston, MA: Little, Brown, 1971).

Wilson, H., *A Prime Minister on Prime Ministers* (New York: Summit Books, 1977).

Witts, L., 'Thomas Jeeves Horder', in E. Williams and H. Palmer (eds), *The Dictionary of National Biography 1951–1960* (London: Oxford University Press, 1971), pp. 501–3.

Wohl, A., *Endangered Lives; Public Health in Victorian Britain* (Cambridge, MA: Harvard University Press, 1983).

Woolton, Earl of, *The Memoirs of the Rt Hon. The Earl of Woolton* (London: Cassell, 1959).

Wrigley, C., *David Lloyd George and the British Labour Movement: Peace and War* (Hassocks: Harvester, 1976).

Wyatt, H., 'Robert Pulvertaft's Use of Crude Penicillin in Cairo', *Medical History*, 34 (1990), pp. 320–6.

Young, H., *The Iron Lady: A Biography of Margaret Thatcher* (New York: Noonday Press, 1989).

Index

Abse, Leo, 131
Addison, Christopher, 27, 28, 30, 42–3, 58, 91, 132
Aitken, Max *see* Beaverbrook, Max Aitken, Lord
Amery, Leo, 24
Anatomy of Courage, The (Moran), 106
approved societies, National Insurance Act, 25–6
Asquith, H. H., 20, 59
Attlee, Clement, 15, 29, 39, 42, 58–9, 93; and Addison, 43; and Bevan, 45; chosen leader of the Labour Party, 45; and Morrison, 45–6; RCP 1945 dinner, 98; support for Bevan, 43–6

Beaverbrook, Max Aitken, Lord, 84–6, 87, 88–9, 92, 102, 121–2
Belgium, 20
Bentham, Jeremy, 22
Bevan, Aneurin: appointed minister of health, 29, 45; approves building more crematoria, 125; and Archbishop Fisher, 134, 135; and Attlee, 45, 58–9; background, 61–3, 135; and Beaverbrook, 88–9; on Beveridge, 16; and Bevin, 40; Cabinet supporters, 42–3, 135–6; at the Café Royal, 99; Churchill's respect for, 9, 10; and the commercialism of the medical profession, 51; composition of the NHS bill, 111; and Cripps, 41; criticism of Labour Coalition Cabinet members, 36–7; death of, 59–60; debating skills, 10; and

doctors, 71; and Horder, 88–9, 121; and hospital consultant staffing, 113–15; housing policy, 29–30; influence of public opinion, 133; leadership style, 59; on Lloyd George, 137; maiden speech, 9; meetings with Moran, 111–15, 133; and Moran, 89, 121; Moran's support, 111; nationalization of hospitals, 47, 112–13; and NHS fees, 137–8; party loyalty, 36, 133; position in Attlee's Cabinet, 38–9, 41; and pressure groups, 132; public popularity, 10; RCP 1945 dinner, 98; resignation from Cabinet, 10, 137; self-confidence, 134–5; as sole parent of the NHS, 4–6, 58–63, 140; wartime criticism of Churchill, 9–10; and the Willink White Paper, 11; and women, 100
Bevan, David, 63
Beveridge, Sir William, 14–16, 16–17, 21; on the abolition of poverty, 17; on Bevan, 15–16; on Churchill, 15; as father of the welfare state, 17–18; and the National Health Service, 18
Beveridge Report, 1942, 4, 11, 14, 16–18, 39, 63
Bevin, Ernest, 14, 39, 39–41, 112, 136; on Bevan, 36
Bismarck, Otto von, 19–20
Black, Sir Douglas, 138
Bonar Law, Andrew, 79
Boothby, Robert, 10
Braddock, Bessie, 100

British Hospital Association (BHA), 118–19
British Medical Association (BMA), 46, 64, 103, 132; acceptance of the NHS, 122; and Bevan, 59–60; campaign against implementation, 118; and the National Insurance Act, 26–8; and the Royal College of Nursing, 100; and the sale of medical practices, 50–2
British Medical Journal, 59–60, 103–4
British Popular Front, 36, 42
Brown, Ernest, 11
Burns, John, 22
Buxton, Sydney, 18

Café Royal, meeting at the, 98–102
Campbell-Bannerman, Henry, 78
Chamberlain, Austin, 24
Chamberlain, Neville, 28, 38, 79–80
Churchill, Winston, 3, 8, 18; on Bevan, 5; on Bevan's housing policy, 29–30; Bevan's wartime criticism of, 9–10; and Beveridge, 15; and the Beveridge Report, 16; defence of Addison, 30; failure to challenge Bevan, 9, 10, 132; and health policy, 10–11; and Horder, 80–1, 84; as leader of the Opposition, 10; and Moran, 84, 98, 120; and the National Insurance Act, 19, 20, 24; praise for Lloyd George, 30; on referenda, 131; respect for Bevan, 9, 10; visit to Lloyd George, 21
Cole, G. D. H., 49, 132
Coleraine, Richard Law, Lord, 9, 10
Conservative Party: acceptance of the NHS, 60; consensus interpretation of creation of the NHS, 3, 4, 8; and the creation of the NHS, 8–11; and the National Insurance Act, 23, 24, 25; opposition to the National Health Service Act, 8–9
cremation, 125
Cremation Committee, 125
Cremation Society, the, 125
Cripps, Sir Stafford, 36, 39, 41–2, 44
Cronin, A. J., 38
Crossman, Richard, 138–9

Dain, Guy, 99, 101, 122

Dalton, Hugh, 15, 29, 39, 41, 44, 87–8
Dawson, Bertrand, 78–9, 86, 119
Dawson Report, the, 78
distinction awards, 113–15
Docker, Sir Bernard, 118
doctors *see also* British Medical Association (BMA); capital investment, 50–1; compensation, 51; general practitioners, 69, 70, 118, 122; hospital consultants, 69–70, 113–15; individual attitudes, 70–1; and the National Insurance Act, 26–8; panel system, 20; role in the creation of the NHS, 69–72
Duggett, Geraldine, 100

Eckstein, Harry, 70, 71
Edward VII, 77, 125
Edward VIII, 80
Emergency Medical Service, 108
Empire Rheumatism Council, 104
Esslemont, Mary, 99
Eugenics Society, the, 102
Evans, Geoffrey, 76

Fellowship of Freedom in Medicine (FFM), 122–3, 125
Fifty Years of Medicine (Horder), 72
Fisher, Geoffrey, Archbishop of Canterbury, 134, 135
Fleming, Alexander, 92, 93
Florey, Howard, 92, 93
Forster, H. W., 24
friendly societies, 25

Gaitskell, Hugh, 88
general elections: 1931, 45; 1935, 45; 1945, 17, 45–6, 132
George VI, 125
Germany, welfare state, 19–20
Gilliatt, Sir William, 101–2
Great Britain, political culture and system, 3, 10, 131–3
Great Britain in the Post-war World (Cole), 49
Greene, Wilfred, 24–5
Greenwood, Arthur, 14, 39
Griffiths, James, 135–6
Griffiths, John, 49
group practices, failure to develop, 114

Hawton, John, 11
Hawtrey, R. G., 22
Health, Ministry of, 22–3, 28
heroin, manufacture of, 10
Herringham, Wilmot, 23
Hill, Lord Charles, 10, 99, 101, 102–3, 111, 112, 122
Holland, Eardley, 101–2
Horder, Thomas, Lord, 75–6, 86, 93–4, 133, 139–40; acquaintance with Labour Cabinet, 91; and Beaverbrook, 84; and Bevan, 88–9, 121; and the BMA, 103; and Churchill, 80–1, 84; and cremation, 125; and eugenics, 102, 103–4; exclusion from the Cafè Royal meeting, 103–4; and the FFM, 122–3; House of Lords attacks, 118–21; Labour Party patients, 88; lack of a party whip, 120; loss of prestige, 124–5; maiden speech to the House of Lords, 94–5; and Moran, 72, 87–8, 103, 104–6, 121–2; opposition to NHS, 71–2, 124; perception of Moran, 124; prime ministerial patients, 78–80; private patients, 77–80; private practice, 76, 105, 125; royal patients, 77, 125; status, 124; view of medicine, 94–5; and women doctors, 99–100
Horder Society, the, 123
hospitals, 69; London County Council, 37–8; Moran and Bevan's discussions on, 112–13; municipal, 37–8, 107; nationalization of, 46–7, 112–13, 118, 138–9; ownership of, 44; teaching, 114, 138–9; voluntary, 50
House of Lords, 71, 91–2, 118–21, 133; Horder's maiden speech, 94–5; Moran's maiden speech, 108; and the National Health Service Act, 8
housing policy, 28–30

Independent Labour Party, 62
Interim Report of the Consultative Council on Medical and Allied Services, 78

Joint Committee on Voluntary Sterilization, 102
Jowitt, William Lord, 39

Labour Party: 1935 general election manifesto, 48; 1942 conference, 49; 1945 general election manifesto, 47–8; 1949 conference, 134; and the Beveridge Report, 4; consensus interpretation of creation of the NHS, 3; credit for the NHS, 60; health policy, 47–50, 58; and hospital ownership, 43; leadership competition, 45–6; and the National Insurance Act, 25–6; policy commitment interpretation of the creation of the NHS, 4, 6
Labour's Immediate Programme (1937), 48
Lansbury, George, 45
Lasswell, Harold, 59
Law, Richard, 9, 10
Lee, Jennie, 42
Liberal Insurance Committee, 27, 132
Liberal Party: and the Beveridge Report, 17; consensus interpretation of creation of the NHS, 4; and the creation of the NHS, 14–30; social policy, 17
Lloyd George, David, 16–17, 18, 78–9, 132, 136–7, 140; and the BMA, 26–8; Churchill's praise for, 30; housing policy, 28–9; and the National Insurance Act, 19, 20–8; visit to Germany, 21
local government authorities, 50; public health programmes, 46–7, 49
Local Government Board, 22
London County Council (LCC), 37–8, 42, 46, 47
London School of Economics and Political Science, 15
Luxembourg, 20

MacDonald, Ramsay, 79
Macmillan, Harold, 4, 29, 39
Mann, Jean, 100
maternity benefits, 21
medical practices, sale of, 50–2
Medical Practitioners' Union, 95
medical research, 23
Medical Research Committee, 23
medical treatment: access to, 21, 22; regional inequalities, 138, 138–9, 140

medicine as social science, 94–5
Members of Parliament, introduction
    of salaries, 25–6
Miller, J. B., 99, 101
Moran, Charles Wilson, Lord, 71,
    91–3, 106, 133, 134, 138, 139; allies
    with Bevan, 111; ambition, 86; and
    Beaverbrook, 84–6, 87, 92, 121–2;
    and Bevan, 89, 121; on the BHA,
    118; and BMA acceptance of the
    NHS, 122; at the Café Royal, 99;
    and Churchill, 84, 98, 120; and
    Hill, 102–3; and Horder, 72, 87,
    103, 104–6, 121–2; and Horder's
    House of Lords attacks, 119–21;
    Horder's perception of, 124; and
    hospital consultant staffing,
    113–15; and hospital
    nationalization, 112–13; income,
    105; introduces bill supporting
    Bevan to House of Lords, 119; and
    the king's 1945 speech, 91; lack of
    a party whip, 120; maiden speech
    to the House of Lords, 108;
    meetings with Bevan, 111–15, 133;
    and military medicine, 106–7; on
    municipal hospitals, 107; primacy,
    101–2; and the Royal College of
    Physicians, 86–7, 103; support for
    a NHS, 106–8
Morrison, Herbert, 37–8, 39, 41, 41–2,
    88, 133; and Attlee, 45–6; attack on
    Bevan's plans, 39; on Bevan, 39;
    and Bevin, 40–1; Cabinet
    confrontation, 44; defence of
    municipal hospitals, 46–7; and
    women, 100

Nathan, Harry Lord, 91
National Birth Control Association,
    119
National Coalition Government, 3,
    9–10, 14, 36–7, 40; and the
    Beveridge Report, 16
National Health Insurance, 18, 21,
    22
National Health Service (NHS):
    consensus interpretation of
    creation, 3–4, 8; enrolment, 60;
    fees, 137–8; income, 59, 137–8;
    Labour policy commitment
    interpretation of creation, 4, 6; sole

parent interpretation of creation,
    4–6, 58–63; status, 60–1
National Health Service Act, 1946, 3,
    42–3, 47, 133–4; as Bevan's cause,
    58; the Cabinet and, 36–46;
    Conservative opposition to, 8–9;
    and the sale of medical practices,
    51
National Insurance Act, 1911, 4, 17,
    18–28, 42–3, 63, 136; amendments,
    22
National Research Committee, 23
National Service for Health, 49–50, 136
Negotiating Committee, the, 99,
    100–1, 111
Newman, Sir George, 79
Northcliffe, Alfred Harmsworth,
    Viscount, 77–8
Norway, 20

Oxford University, 92–3

patients, lack of representation, 101
penicillin, 92–3
pension system, 20
Platt, Robert Lord, 124
poverty, abolition of, 17
prescription charges, 137
*Pressure Group Politics: The Case of the
    British Medical Association*
    (Eckstein), 70, 71
pressure groups, 70, 132
public debate, 132, 133
public health, 46–7, 49, 95

Report of the Interdepartmental
    Committee on Social Insurance
    and Allied Services *see* Beveridge
    Report, 1942
Rhondda, David Thomas, Viscount,
    77
Royal College of Nursing, 100–1
Royal College of Obstetricians/
    Gynaecologists, 70, 101–2
Royal College of Physicians, 70, 71,
    86–7, 94, 101, 123; 1945 annual
    dinner, 98; Moran's domination
    of, 103
Royal College of Surgeons, 70
Royal Commission on Medical
    Education, 60
Royal Northern Hospital, 76

St Bartholomew's Hospital, 75–6, 140
St Mary's Hospital Medical School,
85, 93, 108, 139
St Mary's Hospital Gazette, 106
satisfaction levels, 61
Schmitt, Carl, 41, 120
Serbia, 20
Shaw, George Bernard, 26, 49, 76
Sheppard, the Reverend H. R., 124
Sinclair, Archibald, 36
Smith, F. E., 23
social inequalities, 138
Social Security League, 16, 132
Socialist Medical Association, 48
Souttar, Sir Henry, 99, 101
Standing Awards Committee, 115
State and the Doctor, The (Webb), 48–9

Temple, William, 22
Thatcher, Margaret, 60
Thurtle, Ernest, 9
trade unions, 25
Treasury responsibility, 44
Tredegar Working Men's Medical Aid
Society, 63, 140

unemployment insurance, 18, 20

Virchow, Rudolf, 94

Wales, religious nonconformity,
135
Webb, Beatrice and Sidney, 25, 41,
48–9
Webb-Johnson, Sir Alfred, 99, 101
Weber, Max, 26
welfare state, 5, 17–18, 135; German
origins, 19–20
Welsh Baptist Union, 137
White Paper on health policy, 1944, 3,
11, 58
Wilkinson, Ellen, 42, 136
Willink, Henry, 11
Willink White Paper, 3, 11, 58
Wilson, Charles, *see* Moran, Charles
Wilson, Lord
Wilson, Harold, 37, 38, 41
Woolton, Earl of, 3, 120
Working Group on Inequalities in
Health, 138
Wright, Sir Almoth, 93